THIS MEDIUM'S LIFE

Copyright © 2011 by Joey Crinita
All rights reserved.
ISBN: 0-9641254-2-0
Cover Photograph: Assisi, Italy 1976

Joey Crinita is also author of:

The Medium Touch, A New Approach To Mediumship
From Chains to Wings, The Journey Into Spirit
Healing Poems of Spirit

Dedicated to my Father, Joe and my Mother, Emma and all of the Crinita Clan. My sisters Kay, Sally, Emily, Linda, Irene, Gloria, Susie, and Mary. My brothers Frankie and Paul. To all the people who have made me a better person by simply being in my life, you know who you are and so do I.

CONTENTS

Chapter I	AND... SO IT BEGINS
Chapter II	DESPAIR WITHOUT HOPE. WHY ME GOD?
Chapter III	SPIRIT IS WAITING
Chapter IV	SPIRIT COMES IN
Chapter V	MATERIALIZATION - SEEING IS BELIEVING
Chapter VI	LIGHT AND LAVENDER. BEING SPIRITUAL AND GAY
Chapter VII	PEOPLE I'VE MET ALONG THE WAY
Chapter VIII	SPIRIT WORKER
Chapter IX	SPIRIT TALKS
Chapter X	SPIRIT NUDGES
Chapter XI	THE SPIRITUAL STEPS
Chapter XII	THOUGHTS TO PONDER
Chapter XIII	MEDITATIONS
Chapter XIV	PRAYERS, POEMS, BLESSINGS, SAYINGS... AND THE LIKE
Chapter XV	STRUGGLING SPIRITS. THE GHOST OF CHOM
Chapter XVI	AND... SO IT GOES

FOREWORD

This is a recounting of the experiences which have shaped my life and defined my purpose as a human being, a Spiritualist and a Medium on the never ending journey toward self-awareness.

Indeed, I am blessed. I continue to be spiritually enriched through service to Spirit and through the friendships and guidance of the 'Angels with Dirty Faces' whom I have met along the way, many mentioned herein.

It is my hope these reminiscences serve as inspiration to people who would likewise travel on a life's path in service to others, in whatever capacity you choose to serve God and humanity. I offer This Medium's Life as a walk in the Light, for those who are so inclined.

For the sake of brevity, I refer to God as He or His. This is in no way meant to reflect my view of God as being either male or female. It is solely a reflection of my early Roman Catholic upbringing.

These shared events of my life have helped to anchor my faith and cement my complete trust and belief in the power of The Eternal One, and in the Spirit Helpers who unconditionally guide me along my way. For this, I am grateful. I present them for what they are. These are my beliefs. This is who I am.

CHAPTER I
AND... SO IT BEGINS

I arrived on the planet on Tuesday, October 29, 1940 at the Royal Victoria Hospital in Montreal, Canada.

I have always thought I should have been born two days later on October 31, which would have made me a Halloween baby, in keeping with my mediumistic tendencies. However, that faculty was only to manifest itself twenty-eight years later. Be that as it may, I guess I could not wait to get here.

I weighed nine and a half pounds at birth. My mother Emma who is now ninety-three, recently revealed to me, as she sweetly smiled, that Doctor Henry who delivered me commented that I had a big head. Of course, my sisters who were present in the room had a good laugh, along with my mother. I retorted, "I guess things haven't changed much." I believe if you say something first about yourself, then whatever anyone else says about you, loses steam. I think that it is a Scorpio trait and the equivalent of saying "so what." In her lifetime my mother Emma gave birth to eleven children and we were all born at the Royal Victoria Hospital. Nine survived, seven girls and two boys. We were born within a year of each other. I remember my mother as always having one baby in her belly and another on her hip. My mother never fails to include the two Spirit children when she speaks of her kids. One daughter Mary was stillborn on September 4, 1950 and a son Paul, a miscarriage in 1954. I came to know of their Spirit names from various Spirit messages throughout the years. From an early age we learned how to look out for one another and as within all large families, there was never a dull moment.

We were raised in Griffintown, a Shanty Irish, French Canadian and Italian neighbourhood. People lived in cold water flats with wood burning stoves and ice boxes. Griffintown was a great place to grow up and it had its own special magic. We lived at 1417 Barre Street in a rented small four room bungalow with two bedrooms, which housed eleven people and a cat. There was a stable in our backyard which housed Francis the horse and some mares that were used to pull a caleche around the Montreal streets for tourists. We became quite proficient at cleaning out the stables and feeding the horses, and once in a while we kids would get a ride in the caleche from Mike Kennedy, the owner of the horses.

We were rough and ready and we travelled to school in gangs because there was safety in numbers. If we ran into other gangs there would sometimes be fights between the French and English kids. We learned how to survive on the streets. We made our own fun by playing Hide and Seek and Cowboys and Indians. I was always an Apache Chief, with an old mop handle as my spear. I liked to run fast and feel the wind rushing through me. We played Kick the Can in the streets and drank the popular soft drink KIK Cola. Occasionally we ate steamed hot dogs and drank spruce beer. That was a treat fit for a king. The big event of the day was sitting on the stoop at night-time watching everyone go by. The grownups would stop to talk to each other and everybody knew everyone's business. We listened to Boston Blackie and The Inner Sanctum on the radio. We were poor and we were happy.

Those were the days when front doors were always left open and one could just walk into anyone's home for a visit. I would make the rounds. I visited my Aunt Geraldine and Aunt Cecile who lived on the same block on Barre Street and then walked to the neighbours' homes. This meant I could receive either a cookie, a glass of milk or a soft drink. There was always sure to be something. One of my favourite people was Florrie McKercher, who lived on Lusigian Lane, a side lane off Barre Street where I lived and referred to as "down the lane".

Florrie was a War Bride, a good hearted large blonde woman who loved to talk, and spoke with an English accent. She was a friend of my mother's who had seven children of her own. She was a great cook and would always feed me. I thoroughly enjoyed my visits and liked talking to her. I might add that Florrie was of the Protestant faith. One day whilst making my neighbourhood rounds, I dropped in to see Mary Beauchamp who lived with her husband at the far end of Barre Street. Mary was childless, so I was always made to feel at home and served refreshment. She and her husband lived in the flat beneath my Uncle Henry and my Aunt Cecile, whom we always called Diddles. On one particular day, Mary was not home when I called to visit. As usual the front door was open, so in I went. I was familiar with the house from my previous visits. I sat in the living-room for a while. I then took a look about and went into the bedroom where on the dresser I saw two beautiful religious statues about twelve inches high made of white plaster. I had always admired them having seen them previously. One statue was of St. Joseph and the other of The Blessed Virgin and Child. In a flash of what I considered to be spontaneous inspiration, I scooped up the statues in my arms and headed out of the house and directly down the lane to Florrie's and presented her with these Catholic icons, telling her they were a present from Mary Beauchamp. Of course, Florrie did not believe me, because being Protestant she had no interest in Catholic statues, and she knew that something was amiss. To my ten year old mind, this was an act of repayment to my friend for her many kindnesses to me and because I thought maybe the Saints would do her good because she was a Protestant. That same day, my mother and my Aunt Diddles found out about this caper via a telephone call from Florrie. I was instructed to return the holy statues to Mary Beauchamp at once. I did and Mary graciously accepted the return of her missing Saints and restored them to their proper place. I recall my Aunt standing and smiling as I returned the missing statues and her telling me I could not give away other peoples' belongings without their permission, and not to enter anyone's home when they were not at home. Mary Beauchamp gave me a glass of ginger ale and that was that.

My father Joe was up every morning at 6:00 am, and occasionally we kids would get up early with Daddy and he would make us tea and toast on the flat iron stove top before he left for work. My father worked hard all of his life and passed at sixty-six years of age on August 5, 1980. As we children were growing up, Emma my mother ever the entrepreneur, would take us to the Salvation Army shop on Notre Dame Street to buy our second-hand clothes. She would purchase extra clothing and then resell the items to the neighbours, and thus she came to be known as "Little Eaton's" which was a well-known department store in Canada.

Another one of my mother's monikers is "Bingo" because of her obvious love of the game and the fact she frequented the bingo halls on a regular basis and was at times lucky. There was quite a cast of characters in Griffintown and one of the most well-known was a man named Johnny Fish. He was reputed to be a genius until he banged his head one day and then went a little off. He lived with his mother and sister on Eleanor Street. He was a tall man with short cropped white hair. He would always be decked out in a long brown army coat, a plaid scarf around his neck and a top hat.

However, he also had an aversion to soap and water so you did not want to stand too close. He was a very gentle soul and ever ready with a smile when you approached him. All of the kids knew him. He was like a big child himself. We would stop to ask him about the weather forecast and he would respond with the weather report for the day. If you asked him nicely, Johnny would even sing you a naughty little ditty which he would compose on the spot having to do with one of the local residents. I remember that he liked to pick on his neighbour, Kitty Kearney in his songs. You had to promise not to tell what he said. He would often be seen merrily strolling along Mountain Street speaking to himself on his way to St. Ann's Church. He attended Mass every morning and often stayed for two. He was a fixture in the Church and always sat in the first pew, left hand side closest to the main altar. On St. Patrick's Day, Johnny would be decked out in a kelly green scarf with green streamers around his neck. Often he would be covered in green wrapping paper with bunches of shamrocks on his coat and hat. He would wear this get up for weeks on end. He was proud to be Irish. One day we just did not see him. I later heard he had been ill for several months and subsequently had died of pneumonia. He must have been in his late seventies when he passed.

Another character was named Mrs. Gertie Burnett, who was nicknamed Gravel Gertie. I distinctly remember her because she would make an appearance specifically when there was to be an eclipse of the sun. She was a superstitious woman convinced that an eclipse was always ominous. She was a very pretty and pleasant woman, always made up with long brunette hair and a high pitched voice. I would spot her walking in her high heels down Barre Street attired in black from head to toe, including a big picture hat. Cradled in her arm would be a bottle of booze and the Bible. She would visit with my Uncle Willie Coyle who lived at 1409 Barre Street and we lived at 1417, so I would be on the lookout for her. She would arrive in the morning, seat herself with my Uncle Willie on the front steps of his home, start reading her Bible and be loaded by the afternoon. The crying jags would begin when she got a bit tipsy. "Oh, Mr Coyle, it is the end of the world", she would lament through her tears as she had another drink and read her Bible aloud. Her high pitched voice increased in volume the tipsier she became. As the day progressed she relocated from the front steps into the kitchen. I did not know it then, but as an adult I understand it must have been

Revelations that she read from, because Gertie was surely terrified. She always thought that she was going to go to hell at every eclipse. Why? I never knew, I was just a kid. She would go on until the eclipse had passed and stagger home on her high heels when she realized she did not die. Gertie would show up at other times as well, but the eclipse was the show as far as I was concerned. I witnessed quite a number of these performances through the years and enjoyed every moment. For me, these were some of the simple joys growing up in Griffintown.

I remember my playmate and friend, Mickey Timmons. When he was nine years old, he was playing in the middle of Barre Street in a large empty cardboard box. Tragically, he was run over by a truck coming down the street. No one knew he was playing inside. It was an unbelievably sad experience for the entire block and I felt really sad. I missed my friend.

My school friend Paddy Crane was also an altar boy and a very gentle fellow with a serious heart condition which ultimately took his life when he was about thirteen.

These are some of my childhood memories that I recall now and then.

In 1947 when I was seven years of age I made my First Communion. Thanks to the kindness of the Church ladies who would come to our home to visit, I was able to be confirmed in style. They collected me one afternoon and brought me to a clothing store. They bought me a new blue suit with short legged pants, a new white shirt, a tie, long stockings and a new pair of black shoes.

In 1948 I became an altar boy at St. Ann's Church, an Irish Roman Catholic Church opened on December 8, 1854 and sadly demolished in 1970. The Church was really the heart of Griffintown. It was a magnificent Gothic structure given to the care of the Redemptorist Fathers. St. Ann's was known for the Tuesday devotions to Our Mother of Perpetual Help. There was a beautiful Shrine to Our Mother of Perpetual Help in the Church and people came from all over the city for the services. The City of Montreal scheduled bus service to the Shrine because of its popularity.

The Tuesdays as we called them, would commence at 3:30 pm and continue until 9:15 pm with Benedictions scheduled every forty-five minutes and a Mass at 5:30 pm.

The Church was always full of worshipers and St. Ann's could easily hold as many as eight hundred people. When you first became an altar boy, you would sit in the pews on the altar during services and walk in processions during the religious Holy Days like Easter and Christmas and did not do much of anything else. As time passed you were trained by the older and more experienced altar boys. You then became an acolyte and were now permitted to carry the Mass candles. In time, I was able to serve many of the Benedictions and was happy to be serving God and enjoyed being part of the services. This was my passport to heaven as far as I was concerned. I graduated from being an acolyte to a master of ceremonies, where you assisted at the left side of the celebrant priest during the Mass or Benediction. My favourite was being the censor bearer. I have always liked the rituals and especially the wisps of frankincense. I would swing that censor during the services as if there was no tomorrow. I enjoyed seeing the smoke rising out of the hot censor and ascending into the air, as a prayer, to what I imagined to be the very throne of God Himself.

As an altar boy one had to be very dedicated and devoted to the Church. In my teenage years I would often rise at 6:00 am in order to be at Church to serve a 7:00 am Mass, come rain, shine or snow. These were happy times for me. I was in love with the Church and had hopes of entering the Church to one day become a lay brother. As altar boys we became a close knit group and we did have some good laughs. As children we could be somewhat mischievous at the expense of the newer and inexperienced boys who would come along.

For example, we would advise a new altar boy that we would let him know when to ring the bell during the Mass which signifies the moment of Consecration as the celebrant priest crosses himself with the Sacred Host. Of course we would signal a new boy to ring the bell at the Gospel or at some other inappropriate time that would inevitably result in a glare from the celebrant of the Mass, which would often terrify the new altar boy. On Palm Sunday, Easter or Christmas, there would always be the beautiful Gregorian chants and a soprano to sing during the High Mass. When you have young boys serving Mass and a fat lady up in the choir loft begins to sing in a high soprano voice that fills the Church, in this, the most sacred of places, this possibly could become a cause for great comic relief and it only takes one boy to start with the giggles. That is precisely what happened on numerous occasions. Apologies are in order to Miss Albina McMillan who indeed had a beautiful singing voice.

As experienced altar boys we came to know the idiosyncrasies of many of the priests.

Father Kelly liked two cruets of Mass wine and only a single drop of water poured into the chalice at his morning Mass. Father Murphy, a very pleasant man with a nervous twitch could very easily be made to laugh. He had a habit of rolling his sleeves up and down. He was always fidgeting with his vestments and he never failed to make me laugh. On the way out of the sacristy, as I would approach the altar to serve his Mass, Father Murphy who was walking behind me would often say, "Joe, be good," "Be good Joe." That was all I needed to hear, I would start to laugh and Father would smile.

On other occasions at the beginning of the Mass, Father would start to pray "Introibo ad altare Dei". He would then add, "Joe be good, Joe be good." Many a time when I was pouring the water and wine into his chalice, I would just look at him and I couldn't help myself, I would start to laugh uncontrollably. Father Murphy would sometimes give me a smirk but he would never get angry or cross with me. I guess he just took it in his stride. One could always get plenty of encouragement to laugh during the most sacred moments from the other holy terrors known as the altar boys. There was one very devout and saintly priest, who had an impediment in his speech who shall remain nameless. This priest spoke with a lisp, had a difficult time pronouncing some words, and had a distinct nasal quality to his voice. At the end of the Benediction, when he would recite the Litanies of the Saints, my friend Francis and I would mimic him as we knelt behind him at the altar. So instead of "blessed be God" you would hear "bess be God" and so on, and we would repeat everything we heard word for word, just like parrots, at the top of our voices. This good man never let on that he was aware of our antics.

It could be profitable being a popular altar boy with the congregation, because people would request for you to serve at their Wedding Mass, which always guaranteed a twenty dollar tip from the Best Man. When we were on the altar, we always had a captive audience at all of the services because the nuns from the elementary and the girl's school were in attendance. Traditionally, the sisters would be seated in the first few rows of pews directly before the main altar. Some of these sisters had taught us in school so they knew us. When we were not serving at the Mass, we were seated in the pews at the side of the main altar. My friend Francis and I would roll up our pant legs to our knees under our soutanes and show our legs by flexing them. Some of the other altar boys would follow our example. We had a full bag of tricks and at other times would silently laugh or try to make the other altar boys laugh when they were serving on the altar. This of course was just to show off and be cheeky. There was one young nun whom we called Hawkeye. We would sometimes catch her quietly smiling at our antics and that would make our day. The nuns were also very good to me personally. I was pigeon toed as a child and the nuns took it upon themselves to help. Two of the sisters would meet me at the Church door, each take me by an arm and have me walk down the street between them while instructing me to turn my feet outward. This went on for about six months. I'm happy to say it worked.

The lower level of this old Church was our meeting place. We were allowed to hang out there during a lapse in the services, or when we had nothing better to do. The priests had a huge kitchen in the refectory which was easily accessible from the basement level where we frequently spent our time. The kitchen was run by a recently hired young German woman named Bertha. One afternoon about six of us were sitting around after having finished chores in our hangout. We became hungry and I came up with the bright idea that we should go and ask Bertha the cook for food. We knew there was always a huge cooked ham and loaves of bread left on the kitchen table after meals in case the priests got hungry during the day. We marched up to the kitchen door and advised Bertha that Father Davis said she should give us something to eat because we were working in the basement that day. This is something we often did. We moved furniture and sorted large mounds of potatoes which were dumped by the truckload into the basement. We would sort out the bad ones and put them in garbage bins. There was always about fifty priests in residence, so food was always available. Bertha prepared huge ham sandwiches and gave us Cokes and apples, which we gleefully devoured and enjoyed. However, Father Davis got wind of our shenanigans and called both myself and Francis individually on the carpet. This kindly and gentle young priest who was in charge of the altar boys at this time had to give us a talking-to. Father told me that what I had done was treacherous, to which I responded, "Father, I don't know what that word means," and I truly did not know. Francis was told that he would be penalized and he did not know what that word meant either. I guess in the end all was forgiven. After all, we were hungry young boys and basically good kids.

I have assisted at many Funeral Masses. It is customary for the priest to meet the coffin at the Church door accompanied by a cross bearer and two acolytes with candles who lead the coffin placed on a gurney into the Church. I was an acolyte with a candle and as I passed by the coffin, the sleeve of my surplice became entangled in the handle on the side of the coffin and I started pulling the coffin up the Church aisle with me, until I realized what I was doing. At a subsequent Funeral Mass whilst standing behind a coffin at the front section of the Church, just prior to the final blessing of the coffin with holy water, I held the candle too close to my then spiky hair and singed it. On another occasion I actually did catch on fire as I was leaning over a votive stand at the Shrine of Our Lady unaware my surplice was going up in flames on my back. The flames went through my soutane. Lucky for me I did not burn my back. Some members of the congregation who were praying at the Shrine helped to put out the flames. Brother Andrew ran out of the sacristy and doused me with water. I would later refer to this as my Joan of Arc incident.

In addition to being an altar boy, I have always liked to sing and was accepted into the Church choir. I had a pleasant singing voice. I would sing Gesu Bambino at Midnight Mass on Christmas Eve when I was not serving on the altar. I also would sing solo at the Low Requiem Funeral Masses from the choir loft and I could not see the mourners seated in the Church below. After one such Mass, Father McElliott who was then the Rector, requested I stop whining when I sang the Funeral Mass, because he said that the people felt bad enough without me making them feel worse. I replied, "Well Father, it is a funeral and they are supposed to feel sad." I would intentionally sing the Sanctus in the most mournful way I possibly could, as I felt it was indeed a sad occasion.

Father McElliott once did something nice for me that made me feel good. There was a catered affair held at the Church on a Thursday attended by many people. At the end of the day there were plates of ham sandwiches left over. Father McElliott blessed the food and told me to take it home and tell my mother that we had a dispensation to eat meat on Friday. I could not have felt better if the Pope himself had given us permission. It was a big deal to get a dispensation to eat meat on a Friday.

The Corpus Christi procession was held annually in the Summer. This was a public procession of the Holy Eucharist through the streets of Griffintown. The procession would slowly wind its way from St. Ann's Church down McCord Street, move along Ottawa Street to Fire Station No. 3, which is located at the corner of Young and Ottawa Streets. (It is still in use). The faithful would line the streets and genuflect in adoration as the Blessed Sacrament passed by in a Monstrance held high above the crowd. Each year the firemen would work for a week erecting an altar in an outside corner area of the fire station. The altar was always beautifully decorated with flowers of every hue. Benediction would be held at the firemen's altar prior to the procession making its way back to St. Ann's Church to complete the Corpus Christi ritual.

For the procession of Summer 1953, I was designated as canopy bearer for the procession. The canopy was of a heavy brocade fabric with gold trim, fringes and tassels and decorated with religious symbolism. It resembled a large oversized umbrella weighing at least twenty pounds. My job was to hold the canopy above Father McElliott's head as he carried the Monstrance through the streets to the accompaniment of hymns being sung, the sweet aroma of frankincense filling the air, and the Religious and faithful praying in the warmth of a beautiful Summer's day. To my mind this was heaven on earth and holiness abounded. I considered it a great honour to be so near to the Blessed Sacrament as I walked very closely behind Father McElliott. The procession was over two hours long and at certain intervals my arms would get tired. Inadvertently, I would let the canopy move in a forward motion which caused the good Father Rector unable to see where he was walking. More than once that day I heard one of the other priests discreetly say to me, "Lift the canopy higher." At one point Father McElliott himself said to me, "I can't see. Get that thing out of my eyes." It was the fringes I think! I loved the procession, but I was most relieved when it was over because my arms were sore. I suspect that Father McElliott was grateful when at processions end we finally made it back to St. Ann's Church.

That same year on a chilly November evening on my way home from Benediction, the fog was so thick I could not see an inch in front of me. I was apprehensive as I scurried along Mountain Street in a hurry to reach home. I had crossed William Street and was now one block away from where I lived on Barre Street. I was wearing a jacket and an open neck shirt. From out of the dense fog a man dressed in black wearing a trench coat and a fedora appeared before me. He stood very close to me and seemed to be in his sixties and wore silver rimmed glasses on his round face. I did not know this individual and had never seen him before. I was so petrified that my heart leapt into my mouth. He spoke, asking where was I going. I responded that I was returning home from Church. He gave a wry smile and reached out to touch the small silver crucifix I was wearing around my neck which was clearly visible through my opened shirt. He reached out his hand and held the cross between his thumb and finger. I could feel his hand on my skin. He never said a word and with that, as quickly as he appeared, he seemed to evaporate back into the fog. I was so frightened and shocked that I ran all the way home without a backward glance. I have no idea who this person was. But I do know that after he touched the cross at my throat he disappeared before my eyes. In my teenage mind I felt that the cross protected me from something untoward.

1954 was the Centenary of St. Ann's Church and it was a big affair. The Church was painted and refurbished. New vestments of golden hued material were hand-made by the Church seamstress, Mary Bennett, for the priests. Even the altar boys had new soutanes made. His Eminence Paul-Emile Cardinal Leger celebrated the High Mass at which I was chosen to be the book bearer and to carry the book of the Gospel during the High Mass. I knelt before Cardinal Leger, holding the book as he read the Gospel. It was a very impressive scene with all the clergy in their vestments of gold, the altars lavishly appointed with flowers and palm plants, the people and the choir singing. It was a great celebration indeed. People came from all over the globe and many former parishioners visited St. Ann's on this joyful occasion. Excitement abounded everywhere, all guests were assigned seating. Large printed signs were placed on the pews to indicate the seating arrangements in the Church for the numerous events taking place. My personal contribution was to create my own hand-made sign which read, "Protestant Nuns to the Left" and I promptly displayed it in one of the rows of pews. My work of art went unnoticed for a few days, then all hell broke loose. I did get a good tongue-lashing for that one; I guess I was a little ahead of my time because the Ecumenical Councils were yet to come.

It was not all pray and play and no work. Being an altar boy in my case was a seven day a week affair. There was always something to do around the Church if one chose to lend a hand. I wanted to be near to God and this was the way I could do that. I spent many of my free hours at the Church and became very proficient at decorating the altars with flowers.

I was given the responsibility of caring for the altar dedicated to the Infant Jesus of Prague. This was my pride and joy. The statue of the Infant depicts the Child Jesus as a Little King dressed in a white silk robe and a cape which I changed in keeping with the liturgical seasons. I still maintain a fondness for the Infant Jesus of Prague.

Occasionally I would clean the marble altars with steel wool and Varsol. It was hard on the knees and required plenty of elbow grease and was not my favourite thing to do. One day whilst on my knees scrubbing away at one side altar, four tourists came into the Church. I could tell by their accents they were American. One of the men asked me if I was getting paid for doing this work. I responded, "No." He then asked me why I was scrubbing the altar. I replied, "I am working for the Lord," at which he proceeded to laugh directly in my face. Being a religious person, I was insulted and quite sure in my young mind that he was headed for the hot place.

However, at a later date I did get to replace the sacristan Brother Andrew, when he went on holiday for a month and I was paid forty dollars a week for my efforts. I would have gladly replaced him for free. I was given the responsibility of being in charge of the sacristy which I did for two consecutive Summers. I did want to be a lay brother, so it was good training for me.

In the Summer of 1954 there was quite a stir among the residents of Murray Street in Griffintown where my grandparents, The Bowkers lived. The old houses were built in and around an earthen courtyard. When it rained, the whole outdoor area became mud, consequently everyone had to be careful. My grandparents' home at 203G was two storeys in a building situated directly in the center of the courtyard. This provided Granny with a clear view of all the comings and goings as she sat in her favourite chair by the living-room window. She was quite excited to learn the three flats facing her home on the second floor walk-up were to be gutted and restored as a convent for the Missionaries of Charity, a Religious Order of nuns who dressed in simple white habits trimmed with blue. The sisters were committed to living amongst and serving the poor. The renovations were completed by Autumn and ready to receive the sisters. The neighbours were invited in to see the convent prior to the sisters' arrival. Later that Autumn, Brother Andrew requested I serve Mass one week-day morning at 7:30 for the sisters on Murray Street. It was to be a special Mass to open the convent and welcome the Head of the Order from India. I was yet to see an Indian person and I looked forward to it. I don't recall the Celebrant. All that I recall about the priest is that he was tall with dark hair and was new to the parish. We walked along Murray Street together to the new convent. I was impressed with the cleanliness and sparse furnishings. There were about ten sisters present for the Mass including the Mother Superior. Several of the sisters came from France. When the Mass was over, the sisters offered a cup of tea. The priest and I met the Mother Superior from India. I was surprised because I expected to see an Indian nun wearing a sari and not dressed in a habit. However, the Mother Superior turned out to be a tiny little woman about five feet tall with olive skin, not unlike my grandmother's size and colouring. She spoke with an accent that was foreign, but not Indian. She was nice and thanked Father and I for coming over to celebrate the Mass. Years later I was to recall that morning and it came to me very clearly in a flash. The simple white habit trimmed with blue worn by the sisters and the Mother Superior who had caused quite a stir among the sisters was not an Indian as I had anticipated in my mind but none other than Mother Teresa herself who was the Head of the Order. She had come from India to open this new house among the poor of Griffintown.

One of the tenets of The Roman Catholic Church is the examination of conscience before the confessing of sins prior to receiving Holy Communion. For a young person, going to confession can be heaven or hell, depending on the priest hearing your confession. A priest has the authority to grant one absolution for his sins. There are venial sins and there are mortal sins. As a child I really did not have many sins to confess. So every so often I would make things up, as a child is apt to do. I would say nonsensical things such as, "I got mad at my sister" or "I ate my brother's food". I am sure many Catholics will relate to this experience. Some priests were really tough and made you do heavy penances such as saying five decades of the rosary while kneeling or making the Stations of the Cross two times over. As children, we quickly learned who was the least stern of the priests to hear our confession and we let each other know.

We were most fortunate at St. Ann's to have a wonderful priest in our midst. Father Francis Kearney was a typical affable Irish-Canadian priest, with a ready smile. Everyone loved him, particularly the children. Father Kearney could be found sitting on the Church steps, sometimes having a cigarette and greeting all the passers–by with his most famous salutation, "Hello, honey." This warm welcome was given to all and sundry. To the mothers he would offer to trade two puppies and a kitten for their children. During the Second World War he was a Navy Chaplain. As a result of the wounds he received during the War, he was often in pain. He walked with the help of a cane and wore boots as opposed to shoes. The lines outside Father Kearney's confessional booth were always the longest. People would wait for him. Of course the confession was always anonymous and confidential. The secrets of the confessional were sacred. Even if one knew the priest, you had to pretend that you were speaking to a stranger. That is, except for Father Kearney. When you went into his confessional booth, you would start with the prerequisite "Bless me Father, for I have sinned" then make your confession. When you were finished Father Kearney would inevitably push back the wooden screen which separates priest from penitent, and greet you by name and inquire after your parents. Of course he would make his usual offer in exchange for two kittens or a puppy and let you off with a light penance. Sometimes he would just greet me by name, and inquire as to how I was doing before I began my confession.

This man had great compassion and a genuine love of humanity. Going to confession to Father Kearney was like Christmas compared to some of the other priests. He was always cheerful and reminded one that God loves us and that we were all His children. I surmise that he knew in his heart that the fire and brimstone never worked. I attribute his caring to the fact he had been a Chaplain, and knew what real hardship was. I was particularly fond of Father Kearney and would often rise at 5:00 am to serve his daily Mass at 6:00 am. During the Mass he always moved the missal on the stand for me from one side of the altar to the other. This made it easy for me, as I was not very tall and not too strong. That missal stand must have weighed at least thirty pounds. I would often sit on the Church steps and talk with him. He was a very gentle and spiritual man who truly believed in the goodness of people.

Father Kearney passed away on March 22, 1963. I had already left the Church by then. I recall attending his funeral which was a sad occasion for many people because he was so beloved. There must have been over five hundred people at the Mass. To this day his confessional booth from St. Ann's is preserved and kept in his memory along with a commemorative plaque at St. Gabriel's Church in Point St. Charles in Montreal.

By 1954 I had reached the age of fourteen and with the usual adolescent angst, I was starting to grow up and question my place in the Universe. I had a secret known only to God, myself and Father Kearney because for many years he had been my confessor. I continued to go to confession and that brought me comfort because Father Kearney was my link to God. He knew I was wrestling with my faith and my sexuality. Most of my confessions were about having impure thoughts and losing my temper. I knew I was homosexual and definitely attracted to members of my own sex. Father Kearney never condemned me or ever said a harsh word. We never discussed my personal life outside of the confessional booth as that was sacrosanct. I had always been very religious but now I felt myself to be cast upon the sea of uncertainty.

CHAPTER II
DESPAIR WITHOUT HOPE.
WHY ME GOD?

Although at fourteen years of age, self-loathing, guilt, unworthiness and feelings of utter desolation were frequent companions, they did not take over my life. I knew within my heart I was not a bad person. After all, I did possess intelligence and was able to reason some things out for myself. I knew I was different. I believed who and what I was, was something to be ashamed of according to the precepts of the Church that I so loved. I still harboured the hope of becoming a lay brother in the service of God. I was an average teenager growing up. I played baseball, hung around with the other kids, occasionally got into fights, played pranks on the neighbours by tying door knobs together, ringing both front door bells at the same time and then run and hide and laugh as grownups struggled to open their doors. I went to school, read an occasional book and rode rented bicycles as fast as I could into the wind along dark empty streets.

My father's mother Catherine Ryan had been a school teacher while living in Charlestown in the Boston area. As we were growing up she did not have much patience with us kids and would often scold us thinking that we were too rowdy. As I began to grow up I would visit her on my own. I enjoyed wonderful conversations with her. At thirteen she encouraged me to read books and I credit her for my interest in history. She gave me a copy of Young Bess by Margaret Irwin. This began my lifetime admiration of the Virgin Queen. I still read many books about her life. As it turned out reading books became a lifelong gift from my grandmother.

My grandmother passed in 1954, I was fourteen. We had by then become real pals and I was very sad when she died. Granny was looking forward to giving me a watch for my fifteenth birthday, I was too. Alas, she never made it.

In our religious instruction throughout our Catholic school years, we were inspired by stories about the lives of the Saints. We were encouraged to emulate them in our everyday life. To my young mind, Sainthood was something that one could aspire to and achieve. I was particularly fond of Saint Agnes who was an early martyr. The story goes that she was no more than thirteen years of age. In loyalty to Christ and to protect her innocence, she followed Our Lord to the death. This really impressed me. Incidentally, at St. Ann's Elementary School my favourite teacher was named Sister Agnes Marie. I would often entertain her and the other sisters with my rendition of "Five Minutes More", a hit parade song made popular by Frank Sinatra in 1946. Occasionally, for my efforts I would receive an extra bowl of strawberry flavoured pudding for dessert after the lunch hour meals were provided to us by the good sisters. I always related to Sister Agnes Marie and her kindness, and because of her name she reminded me of Saint Agnes. I would have gladly given up my life for Our Lord because that was an admirable thing to do.

As Roman Catholics we were taught the importance of sacrifice and encouraged to offer things up to The Sacred Heart of Jesus in reparation for the salvation of our souls and for all that He did for us. I took these matters very seriously and totally believed all I was taught. Although I did have my own ideas about the Blessed Trinity, we were instructed about the Father, the Son and the Holy Ghost as three persons in one God. In those days the Holy Spirit was called the Holy Ghost. However, as a child I always thought of the Trinity in the following manner: the Father was God the Father, the Son was Jesus and the Holy Ghost was the Uncle. How I deduced this was because my grandmother Maude and my grandfather Joseph Bowker lived together with my grandfathers' brother Uncle Henry in their house at 203G Murray Street. So, to my way of thinking, the three adults living together in the one house, was as three in one. It was simple. Uncle Henry was like the Holy Ghost.

When I was approximately thirteen, a minor accident resulted in a scar on my right knee. A tiny glass shard became embedded and remains there to this day. Often as a self punishing penance, I would kneel on this knee and offer up the pain while I was serving Mass or while praying before The Blessed Sacrament. I had read and been told that the mortification of the flesh was a way to avoid sins of the flesh and bring one closer to God, because suffering was good for the soul and would please God. Many of the Saints did this. We know from Church history wearing hair shirts was common practice in medieval times amongst pious members of the clergy.

During that same period of time, Brother Andrew who was then the sacristan at St. Ann's told me about the iron chains that some Religious wore around their waist to inflict pain and discipline the body. He showed me what appeared to be a large arm bracelet made of iron with little points on it. He informed me this was worn as an instrument of corporal punishment. The item functioned as a deterrent from sin and was referred to by some Religious as their jewellery. I have since learned the instrument I had seen was indeed a cilice. I was not surprised by this revelation because I knew Brother Andrew to be an extremely devout fellow who possessed a very strong yet simple faith. Brother Andrew frequently reminded me, since Our Lord had suffered so much by dying on the cross for us that pain and suffering made one a good Catholic, and it could be offered as atonement for sin.

Brother Andrew received permission for me to have his old cassock to wear. I was very pleased to have the same cassock a Redemptorist wore in place of my altar boy soutane which had nearly gone up in flames at Our Lady's Shrine. My soutane was now well-patched and frayed from daily use. The Redemptorist cassock comes with a cincture, which is the symbol of Chasity. The cincture is worn about the waist and serves to hold a large set of the rosary beads which is also worn and held together by a large strong pin secured at the side of the cassock. I received the cincture but not the rosary, and I took this token earnestly. Whenever I wore my cassock and cincture, as a further mortification of the flesh, I would stick the pin into my side and offer the pain up to the Sacred Heart of Jesus. If it got to be too painful, I then removed it. No one but myself was aware of my silent gestures. This was between God and me.

The ever present issue of my sexuality was never far from my mind and as a teenager I struggled with this. What was I to do? I would pray and ask God to give me a sign. Was this all a mistake? What is wrong with me? Help me please and change me. Why am I different? Why did you make me like this? Do something!

I did not know other boys like myself and often thought there must be other people like me, but I did not know of anyone. I knew I felt and thought differently. I also knew I had to keep my feelings and ideas to myself. I had no one to talk to, but I did know I was physically attracted to males. To me, that part was natural and simple, but being homosexual was nothing to be proud of in the poor working class neighbourhood where I was raised. I was street wise enough to keep this to myself. Being a queer or a fairy as one was labelled then, was frowned upon by the Church and held in contempt by society in general.

I did have a girlfriend for a while. She always wanted to kiss me and that really put me off. This lasted about six months. I had other aspirations. One was to become a lay brother. I had no interest in girls or for that matter, boys at the time.

I lived with the shadow of my own reality. Not that I was bad, but because I did not know any better and had no other options. I whole-heartedly believed in what the institution of the Roman Catholic Church taught, and not what was in my heart. To me the Church was the only portal through which I would find my way to God. Because I was so young and so religious, I believed a way always remained open to me. I became moody and temperamental, yet still I clung to my faith because it was all that I knew.

On one occasion, out of teenage curiosity I asked Father Baldwin, a good and decent priest whom I liked and respected, "Why was it that many of the young men of the parish go out drinking on a Saturday night and get drunk at the Town Casino?" The bar was located at the corner of Notre Dame and Mountain Streets. It was one block from where I lived on Barre Street and the hot spot to go in Griffintown. I would often see who was going in and staggering out of the bar on weekends. At the Sunday morning High Mass, many of these same young fellows in their late teens and early twenties were present with visible hangovers. I saw them sometimes looking pale and miserable, moving slowly as they picked up the collection and carried the offerings into the sacristy. I was yet too young to experience the misery of a hangover, so I had no idea how they felt. I could not comprehend why they would get drunk on a Saturday and then come to Mass the following morning. I have always remembered Father Baldwin's response. It was, "Joe, the little that they do come to Church does them some good." I thought this a very wise reply.

Retreats were occasionally held to keep the faithful in line. In one of the sermons preached by Father Baldwin during a retreat, Father referred to sinners as debased, degraded and diabolical. The Redemptorists are a Missionary Order. They were good preachers and could frighten the devil out of anyone, especially the young and the impressionable. And that is exactly how I felt as a teenager without guidance, scared out of my wits with no one to talk to about my inner feelings. Father's words remain ingrained to this day.

I felt God had deserted me and wondered why He would do such a rotten thing to a kid. Of course as a Roman Catholic, I believed that God and Jesus and the Holy Spirit were one and the same as defined by the mystery of the Blessed Trinity. Teenage angst was difficult enough to deal with, but this was a double whammy.

I would never pass a Catholic Church without stopping in. I would enter to speak to an invisible and silent God and in my prayers ask for a sign. I was really big on that one. I needed a signal from the Almighty that everything would be okay, and that I was okay. "Why me, God?" was my constant plea.

I would often find myself sitting alone in the silence of an empty Church thinking about my lot in life, and trying to gain some understanding. It gave me little comfort at times but I felt compelled to always drop into a Church just in case God had something to reveal to me. I kept on reaching out. After all I had great faith. But the inner turmoil and guilt were ever present. I wanted an answer from God. I was in for a long, long wait.

By the time I was seventeen and after a few years of seemingly unanswered prayers, I finally got fed up with all the praying and the pleading with God. I came to the conclusion that God had turned His back on me and there was no place for me in the Church. My personal integrity would not allow me to pursue a religious vocation because one had to make vows of Poverty, Chastity and Obedience to God. I felt then as I do now, that if you make vows to God then you had better mean it and be able to follow through. Vows are sacred contracts.

Poverty I could live with because I was already poor. Although I was fairly feisty, Obedience would have been easy enough. I could live with rules. However, I could not take a vow of Chastity. That would be more difficult to handle simply because I reasoned the natural inclinations of a human being could possibly lead to lustful or impure thoughts as I grew older and that would not do. Due to my sexual orientation I was already condemned to a life of a reprobate according to the teachings of Holy Mother Church. I had lost my faith and with that left the Church for good. I stopped praying. I simply did not believe in God any longer. He created me like this.

That is how it would be. I could live without Him and the Church.

And I did.

These were days of deep inner turmoil for me, because all I knew was the Church and I was very religious. So when I left of my own accord, I cut myself off deliberately. This was not an easy thing for me to do. Although it broke my heart, I felt it necessary for my survival in the world.

I had to find out who I was and to fight for my right to be who I was. I did not know what the battle was, but felt in my heart I had been dealt a dirty deal. I had to protect myself and live in my shadows without much hope for a happy future. Life was hard and hope was vague.

All I wanted was to be loved. God did not love me. At the time, I was quite certain of that. Maybe I could find someone who would and I would do it on my own. I had been holding down a job since I was fifteen and that had toughened me up somewhat. Now at seventeen I was anxious to see what life would bring.

CHAPTER III
SPIRIT IS WAITING

There was an excitement about being young as I set about my voyage of self-discovery. I was discovering a whole new world outside of my Griffintown roots. From the age of thirteen, the one big consolation in my life was music and the movies. I always liked to sing and the radio was forever playing in our house. I have fond memories of singing on CKVL's, "Call Me Uncle", a local amateur radio show. Occasionally on Friday nights my mother Emma would bring me to the Fairyland Movie Theatre on Notre Dame Street in Griffintown for the amateur hour. I enjoyed this because it was an opportunity to perform before a live audience. One of my favourite songs was, "If I Knew You Were Comin' I'd Have Baked A Cake". (However, I never won.) The movies held a special place in my heart and like all kids, it was a big deal when one got to go. It was within this milieu that I became aware of the first of two heroines in my life. My first heroine was Susan Hayward. I loved her films and was always excited to see her on the silver screen. My other favourite is singer, Joni James. Through many years of joy and sadness, through heartbreak and my hope of finding true love, Joni was my solace and inspiration through her songs and angelic voice. In their own way, each of these two accomplished artists affected my life on a very deep level and brought me inspiration and joy through their talents. They were a constant in my young life and have remained so through the years. Joni James on a very personal level as a friend, and the incomparable Susan Hayward through her many film roles.

I knew there was more to life than what I had previously experienced, and so life unfolded. My sexuality was a part of me, but it was not all of me. I was a person who happened to be homosexual, not a homosexual who happened to be a person. I accepted the fact that I was born homosexual and it is not a choice. On this I was clear.

For a period of time I wondered if I was the only one in the world with these leanings. I knew instinctively that this was not the case, but I had to find out for myself. So I set about to do so. I initiated my first encounter with an adult gay person. This was the beginning of a long and lasting platonic friendship.

On my own I discovered there were gay bars and certain restaurants where gay people congregated. I also found that the gay and lesbian group was diverse and consisted of individuals from all walks of life and professions. I soon learned not to be shocked by anyone's appearance, behaviour or antics. Each had his or her own story to tell and the discovery that there was a whole gay scene was news to me. I came to know other gay young men and found there were all types of '*enchanted*' people in society. I learned what the word 'camp' meant in a gay sense, and that to have a quick retort and a sharp wit was a very desirable asset in the gay world.

This was 1957 and homosexuality was illegal and a criminal offence, punishable by life imprisonment for practicing homosexuals. There were many raids on gay bars where numerous people were charged with gross indecency and carted off to jail in a paddy wagon. I have never personally had the experience, but I have witnessed raids on gay bars. Occasionally, I was present when uniformed Montreal police officers walked into a gay bar to make their presence felt. It was routine. It was not until 1969 that Prime Minister Pierre Elliott Trudeau said, "I think the view we take here is that there's no place for the state in the bedrooms of the nation. I think what is done in private by two adults doesn't concern the Criminal Code." Hence a revision of the Criminal Code in Canada became law.

Although my social circle was small, we made our own fun. Together, we would go to clubs, listen to music, take long walks and make the best of our situation. We had a good time. Life in general was far simpler then. We were a more innocent generation. None of my friends had come out to their families or friends, so one lived in two worlds. You could be arrested for dancing with a member of the same sex. In the gay clubs, there was a small red light above a door. If the red light flickered it meant the police were on their way. People would then scatter from the dance floor and rush to seat themselves at a table. We truly lived in a time when, "The love that dare not speak its name" was more truth than poetry.

I was young and naive but never obtuse. I approached life with trepidation and caution. I did fall in love for the first time when I was eighteen. Mike was a commercial air pilot who'd take me flying in a small rented Cessna. I sure was flying high. He was twenty-three and looked like John Gavin, the movie star. My first blush of young love quickly turned into a nightmare and lasted for approximately three months. I still lived on Barre Street with my parents. The street was not very well lit at night. The pilot and I would often sit in his parked car in front of our house where we would talk and sometimes kiss before I went in.

Apparently, I was observed by one of our neighbours, Mr. Timmons who would sit and look out of his third floor window late at night and of course had a view of me kissing a young man. Evidently, the cat was out of the bag but the irony of this little tale is Mr. Timmons kept this information strictly within the confines of his immediate adult family circle. My parents, family and other neighbours were never informed of my indiscretion. Hence, no one ever said a word to me. I only found this out about ten years ago, from my friend Francis, who is Mr. Timmons' nephew. To say the least, I was surprised and appreciated his discretion.

As for my first big love, I was later to discover that he was what is termed in the gay world a "chickenhawk." Mike had an appetite for young and innocent gay males who were new to the scene. I learned that after he drove me home, he then returned to a bar to pick up other young men, fresh off the farm, as it were.

This was my first broken heart. It was painful. It seemed love hurt more at eighteen. To help heal my aching heart, I listened to my Joni James records for hours on end, as Joni sang George Gershwin's "But Not For Me" the lyrics took on an all too meaningful significance for me. Her singing brought me solace as I wallowed in self-pity.

Life was beginning to teach me lessons and I knew there would be more life lessons to learn. Still all the while, there was an anxiety deep within. Inner peace eluded me.

Later that year I left home to set up my own apartment. I was eighteen, working, had a reasonable salary and wanted to be independent. My decision to leave home was my own. We were a large family and I wanted some respite from the activity of eleven people in one flat. I wanted to live my own life. I had had my first romance. This is what many did when one was gay in those days. If you could afford to, you left home and made your own way. My little adventure lasted only six months. I soon found myself back at the family hearth.

At twenty, I fell madly in love with a straight young man who worked with me at a delivery express company. He was a strapping, tough talking fellow of twenty-three. We had worked closely together for a couple of years during which time he married. It was a case of unrequited love for quite some time, but I knew he cared for me as much as he was able to. We did become close on a couple of occasions. That was enough for me. I was afraid and shy, enthralled and yet tortured at the same time. This was against all odds and we both knew it. He was always very kind to me and we did have some good laughs together. I thoroughly enjoyed his company. He was a street-wise, quick witted, tough and intelligent person.

He left our place of employment in the Summer and my world came crashing down around me. I was distraught and broken hearted. This set in motion the searing remembrances of my youth that were never quite far from the surface. These buried memories cut into my heart like a knife. The years of pent-up emotion, anguish and self-loathing rose once again to the fore. I decided to end it all. I cunningly stocked up over forty Seconal capsules. On the evening of Friday, August 31, 1962, I swallowed the lot, plus some Aspirin for good measure and went to bed.

When by Saturday evening I had not yet emerged from my bedroom, my family became concerned. Apparently, my breathing had naturally become laboured by that time and I was turning grey. I was rushed to the Montreal General Hospital by ambulance from our family house at 3490 Joseph Street in Verdun where an emergency tracheotomy was performed. It saved my life.

I remained unconscious for six days. It was touch and go for a while. A Doctor later informed me the only reason I survived was because I was young and able to fight for my life. The diagnosis was acute barbiturate poisoning. I remember coming to in the Intensive Care Unit and a Doctor telling me they had to cut a hole in my throat so I could breathe. He also told me I was in very famous company because Elizabeth Taylor had recently had the same operation. In order to make their point, the Doctors conveniently left large bottles of the contents pumped from my stomach on the floor in my hospital room, where they were quite visible to me. They were positioned where I was certain to see the evidence.

The Doctor who performed my surgery was the Chief of Emergency at the time. It was he who informed me of my status when I regained consciousness. Shortly after I was released, a group of friends and I attended a live performance by Marlene Dietrich at Her Majesty's Theatre. In the audience was the same Doctor who had saved my life. We acknowledged one another with a slight nod.

While in the hospital, the resident psychiatrist would visit in an attempt to have me talk and admit that I was homosexual. I took an intense dislike to him. He was always trying to twist my words and trick me. For example, he asked if I had my own room at home, and I replied I did. He then went on to inquire if I spent a lot of time on my own in the room away from the rest of my family. I replied that I did because I liked to be quiet and listen to my music. My room was at the end of the house so it was conducive for reading and playing my records. He proceeded to make a statement to the effect that I did not like my family and did not want to be around them. I simply replied that was not what I said. I would not cooperate with him. One day I overheard him talking to Dr. David Hawkins within my earshot stating I was very cunning. I took it as a compliment because I thought that he was an ass. He finally gave up and stopped bothering me.

Another day I received a visit from the Catholic Chaplain who informed me he had given me Extreme Unction, the Last Rites of the Catholic Church. This was done when I was brought unconscious into the hospital. Well! I was not amused and promptly told him "to mind his own business and leave me alone." The poor man scurried out of my room in a hurry. Considering the conditions in my life at the time, I felt abandoned by God and the Church. I had been living in the depths of despair and thought this was an unwelcome intrusion into my private life, and I was not having it.

Eventually I began a dialogue with Dr. David Hawkins. He was a young physician from Newfoundland. In one of our conversations, he reminded me I was living in a world with other people and could not build a fence around my world to keep out all the people I did not like. Apparently, as I was coming out of my coma, I babbled incessantly and the Doctors knew my whole story anyway. I just wasn't talking when I was conscious. Dr. Hawkins did get through to me. I trusted and respected him and spoke very openly with him.

I had wanted to end my life because of my self-loathing which was a result of my sexual identity and my religion. I felt I was damned anyway. Although I was aware of the gay world around me, I subsisted within my gloom and was not at peace within my soul. There was still a constant pathos and emptiness which lurked deep within but I couldn't put my finger on it. I physically felt the emptiness in the pit of my stomach.

The spark which prompted my suicide attempt was the loss of the man I longed for and adored. Even though I knew the situation to be impossible, the removal of his presence from my life triggered a cascade of feelings over which I had no control. I saw no further point to my life. I remained in the hospital approximately one month. I was released on a Saturday, and no one came to meet me. My parents did not have a car and did not know I was to be released that day. I left the hospital on my own and walking down the long hill to the bus stop, I feared I would pass out because I felt so weak. It was a very sad day for me. I felt very alone but I finally made it home by bus.

Dr. Hawkins gave me his phone number and told me to call him anytime I needed to talk. And I did, for almost a year afterwards. I would be out late at night at a bar and if I was depressed or feeling blue, I would ask a friend to drive me to the hospital. Dr. Hawkins worked the night shift and always made time for me. He was consistently helpful and kind. I am forever grateful to him for his kindness and concern for a young and troubled man.

In the years that followed I would run into my strapping friend on the street and we'd occasionally have a friendly drink. He was not aware of what occurred. My family knew of my attempted suicide but it was never mentioned. The tracheotomy became my battle scar. I had been through my own wars and wear it with pride. During the next few years until I was about twenty-six, I continued to experience the emptiness within. Because of my heightened sensitivity I often struggled with feelings of unworthiness and low self-esteem. I simply did not care and tried to do myself in on a couple of other occasions. The results of these futile attempts were only to make me sick to my stomach and did not require hospitalization.

I eventually realized this was not the way for me to go. These were dark times. I had not yet attained inner peace or found purpose in my life. I still lived in the shadows but unbeknownst to me, the Light was beckoning. I could not see it. Not yet.

I was not a bar person, that scene was never for me. I was not promiscuous, nor had I any inclination to be so. I was and remain a hopeless romantic. I had seen much, was influenced by very little and I was not easily shocked. I have always chosen my friends carefully. If I did not like an individual's personality, I had little time for them.

There was someone whom I did not care for, he was a friend of a friend, so I was polite but reserved with him. He had the following to say about me, "Every time I talk to that bitch, it is like having an audience with Queen Victoria." In reference to my attempted suicide he quipped, "He has a peaches and pills complexion". I loved it. I appreciated his wit.

When I was twenty-two, I was granted a Green Card to the United States and moved to New York City. The New York experience lasted ten months only. The highlight of my time in New York was that I was able to see my idol Joni James perform live at the Wildwood Manor in Wildwood, New Jersey. I was overjoyed. Joni dedicated a song to me during the show, she sang, "Too Marvelous For Words" to me. During this same period I saw Judy Garland perform at Forrest Hills.

One evening I received an urgent telephone call from my mother, Emma telling me my father was to undergo a serious operation and I had better come home. He was scheduled for a mastoidectomy surgery and there was a possibility he could die. My father had been afflicted with hearing loss for as far back as I could remember. My mother's call scared me. I liked living in New York but it wasn't a big deal for me to come home. I did not know many people in the city and I did miss my family and friends. I was the eldest son, so I returned home to be with my family in case something happened to Daddy. This was my duty because there were still five younger siblings at home and I would be responsible for them.

My father survived the operation. I remained with my family for less than a year. I then accepted an invitation from my friends, Dick Hillrich and Howard LeMessurier who had recently rented a large penthouse apartment at 4545 Walkley

Avenue. They offered me room and board. They had been a couple for over twenty years, so we were like a little family. I secured employment with Cunard Steamships, thanks to the kindness of a neighbour who lived in the apartment beneath us. She quizzed me one day in the elevator, enquiring if I was the one who at night dropped my shoes on the floor above her head. I confirmed it was indeed me and promised to be more aware. She was a lovely woman who just happened to work in the Cunard personnel department, hence the job.

In those days there were taverns in Montreal designated for men only. Beer was the only beverage served. I along with friends would frequent the Altese Tavern in the city's east end. I preferred Molson's ale and when in the mood, would have a couple of beers. I did not drink often so it did not take much for me to get a tad drunk.

My good friend and trusted confidant Alvin Cohen knew me very well. He also knew when I was tipsy. My hands would become very hot and red. I would sit holding my hands before me, staring at them like a drunken fool, sometimes for hours. I recall telling Alvin that someday I would do something with these hands. However, I had no clue as to what it was.

A few years later I finally figured it out. My mediumship is in my hands and it is a signal Spirit is near to me. Now when I do message work and readings, I feel everything with my hands. So unbeknownst to me, even in those days, I was being set-up for my future work. In essence, I had turned my back on God, but God had not turned His back on me. He was waiting for me to catch up, but I was not yet prepared.

The gay world was a tough one and contrary to what some people believe, not a place for sissies. You had to be able to stand on your own two feet and keep your wits about you.

At twenty-five I was still living with Dick and Howard. After so many years together they decided to go their separate ways. This meant I had to move and secure new accommodation. I was working at Cunard and as fate would have it, was laid off from my job. I had just signed a lease on a small apartment in Verdun and was soon scheduled to move. From out of the blue I contracted Hepatitis A, apparently attributed to Chinese food that I had recently eaten. My liver was seriously compromised. The Doctor informed me I needed to be on complete bed rest for perhaps one year and it would be necessary to go into a Convalescent Home for recovery.

Here I was at twenty-five without a home, job or money and I was going into a Convalescent Home for one year. I will never forget a drizzling and cold November evening in 1965 when my friends Bob Forrest, Ronnie Glenn and Jean St-Pierre rented a U-Haul to move my furniture into the basement of Jean's father's house on Marcil Avenue for storage.

I remember sitting on the curb utterly overwhelmed and desolate. I was headed to the Convalescent Home the following morning. Upon my arrival at the Convalescent Home, I received a telephone call from the landlord of the Verdun apartment I had committed to. I had signed a lease with his sister and as it turned out, he was a Monsignor in the Church and threatened to sue me. I told him to go right ahead. I was in a hospital, had no job or money, so he could please himself. I was not to hear from him again. I guess he must have been inspired by the Holy Spirit. My time in the Convalescent Home lasted nine months. I was confined to bed rest for the period of time. It wasn't so bad though. I read books and my family and friends visited. I recovered and was reinstated by Cunard, so I was able to support myself, find a new apartment and get on with life.

I had become very cynical however, every so often I would find myself stopping into a quiet Church to think and meditate. There were stirrings within my being, but I was not sure what they were. I was still an anxious, unsettled soul.

In December of 1966 my friend Carol Tucker, who was employed by Eastern Airlines suggested I apply for a job at Eastern. The company had recently opened a reservations office in Montreal. I wasn't certain I would get a job, but I did. I was hired on December 12, 1966.

Whilst at Eastern I met Terry Martel who was a friend of Millie Gordon, the woman who was destined to become my first spiritual teacher and help place me on the path of understanding.

My true work was about to begin. Spirit was waiting.

CHAPTER IV
SPIRIT COMES IN

At the age of twenty-six my life was beginning to change for the better. I thoroughly enjoyed my job at Eastern Airlines. I was soon to determine airline people were a breed unto themselves. I liked being part of the industry. The office was centrally located in an older second floor walk-up building on Mountain Street in downtown Montreal. It was never quiet on weekends and we could always hear the racket from the street below. Montreal was a happening town and it all seemed to be occurring right on Mountain Street. Frequently we looked through the window to view the passers-by below us, in between taking telephone calls of course.

Eastern was a whole new world to me. I had come from working at Cunard Steamship which was a typically British well-run 'stiff upper lip' class conscious office environment. Everyone was very polite and proper. We all knew our place. However, I did enjoy the work and the fine people with whom I worked.

By contrast, working in the Eastern Airlines reservations office was akin to entering a Fellini movie. We were quite a varied and eclectic cast of characters. Montreal has always been known for its beautiful, chic and stylish women. I found myself in the midst of several of these fabulous dames, right in my own office. The staff consisted of beautiful ex-models, Joanne Munro, Lise Ouellette, and Carole Stevenson to mention but a few. A number of these colourful and cultured women in the office were former flight attendants. In those days you were not permitted to wear blue jeans to work. A strict dress code was in place for all employees. Business attire was the rule. There was never a dull moment in the office. We worked in shifts and were constantly busy. We knew how to party and we did. It was always fun and very social. Subsequently, many enduring friendships were forged.

One of the more memorable personages was Ms. Denise Belair, a former telephone operator with Bell Canada. Denise, a charming and delightful creature came to be known as "La Divine." When she was fed-up with a client on the line, she'd throw her headset down on her desk upon the completion of the call and say; "J'ai mon voyage" (loosely translated in English, "I've had enough"). She was our own Sarah Bernhardt, well groomed, gracious and professional.

Carole Roherty was our chain smoking gal with a heart of gold. Originally from Beldoon, New Brunswick, this earned her the moniker "Bertha Beldoon." When a new reservation agent (myself included), fresh out of training would initially begin to answer the reservations line, as a rite of passage Miss Roherty would call we newly minted and unsuspecting agents from her home, usually near nine o'clock in the evening. She would pretend to be a travel agent with a mean streak and give us a rough time over the telephone. She would frighten the wits out of us by asking questions she knew we could not answer or have us book itineraries to far and out of the way destinations almost impossible to get to. She would then rebuke us because we were too slow. As soon as one answered the line she would intimate the individual by asking "what's your name" or "who am I speaking to" in her most aggressive manner, but always in a very low voice. In this way she would gain the upper hand and the stage was set for thirty minutes of dread. We did not know if and when our calls were monitored. So one always had to be polite and courteous, this was our job. You would not dare to be unresponsive to her demands. Bertha Beldoon loved it all and few new agents were spared her prank calls. During working hours she would request I sing, "How Important Can It Be" while she puffed away on her cigarette. This would be either in the lunch room or at her work station. I did the latter very quietly because we were not allowed to sing in the office. Joni James was her favourite singer, so that was all right by me.

Miss Carol Tucker, my stalwart friend who encouraged me to apply for the job and whom I still refer to as "Miss Tucker", was 'camp' with a capitol C. She was beautiful and cheeky, had a million dollar personality and the brains to match. When she gave her name to the passengers she would say; "That's Tucker with a T". In 1967, into this crazy world at nineteen years of age came the innocent Gloria Gari with her long flaming red hair. We became fast friends. The Blonde Bomber, Noella Martinez joined us soon after. I would often stop and chat to Noella as she worked the teletype machine. This was the beginning of another lasting friendship.

One grew up quickly at Eastern. Our office was an exciting and wonderful place to work. No one cared if you were straight, gay or indifferent. And I wasn't the only gay in the village! I was destined to spend twenty-three years of my life there. We were all part of a huge family at Eastern and proud to be a part of "The Wings of Man", Eastern's tagline. Our work environment made the job pleasant and fun. Travel opened a new door to the world for me and it afforded many opportunities for my personal growth in the years to come. Particularly as time went by, it enabled me to travel for my spiritual work, and travel I did.

Millie Gordon and I finally met on a cold February evening. We hit it off immediately. I listened in rapt attention as she shared her many spiritual experiences with this eager young man, interested to hear her every word. This was the start of a long friendship.

On my visits with Millie she would read my palm, we would drink tea and she would then read the tea leaves for me. She sometimes read my cards. Who could ask for anything more? There was so much to learn and to know. This was the beginning of a lifelong adventure. Le Mystique was a popular gay bar on Stanley Street where friends and I would sometimes go. Ironically, a few doors away was a Spiritualist Church located in the basement of an office building. I would wait around outside the building watching the people go to a Sunday night meeting. I did not gather the nerve to go in and I did not know what to expect, so I was reluctant to venture forth. Finally, one Sunday evening after three weeks of scouting the place out, my friends went into the bar and I went into the Church. On this first visit, I stood at the back of the room observing the service. I was a little put off because they were reading the Bible. They were obviously Protestant. Coming from my Catholic background, I wasn't yet ready for that. I was still not on the best terms with God at that time so the Bible bit threw me off. The medium was a smallish woman who spoke at quite a clip as she conveyed Spirit messages. Although her diction indicated she was not an educated woman, I surmised she was a good clairvoyant as I listened and paid attention to the messages she gave to the members of the congregation. They seemed to understand and accept them. I went back for a couple of weeks, but never received a message. One evening after the service I asked the medium if she could recommend books for me to read. She replied "Oh no, don't you read no books, come to us and we'll teach you all you need to know." I knew she meant well but I needed to be conversant about Spiritualism. I had been reading all manner of books I could obtain on the subject. So this would not do for me and I never returned to the Stanley Street Church.

I heard of another Spiritualist Church on Guy Street. This Church was run by the Reverends Charles and Janet Graydon, a Scottish couple in their sixties. Charlie Graydon was a very good medium who worked with a Guide named Lusing. Mrs Graydon was a Spiritual Healer who also conducted Spiritual development classes for beginners. As I was wont to do, I was cautious when I first started to attend the Graydon's Church. I am by nature reserved and shy, therefore I would sit at the back of the Church hall and listen to other people's messages, taking it all in. I observed this was a much larger congregation than the previous Church on Stanley Street.

Something was changing within me. I began feeling a semblance of inner peace. Since my spiritual talks with Millie, my faith in the Almighty was slowly being rekindled and I was earnest in my search. After attending the Church for a couple of months, I started receiving messages from Lusing through his medium, Mr. Graydon. He would tell me to be patient and advise me Spirit would work with me one day. It was always the same message. As an added incentive he'd say, "Remember, Rome wasn't built in a day." This became a standing joke with me. I would eventually repeat the words in singsong fashion along with him. I was not really interested in developing psychically. All I wanted was inner peace. I truly had no desire to become a medium. I was beginning to acquire some stillness within. That was enough for me.

During a service I would at times feel energy and warmth around the crown of my head and occasionally feel what could be best described as little shots of electricity. I liked the sensations but was not yet aware of what they were.

As it turned out my friend Gloria Gari expressed an interest in Spiritualism. We would attend the Sunday evening services together. On one such occasion, Gloria turned to me during the service, pointed to the raised platform where the Reverend Charlie Graydon was standing giving messages to the congregation and said, "I see you up there one day giving messages." I looked at her and said, "Are you nuts, that will never happen." In response Gloria simply smiled.

I was invited to participate in Mrs. Janet Graydon's development class and accepted. At the class Mrs. Graydon seated me next to her. Directly above me a floor lamp remained lit during the class. It would get on my nerves because it is not easy to meditate or concentrate with a light shining in your eyes. I would have preferred to sit in total darkness. I would sometimes close my eyes and feel energy covering my whole head. I could feel the power and I knew it was not my imagination. It was the only experience I had for quite some time. However, Mrs. Graydon would insist I was receiving impressions, which I never did. At the time I was not receiving any thoughts or impressions in any way, shape or form and would not make things up.

During the classes, I did notice my breathing was becoming much heavier than normal. My legs seemed to stretch and become much longer than they normally were. I was aware of other physical sensations as well. My hands would get hot and I could feel the energy around my head. It felt heavy and I would feel as if I wanted to doze off. I would sense Spirit was near. I would totally relax and enjoy a feeling of serenity and peace when this would happen. I remember the joy I felt within my heart combined with a sense of wonderment and anticipation as I began to discover I could feel the presence of Spirit about me. I was very pleased by this turn of events.

This was a far cry from the years of anguish and spiritual desolation that I had become accustomed to. At times, I could faintly see another person in the room being transfigured. My psychic centers were beginning to open. I had no fear, I trusted in Spirit and knew I was protected. I would surround myself with a white light and pray before every class. I was re-establishing a personal relationship with The Eternal One. I witnessed the spiritual growth of the other students in the development class as they became more confident in the impressions they received and shared with the class. This was not the case with me, my primary consideration was to feel spiritually alive and to become more aware.

As months passed during the development classes, I began to experience sensations in the throat area and my throat would become very dry. I sensed and felt that someone was trying to speak through me. It was as if they had to learn how to speak first. One evening I sensed Spirit come closer than ever before. Mrs. Graydon was aware that Spirit was trying to come through me. She lifted me to my feet whilst holding my hands in hers to give the Spirit entity more energy. I could feel the power surging throughout my body. It felt like little jolts of electrical shocks. I did not shake, it was a very gentle sensation and I felt impressed to speak. I seemed to gag on the words and could not get anything out. I remember making a sound akin to "ah ah ah." This became a weekly occurrence as I was concentrated on. Spirit was coming closer.

I was aware of what was taking place yet I seemed to be observing myself from afar. In the following weeks when it was my turn to be concentrated upon, I would receive impressions and be encouraged to speak. It took some time before I could actually get words out. I was advised by Mrs. Graydon that Spirit was building a voice box within my throat which made it easier to project my voice. I am naturally soft spoken, however to this day when I speak in public, I do not need a microphone to be heard. This was the beginning of Spirit using me in an inspirational manner. I would sometimes open with a quote such as, "Consider The Lilies of The Field" from the Scriptures. The thoughts came quickly and the words flowed out. It was like turning on a spigot. I would not have time to think and talk at the same time. I was not very articulate then. This was quite an experience. There would often be an inflection in my voice and my vocabulary seemed to considerably improve when I was in this altered state of consciousness.

This condition is referred to as working in control, which means exactly what it implies. It is a slight trance state and a discarnate entity is controlling the medium's body and voice box; similar to a puppet on a string, in a very gentle manner of course. The first entity who actually identified himself when he was speaking through me whilst I was in control was Mr. Wong. As I sat in class, I would begin to feel a tightening around my forehead as if I was wearing a headband. At other times the energy would cover not only my forehead but also the complete top of my head. It felt as if I was wearing a helmet or a cap placed very tightly against my skin, not unlike a bathing cap. There was a weight to the energy and I felt as if it was superimposed over my entire body. It was palpable. I would concentrate on my breathing. A feeling of serenity and complete peace would ensue. I realize now the center of the forehead (my third eye) and the crown chakra (top of the head) were being manipulated and worked on by Spirit. I had begun to feel these sensations at night-time when I went to bed. This was not my imagination. There were adjustments being made to my etheric body and I sometimes physically registered them. This experiment from the other side went on for quite a few sessions. The same physical sensations would manifest each time. I'd sit in the chair and open myself up to the energy. I could feel the energy in my body shifting.

I would often appear to be and feel much taller than I am at 5'7 ft. The other members of the class and I could tell the difference as Spirit overshadowed me. I would be in what I later came to know as an altered state of consciousness. Heretofore, I had never in my life experienced anything like this and I knew I was not hallucinating. It was all a little bewildering and unusual, but never frightening. I actually looked forward to these sensations. This was a new adventure for me and it was evident that something was occurring.

I was regularly attending the Church. To be of service I offered to vacuum and clean the Church on Saturdays. Upon completing my chores, I would now and again sit in the quiet of the darkened meditation room.

I would relax, breathe gently then wait to ascertain if I could feel Spirit coming closer to me. I wanted to become familiar with the sensations I was experiencing whilst in the development class. I always thought of these moments as practice sessions for Spirit to come closer to me physically. The room was pitch black and I would see billows of energy which appeared like little white puffs of smoke. I could see what appeared to be static bolts of electricity as well. The occasional Spirit Light would appear and disappear quickly in a flash. Spirits manifest in the form of tiny pings of silvery white or blue light. I understand that even in normal circumstances while a person is sitting in a dark room, one can detect some form of energy in the ether.

I desired to become accustomed to Spirit and to have a sense of when they were around. I would sit and pray and talk to Spirit and pour my heart out. After all, I was trying to find my way back to God after years of ignoring Him.

I wanted to be free from the suffering I had imposed upon myself due to my natural inclinations and misguided religious beliefs. I would talk to Spirit in the darkness. I could not see clairvoyantly at the time but I sensed in the stillness of the room someone was listening. I put myself out there and fervently sought to get in touch with my inner self. I began to notice slowly but surely that the anxious and unsettled feelings which had been my constant companions for years were beginning to dissipate. I was starting to feel better about myself as an individual; and to feel complacent and natural with the presence of Spirit as I sat in prayer and meditation during these moments of solitary communion.

I would pray to God, addressing Him by the name of Great Spirit, which I was totally comfortable in doing. I continued to read, informing myself about Spirit and Spiritualism. I was slowly regaining my faith. Not unlike a leery child, I was hesitant in my personal dealings with the people at the Church who were in the know, and for the most part, experienced Spiritualists. I took everything in, asked questions and said little in response. This was all new to me and I was determined not to make any blunders. I had been out in the cold for much too long and I wanted to be sure. I was very forthright in my questioning. I instinctively trusted Spirit, but as for people, I waited and I watched. I wanted this to be real. This was my inner life I was dealing with. I was always circumspect and kept my own counsel, until I got to know and felt comfortable with someone.

I was elated as I started to further develop and was able to feel Spirit coming closer within my aura. It was a discernible feeling for me. I experienced true peace of soul for the first time in years. I had had a sense of unworthiness since my youth. So I was blissful, amazed and grateful that Spirit was coming close to someone like me. The abject years of wondering, of asking for signs and of self-contempt were slowly coming to a close. God was responding to me after all. I never believed it would happen.

I was a child of the Great Spirit and I was reconnecting. A few years later during a service at Camp Lily Dale in upstate New York, I heard the medium, Harry Malesi deliver a message to someone in the audience stating, "The Great Spirit does not care who you are or what you are." I thought to myself, if only I had heard that message when I was a teenager.

One evening during our development class an interesting event occurred. Spirit was slowly beginning to manifest through me and I was being concentrated on by the class. The usual members were present, we were eight in the room. I was working in control. Spirit had raised me to my feet with the help of Mrs. Graydon who held both my hands and then released me to stand on my own. I was standing in the center of the circle, about five feet from my chair. My eyes were closed and I was in an altered state of consciousness. My chair rested behind me a few feet away. The Spirit entity known as Mr. Wong began to speak through me. From out of the blue, another male member of the class, allegedly in a trance state, rose to his feet and started to berate me in a hysterical voice screaming at my Guide, "Your instrument is unworthy, he is unworthy." Well... pardon the pun, all hell broke loose!

In a split second Mr. Wong had stepped aside and I could feel a forceful shift of energy and strength entering into my body. My Doorkeeper, a Guide (who shall remain nameless) is an Aztec Warrior. He is responsible for my protection and he instantly took over my body. I could feel the shift because he is over six feet tall, very powerfully built, and I was familiar with his vibration. In a loud and booming voice he commanded the so called entity to stand down. He addressed the other student in a voice filled with fury and said, "How dare you attack our instrument. We will prove to you we are here and our instrument is worthy. We are working through him. I am now going to place him backward in his chair." I was standing about five feet away from my seat in the center of the circle. With that, I was suddenly returned to my chair in a backup motion. My eyes were still closed and I remained under Spirit's control. I was then unceremoniously plunked backwards with a thud into my seat. I was startled. You could feel the tension in the room. Mrs. Graydon was beside herself and let it be known that she had never witnessed anything like this in all of her years in Spiritualism. I gathered my composure, got up from my seat and walked over to the individual to inquire if he was alright. He was clearly shaken. Suffice to say, I have no further comment on this incident. It is a known fact that in a well-run development class with an experienced teacher, such as Mrs. Graydon was, this sort of incident does not occur. Spirit knows the rules, and adheres to them.

It is very unusual that two Spirit entities would take control of different individuals, particularly neophytes, at the same time in an everyday development class. For the record, development classes are conducted to train the Spirit entities as well as the student medium. There is a code of behaviour on how to approach a medium from Spirit side. The leader of the development class always issues clear instructions to the Spirit entity to insure all is conducted in a smooth and respectful manner, without risk to any individuals concerned. This is often a learning experience for both the budding medium and the Spirit entity.

There are specific circumstances when such events could occur, when two mediums are entranced at the same time. This would be in a rescue circle. It is not uncommon in that instance for two individual mediums who are trained and experienced as rescue mediums to be in trance at the same time. This allows the lost or struggling Spirit entity to enter their body (in Spiritualist circles this is referred to as taking the rescue). The second medium also enters into the trance state which enables their personal Spirit Guide to use the medium's body and more specifically their vocal cords, to converse with the lost or confused entity. The entranced medium's Guide will open up a conversation to encourage the struggling Spirit to look for and to see the Light. Another Spirit entity would then guide them into the Light. These conversations may take some time depending on the level of awareness and the willingness on the part of the lost or struggling entity to move towards the Light. Rescue circles are not a spur of the moment thing and at times can become quite long and involved affairs. Frequently, the lost entity may not be aware that they have died and possibly would not have any concept as to where they are or what is taking place. Rescue circles are often comprised of three experienced mediums and other Spiritualists who function as batteries for the entranced mediums and as observers of the rescue. This subject is detailed in Chapter 15, Struggling Spirits.

After this episode, I believed the harmony of the group had been compromised. This was not a game to me. I took my spiritual development very seriously. I was beginning to feel a semblance of inner tranquility and I was not about to have it disturbed. I had waited too long for this and I began to feel a glimmer of hope I was on to something that was real for me. This incident put me off on one hand, but on the other, I then knew for certain I was truly protected by Spirit and that gave me great comfort. I sincerely appreciated what I had learned at the Church but I would soon leave Mrs. Graydon's class to continue my spiritual unfoldment on my own.

I had complete faith in Spirit and I decided to start a spiritual development circle in my home. I invited several of my work colleagues who had an interest in Spiritualism and related spiritual matters to join me. Gloria and Noella agreed and two of my classmates from the Church, Gwen and Jack requested to join us. My friend Eddie Barr who was developing as a medium also joined our class. Carl Cormier, another Eastern Airlines colleague came to our class at a later time and remained with us for several years. The conditions for our group were simple. Be clear and sincere in your motives. Show up. Be on time. Be in harmony with the group and remember this was not a competition. I believed I had gained enough experience and basic knowledge to conduct a class and I knew Spirit would lead us where they wanted us to go.

We would open our class with The Lord's Prayer and ask that a Light of Protection be placed around the group. In order to raise the vibrations we sang hymns and other songs when so inclined. We would also chant the Om Namah Shivaya mantra from time to time. We concentrated on each individual in turn. We discussed spiritual matters, shared experiences and always concluded with a prayer of thanksgiving for blessings received. We acknowledged our Spirit Associates for their guidance and direction. I conducted the class intuitively and never encountered problems.

By this time I had made peace with God and had complete faith in His power and in His guidance. I also became aware of the First Spiritual Church of Montreal located at 2186 St. Catherine Street, West. This was the largest Spiritualist Church in Montreal. I started to attend and later became a member.

Working at the First at the time were two very talented mediums, namely Mrs. Margaret "Peggy" Eaton and Elizabeth McIntosh. Our development class had been meeting for well over a year when I asked Peggy to come as a guest to see how we were doing. She graciously obliged and stated she was very pleased with how the class was conducted. We were doing just fine. After her initial visit, Peggy would come as a guest every few months. We were always happy to see her. Elizabeth would also visit on occasion. It seemed Spirit had guided us along and we actually developed without the assistance of a fully trained medium.

Initially my Spirit Guide, Mr. Wong would work through me while I was in the control state and he would address and often teach the group. As the years went by, various other Spirit entities, each with a recognizable vibration and distinct personality were to come through to speak with us and bring teachings. Some members of the class were able to see them clairvoyantly as they overshadowed me. I never knew who would manifest during any given class.

The following is a recollection from Noella Martinez who shares her experience of one of our development classes:

Joey and I were colleagues at Eastern Airlines in Montreal when he introduced me to Spiritualism in 1968. He informed me of a Spiritualist Church on Guy Street founded by The Reverends Graydon. On Sunday evenings I attended services accompanied by my husband Jose and my nephew Jean, who had a lung condition that affected his breathing. After the Sunday service, Mrs. Janet Graydon would give him Spiritual Healing by the laying on of hands. As I observed Mrs. Graydon working, the thought came to me that I could be used as a healing vessel. This was later confirmed by Spirit via various messages I received through mediums and within our development class. As a result I have been practicing Spiritual Healing for a number of years. This was to be my gift from Spirit, although I was not fully aware of it at that time in 1968.

When Joey started to hold his development classes at his home, he invited me to attend. Our meetings were held on Tuesday evenings at 8:00 pm. There would be at least eight people in attendance. He always stressed the need for harmony within the group. Consequently, if someone was invited into the class and it became apparent they were not there for the right reasons, or if their energy was not in sync with the rest of the group, they seemed to leave quite rapidly. I do not know how Joey did it, but he seemed to know quickly who would stay and who would go.

I now had been attending the class for three years. I was not a disturbing influence, however it seemed I was just sitting there like a bump on a log. I never received any impressions or saw any Spirit. Joey was very patient with me.

I had informed Joey when first asked to participate that I would not believe anything, until I got a miracle.

I certainly did not see anything clairvoyantly. I have difficulty seeing in normal everyday life. I have had weak eyes since childhood and cannot see at all without my eyeglasses. In addition, I have difficulty seeing things which are right in front of me. I wanted a miracle. This was not a bargain with God, simply what I wanted if I was to be a part of a Spiritualist group. I was raised a Roman Catholic and that was my religion.

Depending on the number of individuals in the class, (generally six or eight), I would sit directly across from Joey. One night after waiting patiently these three years, I saw someone. It was Brother Andre. To me, this was my miracle. I had never seen anything clairvoyantly in my life. I could sense other things and by this time I had developed my healing abilities. But to see Spirit? Never. I was sitting quietly with my eyes closed in meditation. All of a sudden I opened my eyes, and who was standing there before me? A life-sized Brother Andre. I could see the separation in his hair, his eyes and the pupils in his eyes. I cannot see that clearly in daytime wearing eyeglasses when someone is looking me directly in the face. But I could see him. I saw his collar and the top button of his black cassock. I was in my seat and he was looking down at me. He had this fatherly smile on his face as seen in photographs, and there were not that many photographs of Brother Andre around.

I felt such a sense of peace, it was unreal. He had a gentle smile. It brought a feeling of serenity. I was aware I was seeing an apparition and that I was receiving my miracle. For one split second I closed my eyes, when I reopened them, he was gone.

When the period for concentration was over, Joey turned on a light and began to go around the circle asking each person if they had received impressions, saw or felt anything during the concentration period, or had anything to share with the group. This was usual procedure in the class. Finally, he came to me. My usual response was I had nothing to share. This time I started to say "I saw" and Joey quickly cut me off by saying, "Okay Noella, hold it, I'll come back to you." He addressed the people to my right, and then turned to Elizabeth McIntosh who was sitting to his left, which was on my far right. (Elizabeth McIntosh is a brilliant medium from the Church who was visiting this evening as a guest.) Joey asked Elizabeth what she had received and she replied, "From the side, I saw the priest from the mountain, standing in front of Noella." Of course Elizabeth not being Catholic originally would not know who she saw. She saw a religious figure in a black cassock. It could have been a priest or a brother. To her they all looked the same. Then Joey came back to me and asked what I had seen. I replied, "Believe it or not, I saw Brother Andre." Joey responded as he always did, "uh huh." Joey then advised me he also had seen Brother Andre from the back, as he stood before me. The class was very excited for me, this was my first clairvoyant experience.

Joey always looked for his double-checks. That is why he often asked us to wait when he knew we saw something or someone. He would first check with the rest of the class to see if they also clairvoyantly saw the same thing.) We three saw Brother Andre from different angles, meaning that he was really there in the room with us, in all of his dimensions. I saw him from the front, standing before me. Elizabeth saw him from the side and Joey saw him from the back. This was a great joy to me. Because of this apparition, I felt very safe working with Spiritualist people. I sat in Joey's weekly classes for at least ten years.

For the information of the reader, Brother Andre was a lay brother of the Holy Cross Congregation. He was the founder of Saint Joseph's Oratory in Montreal, Quebec, Canada. On October 17, 2010 Brother Andre was canonized as a Saint of the Roman Catholic Church.

Gloria Gari was also part of our development class for many years along with Noella. I resided at 4560 St. Catherine Street in Westmount. The classes were held in my master bedroom. I would arrive home from my job at Eastern, set-up the room by pushing my bed against a wall and arranging chairs in circle formation. The one thing that I never moved was the dresser because it was too heavy. It was positioned in the right hand corner of my bedroom, against a wall and out of the way.

We opened the class with a prayer. We would then enter into the silence for a few moments to clear our minds from the concerns of the day. This was our sacred time to commune with Spirit. I would be seated at one end of the circle which was away from the dresser. Gloria sat on the left side of the circle, the dresser was against the right wall on the other side of the room. Without fail, when we were all gathered in the silence, Gloria would sense when Spirit was about to enter within our group. She would announce; "Good Evening Mr. Wong" and as if on cue there would be a loud knock on the dresser, which we all could hear. I had already sensed his presence as his energy entered into my aura in preparation for the evening's teachings. Mr. Wong has a special affinity for Gloria and his first words through me were always, "Good evening Gloria." For years I worked in control and Mr. Wong did much of the inspirational teaching in the class. We always looked forward to his knock on the dresser, this was our phenomenon.

    I was being transformed and my life began to change. It was not my desire to become a medium; that was way beyond my reach. My desire was to be happy within myself and attain inner peace. I longed to establish a loving relationship with The Eternal One and nurture my soul which had been troubled for so long. I could feel the cynical and untrusting parts of my personality slowly begin to crumble. For years I was like the proverbial lamb lost in the woods. The difference is that I am not a lamb, I am a Scorpio and I am far from being weak-willed and easily led. I was in the process of becoming a stronger and more positive person.

    Soon I was invited to speak at the First Spiritual Church and did so for several years. I became an inspirational speaker and during my early years, never prepared a talk. I closed my eyes and Spirit delivered the discourse. This was the beginning of my public work. It would be years before I was given the gift of clairvoyance. As the years progressed, as I grew and became more confident, I worked less and less in control because I felt the need to be totally responsible for the words which came out of my mouth. Spirit continues as always to inspire me. I preferred to work consciously with my eyes open to see people's faces and look into their eyes when I was speaking. Mr. Wong is still around and occasionally slips in to let me know that he is about when I am teaching at seminars or at other times when I am reading for certain individuals.

    As I write, I am reminded of Mr. Eddy DeBanks, a genuine trance medium who served at the First Spiritual Church. A lifelong Spiritualist, he was a very quiet and unassuming gentleman. Whilst in the trance state, when he delivered a discourse under the influence of his Spirit Guide, he was transformed. There was no doubt this was a highly evolved, intelligent and wise disincarnate entity addressing the congregation. Based solely on the calibre and the content of his talks, it was obvious to those listening that his discourses were out of his normal frame of reference. He was not so very articulate in his daily expression. This was definitely not Mr. DeBanks speaking. One could easily discern this by simply being attentive. In my experience throughout the years, I have witnessed enough trance speakers to determine the real from the imagined. Mr. DeBanks was the real article. It was an uplifting experience to hear him.

One evening as I was seated in the First Spiritual Church with Gloria, she turned to me and said, "I see you as the President of this Church one day." Again, I looked at her as if she were crazy and said as much. However, it did come to pass a few years later. I was elected President and served approximately four years.

My lifelong friends are part of my spiritual family. Gloria and Noella are in attendance when I occasionally hold a Sunday afternoon, "Walk In The Light" seminar.

As for myself, Spirit truly did come in.

CHAPTER V
MATERIALIZATION – SEEING IS BELIEVING

As an integral part of my search for knowledge, I was able to attend a materialization séance in July 1970 accompanied by my friend Gloria Gari. I did not have a preconceived idea of what to expect. By this time I had been involved in Spiritualism for almost five years and was aware of some of my Spirit Guides. Gloria and I looked forward to this experience with great anticipation and much curiosity.

MATERIALIZATION

The rarest and most difficult phase of physical mediumship, the medium enters into a very deep trance state. With the assistance of the Spirit Guides and Chemists, the Spirit entity is able to temporarily manifest, visible and palpable, a replica of its former physical body, and is able to move about freely and converse exactly as it did on the earth plane providing accurate and detailed information about themselves and their life on earth. The materialized figure will possess physical characteristics: limbs, face, hair, eyes, head; in short, a complete body built of ectoplasm. As the ectoplasm issues from the medium's body, it is formed by the Spirit Chemist within the cabinet into the temporary body which the manifesting entity will use. The medium is entranced and quite helpless as he sits in the cabinet which is specially constructed for the séance. It is a box-like cupboard covered with a black cloth. The only article of furniture in the cabinet is a chair on which the medium sits. The Spirit is attached to the medium's body by a visible ectoplasm cord drawn from the medium's body. Should there be a sudden flash of light, or should someone touch a Spirit unexpectedly, startling the medium in any way, it might result in serious injury or perhaps death to the medium through the nervous shock to the system and the rapid recoil of the ectoplasm back into the medium's body. One should not touch them unless given permission to do so by the materializing Spirit, certain precautions must be taken to protect the entranced medium. On occasion there may be three or four Spirits materializing at the same time and a materialized figure will frequently walk through you and dematerialize right before your eyes, seemingly to evaporate into the ether or disappear like a small pool into the floor.

Gloria and I flew from Montreal to Muncie, Indiana and then made our way to Camp Chesterfield by taxi. We were booked into the Sunflower Hotel which was on the grounds. The day after our arrival we attended an outdoor demonstration of clairvoyance. The medium was Marie Perkins. She addressed me, relaying a message from my brother in Spirit who had never touched the earth plane. She advised me that he had grown up in the Spirit World and that he was named Paul. He wanted to communicate the fact to me that he was around and interested in my spiritual welfare. This was the first time that he had given his name. Marie, who was later to become a close friend and spiritual mentor, was a stranger to me at the time. I happily accepted the message from my Spirit brother. Gloria and I were new to the camp and busied ourselves for the remainder of the day walking around and going into Muncie to have a bite to eat.

We had booked ourselves into a trumpet séance for that evening and looked forward to it. For the benefit of the reader, the trumpet is another form of physical mediumship which is usually conducted in a room with infrared lighting. The trumpet is a cone shaped instrument usually made out of tin or aluminum which can be made to float about the room by Spirit, totally independent of the medium. The trumpet should never be handled during a séance. The sitters are able to converse freely with the communicating entities who will manipulate the trumpet, sometimes touching the sitters on the head.

This trumpet séance turned out to be an experience that I would sooner forget. It has always been my experience to test the Spirit as I am skeptical by nature, so I am on the lookout, particularly in dealing with physical phenomena. As fate would have it, during the séance that evening I was able to see the 'male medium' walking about the room and speaking through the trumpet. I was obviously very upset, so I waited for an opportunity. As the medium approached my chair, he walked near enough that I was able to put my foot out in an attempt to trip him. He stumbled for a second and quickly regained his balance. Gloria who was seated beside me did not know what happened. This was my first trumpet séance and I was not at all happy. I was so livid and upset at the deception that I wanted to leave The Camp that night. Between my tears and disappointment, I kept Gloria talking the whole of the night until the light of the dawn. I was broken-hearted by what I had witnessed. I was ready to abandon Spiritualism. It was incredible to me this could take place. Gloria finally convinced me to stay for the next day because we had signed up for a materialization séance. By this time it was morning. I was still beside myself with anger and dismay and ready to fly back to Montreal. My heart was broken but I stayed and we went to the séance.

The medium was James Tingley. Naturally I was very excited to witness my first materialization, however I remained a little wary. We sat next to Marie Perkins who was the cabinet attendant. Her function was to protect the medium and see that no harm came to him during the séance while he was in a trance state. We had a perfect view of all the activities and were not about to miss anything. I was not going to be fooled a second time. As the séance progressed, the Spirit entities manifested. They were recognized and welcomed by their relatives and friends. It was quite impressive particularly when in some instances the Spirit forms disintegrated in the centre of the room and disappeared through the floor. At other times, the Spirit would face the people who were standing, walk through them, and tap them on the shoulder from behind. At one point there were five entities manifesting simultaneously. I witnessed many happy reunions that evening and recall thinking to myself there was indeed a God, and my doubts were removed. I saw that this was real. Gloria and I were both thrilled. This certainly made up for my experience of the previous night. It was like a party atmosphere in that room. I was invited to stand in the center of the room by Doctor Taylor, one of James Tingley's Guides who was the Master of the Séance. It was now my turn to meet Spirit. The first entity to materialize was my father's father whom I did not know. Grandpa Nicola Crinita died April 1941, six months after I was born. I welcomed him and joked, "Grandpa, you must have taken one look at me and dropped dead." I was not afraid of Spirit and I was very happy to meet my grandfather. I thought I might as well have a good time, everyone else was.

'Doctor Milton Price' identified himself as my Doctor. He told me he was from Wales and spoke with a Welsh accent, frequently using the word; "Indeed." He placed his hands over my head and said, "One day the bubble of a great mediumship will burst." I thanked him and replied, "I am grateful, but I only want the highest and the best of Spirit, and I don't want any garbage. I only want the best." To which Dr. Price patiently responded that I would only receive the highest and the best of Spirit. He touched my head in a blessing and evaporated. In hindsight, I can't believe what I said to Doctor Price. I was cheeky but I wanted to be sure Spirit understood I took this all very seriously. I was still smoldering within because of the shenanigans of the prior evening. I wanted Spirit to be aware that I would not accept anything less than perfect. And I was not kidding.

Then 'Wana' made her appearance. She materialized as a little girl full of life and very energetic. She invited me to sit with her in the centre of the room, cross-legged on the floor, which of course I did. She informed me she had frozen to death at twelve years of age. She was Lakota Sioux and the daughter of a Chief, and was now over two hundred years old. She was very playful and informed me whenever I needed her, to just think of "what I wana" and she would be there. We had quite a nice chat and she told me that she would be my Message Bearer, which was news to me because at the time I was not yet clairvoyant. I was to develop that faculty about two years later. However, true to her word, Wana has been working diligently with me now for over thirty-five years. When she is around my hands become very active because as it turned out, this is where my mediumship resides and how I sense and feel things.

I was having quite a time of it that evening and I was elated when a Native American entity materialized before me. He introduced himself as, 'Red Feather'. I acknowledged him by saying "how", he was not amused and responded, "I can speak English as well as you do." It seemed I had watched too many Hollywood Westerns in my youth. Truly, my ignorance was unintentional. He put me in my place and that settled that. Red Feather proceeded to tell me he was an Apache and my Healing Guide. To prove to me that he was really here, he said, "I am going to walk through you and then tap you on the shoulder", which he immediately proceeded to do. He was standing before me and walked right through my body. He then was standing behind me, tapped me on the back of my shoulder and walked through me again to stand before me. I was very impressed. By this time the séance was in full swing and I did not know what to further expect.

James Tingley's Guide, 'Snow White', whom I erroneously referred to as 'Goldie Locks' in my book, The

Medium Touch, (and for which I sincerely apologize) was running around the room singing and playing with people. I was taking it all in. When the black curtain was opened, I could see James Tingley sitting in his chair in a dead trance with billows of ectoplasm flowing from the orifices of his body. I plainly saw the ectoplasmic cord from his solar plexus which was attached to the manifesting Spirits.

Another Spirit manifested before me and addressed me by saying, "Good Evening Joe, I am Amelia Earhart." I was quiet for a moment and did not immediately respond. The entity continued, "You do not know who I am, do you?" That was the truth, I had no idea who this person was, but I thought to myself, judging by her name she must be some old time movie star. The other people in the room responded to her immediately. Many called out, "We know who you are Amelia, we know who you are." This went on for a few moments. The Spirit of Amelia by this time was walking around the room and had now come to stand beside me. She addressed the other sitters who were very excited and calmly said to them, "I have come for the boy." She then turned to me and said, "I was a pilot and my aircraft went down in the Pacific. There will be many stories about me, but do not believe them. This is what happened: My plane went down. Do not ever be afraid to fly because I will always be with you to protect you in the air." (I was working at Eastern Airlines and travelled frequently by air.) And that as they say, was that. As I said earlier, I had never heard of Amelia Earhart until that time. Her appearance did cause quite a stir amongst those present. So much so that after the séance some of the people who were present in the room came up to congratulate me and to tell me more about Amelia Earhart, she is after all a Great American Legend.

As the months and years went by, things certainly changed. People gave me books on Amelia, I got messages through mediums and was given photographs by others. Most importantly, I am never afraid to get on an airplane. I always look for a Spirit Light whenever I board an aircraft and call on Amelia whenever there is turbulence. In Chapter 10 of this book, I will share an experience related to this materialization of Amelia Earhart.

The final Spirit to materialize for me was my brother Paul. He greeted me warmly telling me that he was happy to come and speak with me at last. He thanked me for giving him the opportunity of being able to work with me from Spirit side. He advised me he was helping in my spiritual search. He had a fine sense of humour. I quote his words, "You know I look just like you, except that I am handsomer and taller." (Which was true, I am 5'7", but as he was standing before me he appeared to be taller by a few inches.) He remarked laughingly, "I'm also not quite as chubby as you, my face is thinner." Since I do have a tendency to be overweight, he was not wrong. However, this was not the end of it. I firmly believe in doing double-checks and I relate the following experience which I have also covered in length in The Medium Touch, Chapter 9.

I have seen Paul clairvoyantly several times. I have awakened from sleep to see him standing over my bed, tall and smiling. He has a beautiful countenance which radiates Light. I must concede that he is far more handsome than I, but he is an angel and I am not! I have since the time of the materialization received further verification of his presence from various other mediums. I was invited to demonstrate clairvoyance at the International Spiritualists Federation of Healers Congress held in London, England, in September 1975. Whilst there, I had arranged for a private consultation with Mrs. Jessie Kessen, a medium from Scotland. We were strangers to each other; in fact, she was not aware that I was a scheduled worker at the congress. I recorded my reading, of which the following is an excerpt:

J.K.   Have you a brother in Spirit?

J.   Yes, I have, God bless him.

J.K.   He's had a very wonderful education in Spirit because he's been through the Temples of Learning. Did he pass over young?

J.   He never touched the earth plane.

J.K.   That's right! Because he's telling me he was educated on the other side and you will believe him when he says, "Until you extended along the time when you were of that age, twenty-eight, I was literally dead. I was just a thought, just a memory, there was nothing concrete about me, but you have brought everything to me as the branch of a tree needs the sap, and I'm

	alive again and part of the family. I think I could give him height, I think I'm just that little bit taller."
J.	I was told that before!
J.K.	And he's just not so, so could I say…
J.	Fat!
J.K.	No, chubby in the face. That's true, he's overshadowing me. No, I'm not laughing at you, and you're not laughing at me. His whole purpose today in coming is to say, "I'll walk beside you." Has music anything to do with you? Because he wants to sing, "I'll Walk Beside You." I could cry emotionally because this is his opportunity through you to reach his Mum. He's not on the outside looking in anymore; he's part of the family. You know he was very lonely on the other side until you came along and you started your search and now he feels he's not intruding on you if he says, "I'll walk beside you," and you'll be companions, but he'll not intrude upon you. You'll be pals." When he was educated and passed through the Temples of Learning, he pleaded with them that one day he would be appointed to watch over you, because the material world holds more shadow than where he is. He can see God in all things and glorify His works and so you must learn to do the same. Your brother is helping you with philosophy. He is here again saying, "I'll walk beside you."

I find it noteworthy that Paul used his height and weight to confirm his identity as these were his exact words when he first materialized five years earlier.

He again confirmed his presence one evening in the Fall of 1979. I had finished taking a service at our Church and whilst standing at the back of the Church engaged in conversation with Arthur Luke, when all of a sudden he stopped in mid-sentence and asked if I had a younger brother in Spirit who resembled me. I replied that I did. Arthur had seen him standing beside me. Mr. Luke was not a clairvoyant medium in the sense I am, so this made Paul's appearance all the more evidential to me.

Gloria Gari relates her experience of the evening:

I was twenty-three at the time of the James Tingley materialization séance. I had been involved in Spiritualism for about four and a half years and was also sitting in Joey's development class. When the opportunity arose to visit Camp Chesterfield with Joey, I took it. We were both excited at the prospect, however after the alleged trumpet séance of the prior evening, I believe Joey had to see the materialization. Based on our personal experiences within our classes and messages at the Church, we knew that Spirit did exist and I am happy I convinced him to stay. I just knew that he could not leave Spiritualism because of one bad experience.

I did not know of any relatives in Spirit so I was pleased when I was presented with one of my Spirit Guides. As Joey described, the evening was a revelation and there was no question in my mind that we were witnessing the real thing. You could see James Tingley in a dead trance state in the cabinet. There was much ectoplasm coming from the orifices of his body, mouth, ears, etc... and the Spirits were walking through people. The first entity to materialize for me was a little girl who introduced herself as 'Lotus Blossom'. She sat on the floor in the center of the room and tickled my toes with her tiny hands. She said this was how I would know when she was around and would help me with my clairvoyance. I have felt her presence many times since then and have had her identity confirmed by many mediums. The next entity to manifest was a nun called 'Sister Maria'. She addressed me and then as proof, she walked right through my body. I could feel the energy and her presence as she passed through my body, stood behind me and then passed through me again to stand before me. She is a Healer and has been with me for many years. Whenever I have received a reading or sat in a circle, Sister Maria always comes through for me. The next entity introduced himself to me as 'Red Wing', a Native American who functions as my Protector and Door Keeper. I am aware I am protected by Spirit and that they are always around watching over me. I can say this experience was one thousand percent authentic. I could feel the entities as they walked through my body in addition to the experiences of all the other people in the room.

Within the next year, Joey and I visited the Spiritualist Association of Great Britain at 33 Belgrave Square, London, I received a private reading from a medium. Not one relative came through, only my Spirit Guides who wanted to prove they were still around me. I thought that was terrific! This experience solidified my belief in Spirit and I am grateful to James Tingley for the gift he gave me. Through the years, Spirit remains a constant in my life.

I am grateful that Gloria encouraged me to stay and attend that particular séance. I feel it was Spirit's gift to me. They wanted to ensure I was truly aware of their presence in my life. That evening, I was introduced to my Band of Guides in addition to the Spirit entities that had already been working with me. This is the first time I have ever revealed the names of some of the Spirit Guides who have led me along the way, through the good and the bad. Let me state it is not necessary for one to know the names of their Spirit Guides. This is not something that you should become concerned about. If Spirit wishes for you to know their names, they will reveal themselves in due course. This event had an extremely profound effect on me. I believe Spirit set it up that way to solidify my faith and to encourage me in my mediumistic development and to prepare me for the coming years.

Elizabeth and Bill McIntosh

This is a recounting of the visit of Dr. Richard Ireland to the First Spiritual Church in Montreal in the early sixties as told by long-time Spiritualists and highly gifted mediums, Elizabeth and Bill McIntosh.

Dr. Richard Ireland was a well-known physical medium from Phoenix, Arizona. Although at the time of his visit to the First in Montreal, he was not known to Elizabeth and Bill. They had not met nor had they ever heard of Richard Ireland. He was invited to the Church by the then President, Mr. Reg Sharpe. During this visit Dr. Ireland demonstrated the varied aspects of physical mediumship such as materialization and he also conducted a trumpet séance which took place in the Church.

Prior to the actual materialization séance, Dr. Ireland spoke at a Church service and gave a demonstration of clairvoyance from the platform using billets (pieces of white paper on which people would write a question or address a note to loved ones in Spirit). What impressed Bill McIntosh about Richard Ireland was that prior to the service he would not come into the Church building. He kept himself isolated from the congregation by standing outside of the Church on St. Catherine Street. He spoke to no one. People wrote out their billets. They were collected by Reg Sharpe, then President of the Church and the folded billets were placed on the platform and not seen by the medium until the message part of the service began. A blindfolded Richard Ireland gave an accurate and most impressive demonstration of billet reading. He walked back and forth on the Church platform as he read the billets without opening them and threw them into the congregation to the individual who had written the particular billet. He replied to the question or gave whatever messages he received from the vibration of the billet.

The materialization séance was held the next day. There were forty people in attendance. The group was divided into two groups of twenty. One group was seated in the main part of the Church. The second group of twenty sat in the Healing Room. Elizabeth and Bill were part of this second grouping. The Healing Room is approximately twelve by nine feet and is connected to the main Church by a narrow hall about twelve feet long. A small cabinet was erected in the Healing Room. The cabinet was empty except for a chair. The entrance was covered with a black curtain. Prior to the séance, Richard Ireland removed all of his clothing and Reg Sharpe provided him with a pair of new underwear. This is what he wore as he sat in the cabinet. The room was inspected before the séance began to ensure that there were no hidden apparatus, et cetera. All was clear for the séance to begin.

At the start of the séance, Richard sat in the cabinet. He advised the group that he was going to do some deep breathing and he went into a deep trance. As the séance began, Richard Ireland's Guide appeared and spoke to the group. He requested we sing songs and said, "I do not want holy songs." So we sang popular tunes for a while. The black curtain split and we could see the ectoplasmic cord attached between Richard Ireland and the Spirit. We could also see him sitting in the chair, in a deep trance state.

As the séance progressed the next entity to materialize from the cabinet was a nun, in full habit. She said hello to everybody in the Healing Room and walked down the hall into the Church Hall to say hello to the people down there. Richard Ireland was still sitting in trance in the cabinet as this was taking place. When she walked back into the Healing Room, she dematerialized into midair. None of the manifesting entities went back into the cabinet. They all disappeared right before our eyes into the floor as it were, and all present saw this happen. Everyone in the room received some evidence from the Spirits who materialized for them. There were two materialized Spirits for each person present in the room. Mainly, it was relatives and people whom they would have known because not everyone knew who their Spirit Guides were. These were not just Spirits nodding their heads and going down through the floor. Everyone received a message and words of encouragement from the manifesting entities. The Spirits always mentioned a memory or something that was connected to whomever was coming through. So there was no question as to their identity or that this was real. The entities would touch us but we were not permitted to grab them as that could have caused injury to the medium. Bill relates that his grandfather and an uncle came through to greet him. He could make out their recognizable features as he chatted with them.

For Elizabeth, her grandmother Fannie Steele materialized. When she first came out of the cabinet, she walked directly over to Bill and tapped him on his head two times. She was as solid as if she were in the flesh. The Spirits looked exactly as you remembered them. Elizabeth recalled, "My grandmother was an older lady and she dressed older with a cameo brooch at the throat with her hair worn up in a roll as we used to call them. The proof for me was that she looked exactly like my grandmother. The first thing she said was, "Hello Betty, it's lovely to see you." She is the only one in my lifetime to ever call me Betty. This was proof for me that this was my grandmother. Then she said, "I have to apologize about your mother", because my grandmother had gone to live with my mother when she became a widow. When my grandfather died, my grandmother was already more or less bedridden. So when she came to live with her, my mother had to lift my grandmother to change the bed sheets. This caused her to damage her back. As a result of my mother's diabetic condition, which resulted in wearing calipers (leg braces) and brought on other ailments leaving my mother in very poor health. This was my grandmother apologizing for what she had caused my mother to go through.

Elizabeth continues, "I was aware of 'Chief Running Water', who has been my Guide for a long time. He is a very tall Indian. He materialized in his tanned deerskin and an elaborate headdress and stood before me with his back to Bill. Whenever I had received any impressions from him, he never let on that he was a Chief. He did not boast about that. Running Water and I spoke to one another in a Native American dialect. Then we spoke in English and he said, "I have something for you." With that, he reached for something at the back of his head. He then said, "Put your hands on top of mine." His hands were close together and I put my hands on top of his. He then withdrew his hand. I had a feather from his headdress. He told me I would have it for a while. It was a gift from Spirit and it would go back to Spirit. I kept it in my Bible for a long long time. Years later when I went to show it to someone, it was no longer there. It had dematerialized and gone back to Spirit, (as all authentic apports do).

Bill remarks: "Running Water materialized facing Elizabeth. The interesting thing about Running Water was that as he stood facing Elizabeth, I was standing behind him and was very conscious of the many feathers which made up his headdress. He was very tall; which really struck me because I had been reading about materialization and had read that the figures which materialize were frequently the same height as the medium. However, this fellow was much taller than the medium Richard Ireland, who was not a big or tall man. I was really blown away by Running Water's appearance."

The final materialization of the evening was Brother Andre. When he materialized he requested we all stand up, which we did. He appeared to be about five feet eight inches in height and wore a black cassock with buttons all the way down the front. He spoke in French, mingled with the people and gave us permission to touch him. He blessed us all. We knew that Richard Ireland did not speak French. Brother Andre walked out of the Healing Room and along the hallway into the Church to speak with the people there.

After the materialization, we all hopped into our cars and hightailed up to Saint Joseph's Oratory to verify what we had seen was what we knew of Brother Andre. Elizabeth continued: "And you know how they have the black cassock with all the buttons, a black coat, that is how he appeared and it was exactly like the statue of him at Saint Joseph's and it is as he came through.

We were quite elated at what had taken place. The two hour materialization séance that we experienced at the First Spiritual Church through Richard Ireland's mediumship was beyond a shadow of a doubt, genuine.

In addition to this séance, we also had a trumpet séance with Richard Ireland at that time. It was held in the Healing Room. Richard did not have trumpets with him so we provided them. The Spirit voices that came through the trumpets were really something. The trumpets would tap you and they would knock you on the head. When it was over, Richard just got up and went out of the room, but we still had the trumpets in the Healing Room. Although the medium had left the room, the voices were still talking through the trumpets. Quite, quite definitely, the voices were still talking.

Elizabeth stated: "I also witnessed a materialization in Glasgow, Scotland. I went with my sister-in-law, Dorothy and it was in the Glasgow City Chambers, downtown. It was a woman from London who came, a well-known medium. This was a hall with a couple of hundred people in it. Some people were in the balcony, others down on floor level. The medium was on the stage and she was in a cabinet too. The medium gave messages and direct voice. She would say she was looking for this person, let's say the name was Emma and she would say she is in the sixth row back, and she was so many seats in. After the person's name was called, a materialized Spirit would come down from the stage through to the person at their very seat. At the end of the evening before she left the stage, the medium materialized a bunch of flowers, directly from her body. They were solid flowers, and she threw them into the audience. She most certainly materialized these fresh flowers from her body. What I saw in Glasgow was very real."

In conclusion, for the information of the reader there are websites on My Space and You Tube which show clips of Richard Ireland reading billets on the Steve Allen Television Show in 1969. There is also a website created in dedication to Dr. Richard Ireland by his son, Mark Ireland.

An authentic materialization is indeed a thing of beauty. For it truly bridges the gap between this world and the next. Mediumship and Spiritualism have frequently been tarnished by the brush of insincere charlatans that betray the trust of individuals who seek them out. During my experiences as a seeker, I have witnessed my share of "phony mediums" and their shabby tricks.

In addition to my first "faux trumpet" séance, I also witnessed a materialization where the medium who was very well-known and clearly identifiable to me by a gap in her front teeth, paraded about the séance room in the guise of a disincarnate Spirit. Fortunately for me, I believe that my own Guides clue me into these people in addition to my own common sense. Some credulous people are willing to believe anything and can delude themselves into seeing and hearing what they need. I believe in personal responsibility and in karmic retribution. Those who knowingly deceive the unsuspecting will have to answer for their behaviour, possibly in this life but most assuredly in the next. The Law of Spirit is the Law of Attraction and like attracts like. If a gifted medium abuses their gift, then eventually the calibre of their mediumship will diminish. Their Guides will leave and they are left to the whims of lower entities, because their inner Light will slowly dim. It is indeed a slippery slope.

These are solely my personal experiences which took place in the 1970's when I was relatively new to Spiritualism. This is not a condemnation of the Spiritualist Camps of today. I am confident that much has changed for the better over the past thirty years. Elizabeth McIntosh relates her experience at a materialization séance at one of the Spiritualist Camps.

"I attended a materialization séance. The medium was well-known. She was a tall stout woman. I was invited to come and stand in front of the cabinet. The materializing Spirit then appeared out of the cabinet and proceeded to hold me in a tight embrace stating that it was my Guide, Running Water. As she drew me closer, she said, "You not know who I am, I am Running Water." I in turn replied, "Not with boobs like that you are not."

Needless to say, I was not impressed.

The adage that all that glitters is not gold is indeed a fact of life. However, if we did not have hair, there would be no need for wigs. If the authentic and real thing did not exist, there would be no need for imitations. For myself, incidents such as these have not weakened my faith and belief in Spirit. Some of these types of experiences have caused me great pain and at times, made me cringe. I will further add that the positive experiences I have been witness to through the years, far outweigh the negative ones which I have always viewed a test of my faith. As a medium I feel this was necessary for me to see both sides of the coin.

I have seen so many more good and beautiful manifestations of Spirit than not. I have known and still know brilliant and sincere mediums and workers in the field.

Like Doubting Thomas, I have seen with my own eyes.

I conclude... Seeing is Believing!

CHAPTER VI
LIGHT AND LAVENDER.
BEING SPIRITUAL AND BEING GAY

My spiritual quest had begun in earnest. I was overjoyed and ecstatic to think that Spirit would even come close, let alone work through one such as I. For years I thought of myself as contemptible and unworthy in the eyes of God, the Church and society. The stigma of being "one of those" cut far and deep into my psyche. I placed little or no spiritual value on myself which I felt was a result of the Catholic indoctrination in my formative years. As a young boy I had learned that if you are different, then some people do not like you. I was off to a head start by being gay and for some time I was not comfortable in my own skin, until I figured things out for myself.

During my youth and well into my teenage years, religious fervour ran through me to the very core of my being. I wholeheartedly desired to be a part of God's Church and to dedicate my life to the service of humanity in His name. Even though I was blessed with good common sense, I did not have the mental acumen or life experience to truly reason for myself. I was a child of faith and took everything literally. It took years of painful soul searching for me to finally accept myself as I am.

This brings to mind the variations of the proverb which is attributed to the Jesuits. I much prefer Muriel Spark's interpretation from the play and the film of "The Prime of Miss Jean Brodie" in which the formidable Miss Brodie proclaims, "Give me a girl at an impressionable age and she is mine for life."

In 1953 a visiting lay brother was assigned to St. Ann's Parish. He was in charge of vocations and part of his duties was to have "the talk" with young people, which consisted mainly of the altar boys. I was thirteen at the time and the brother invited me in for a chat. As I sat and squirmed in my chair, he quizzed me on what I knew about sex. I must admit at that point in my life, my knowledge was next to nil. He got right to the point telling me all about sex between a man and a woman. He advised me in very plain street language what men and women could do in bed. They could perform all sorts of sexual acts with each other (which I thought at the time would happen only in French films, what did I know?) He told me that they could pleasure themselves in any way they so desired and for as long as they wanted, provided they completed the sex act for the purpose of procreation. I think my jaw dropped to the floor. He used words I will not repeat here, but they were most explicit and left very little to my imagination. He then got around to the big question which is a part of the Catholic interrogation process utilized in the confessional box, or in these little talks. "Have you been abusing yourself?"

Here is one of the tools of ultimate Catholic guilt. Many Catholic children have had this question put to them at one time or another, on some occasion. (I would think boys in particular, for obvious reasons). The word "abusing" conjures up all kinds of imaginary demons to the young and impressionable mind, and often can be quite frightening to credulous children. I answered him truthfully that I was not. However, I felt that it was none of his concern whether I did or not, and I was sure not going to tell him. I was relieved when our little chat came to an end. I was still fairly naive at that time and being so religious, I knew some things were bad. I regularly went to confession to Father Kearney and he had never asked me that question, or anything similar to it.

Much to my chagrin, in the years to follow my life would turn out to be contradictory from what I understood to be what God expected from me as a good Catholic boy. Through religious instruction and general information I was made aware that homosexuality was not to be tolerated. Not unlike many other young people, I turned against myself in self-contempt and I derided myself for simply existing. I was not a happy camper... pardon the pun!

During the Mass, in preparation for Holy Communion, the well-known hymn, "O Lord I am Not Worthy" was always sung. These words were embedded into my mind and summed up how I regarded myself. As I struggled with my sexuality, trying to determine where I would fit in, I knew these dark years from my teens and early twenties very well. I had lived with these shadows for lengthy periods during my self-imposed years of spiritual deprivation. I had yet to come to a clear understanding that people were both spiritual and sexual beings. Nor had I arrived at the perception that being gay and being spiritual were compatible. This would become clear to me many years later.

As a result of becoming involved in Spiritualism, my confidence grew along with my commitment to Spirit. I was an active member of the First Spiritual Church of Montreal, and I often spoke at the services. I continued to hold a weekly development class at my home and travelled to attend metaphysical seminars. One thing led to another and I was invited to conduct workshops with various psychic and spiritually minded organizations in other cities. This afforded me the opportunity to meet other kindred souls and broaden my spiritual and personal knowledge.

My inner life was very important to me and I realized that I was most fortunate. I judged by the peace I was experiencing within, that I was well and truly progressing on my spiritual odyssey. This was my life to be and Spirit was guiding me along the way. As I approached thirty, I had found my way. I had a sense of purpose and knew I was making a difference. In this manner Spirit was able to reach people through me. My job at Eastern Airlines paid my rent and my living expenses, and most importantly provided me a means to travel.

I have always referred to my mediumistic responsibilities as my work. I was working to serve Spirit and hopefully bringing a glimmer of Light into the lives of those with whom I came into contact. Granted anyone can be psychic, and that qualification alone is not an indication or a guarantee of spiritual awareness or development. Being psychic does not make one spiritual. This is solely a personal and individual choice. However, mediums who generally develop their gifts within a spiritual framework have a tendency to be more spiritually inclined in pursuit of their spiritual activities. They strive to work in concert with ethereal beings that are of a higher spiritual essence.

I am very conscious of working in the Light and through the years, I have on occasion referred to myself as having a "dash of lavender". I think it is a quaint turn of phrase and has a nice ring to it. Actually, I really do see myself as having more of a splash, as opposed to a dash! I do like the connotation of Light and lavender.

A friend of mine once remarked that I was a walking contradiction because I can be so reserved at times and a little outrageous at others. In 1975 the Annual Eastern Airlines Christmas Party was attended by well over a hundred people: employees, spouses, girlfriends and boyfriends. It was quite a lavish affair held in the huge foyer of our office in beautiful Westmount Square. The employee party committee did an outstanding job of planning the bash. There was plenty of wine, women and song, to coin a phrase. Also in attendance were a few gay blades, thrown in for good measure.

I had now been with Eastern for almost ten years and our office staff had grown substantially by then. We had recently hired many new employees. Amongst them, a good sprinkling of straight macho young men of Italian descent and some very beautiful young ladies, also of Italian descent. They added plenty of colour to the atmosphere and were always fun. Surprisingly, some of them turned out to be quite camp in their own way, (as in quick-witted, not gay). However, at the time I do not think they were quite ready for what was to transpire that evening. The party was well under way when I asked my boyfriend to dance. We took to the floor.

One would think that someone had dropped a bomb in the middle of the room. Some of the new hires just stood there and stared open-mouthed. The silence was deafening. I did not care. My colleagues knew I was gay and in a committed relationship. My partner and I continued to dance until the end of the waltz. As the song concluded, I felt a tap on my shoulder and turned to see my friend Elaine Philips standing before me with a huge grin asking... "May I have the next dance." It was a very gracious gesture on her part. This diffused the shock effect. At that time, two males dancing together at a company party, quite frankly, was indeed shocking. Elaine was very smooth as we waltzed off into the crowd leaving some people staring in stunned silence. Anyway, they got over it soon enough. I received a few pats on the shoulder that night from many of my fellow workers and friends. I was an adult and not ashamed of who I was. I wanted to make a statement, and I did. I had as much right to dance with the person of my choice as anyone else.

In the late eighties Eastern was in dire straits and there weren't many funds available for the Employee Christmas Party. I taught a few Psychic Workshops over several weekends at the office for employees, their families and friends. The proceeds went to the Employee Christmas Fund. I am a lapsed Catholic, but be that as it may, I do frequently drop into a Church to pray, meditate or light a candle for people in Spirit, or just to have a chat with God. I have no problem with this. I feel very at home and enjoy the stillness and peace of an empty Church. Through the years I have attended many a Midnight Mass on Christmas Eve with my family. I am quite comfortable in any type of house of worship.

I felt extremely honoured when on my first visit to Assisi in 1976, I was invited by a Franciscan friar to read the Gospel at a Mass in the Portiuncula which is a little chapel located within the huge Basilica of St. Mary of the Angels. I felt very blessed to be able to do the reading in the Portiuncula which is known to be St. Francis' favourite chapel which he had restored in the year 1209. I took this as a sign that St. Francis had no problem with me doing so. Through the years, I have met many holy and devoted priests and I am always at ease with them and enjoy their company very much.

Although I had been hurt by the dogmatic pronouncements of the Roman Catholic Church, I did leave on my own accord. I have long since let go of traces of Catholic guilt and my sense of being lost without the Church. I have made my peace with God and I am quite content with my lot. However, I owe the Church a debt of gratitude because of my early religious training. I believed in God, angels, saints and the concept of the afterlife. Spirit was not foreign or strange to me, and I do personally believe that Catholics make good Spiritualists, because of these teachings.

I shared an ongoing joke with Monsignor Michael Regan, who was the parish priest of Our Lady of Perpetual Help Church in Carrollton, Georgia. Whenever we would meet, Father would say... "Now Joe, there is only one way" and I would finish the sentence for him... "Yes Father I know, through Holy Mother Church." He was a good priest and always wanted me to go to confession and return to the fold. He was doing his job and I always humoured him. This just goes to prove that Catholic teachings once ingrained, are not easily forgotten.

During the Summer of 1979, I did have the opportunity to verbalize my feelings about the Church to a priest. This priest had been a missionary in Haiti and had recently returned to Montreal. My friend Andree Duquette knew him and told him about her friend, a Spiritualist medium who had been a former altar boy. He was interested to meet me. I knew he wanted to check me out and this was agreeable to me. I was invited to his home and we had a very pleasant evening. He was aware of Spirit and of mediumship from his Haitian experience. He knew I was no longer a practicing Catholic. We spoke for several hours in an open and honest manner. I related everything to him, including the past hope I had had of becoming a brother. We spoke of homosexuality and how I felt about the Church's position on this issue. We spoke of how I turned my back on God and left the Church. He got who I was. At the end of the evening Father asked if we could join hands in prayer. As we prayed together he asked if I would forgive the Church for all that She had done to me. I replied, "Of course, I had done so years ago and it no longer mattered to me at this point in my life." I knew that I was doing good work and making a difference and my sexual orientation had no bearing on the matter.

One of the things that irks me about major religions is the patronizing attitude concerning homosexuality and in particular, when they make the pronouncement: "They love the sinner but they hate the sin" - My response to this comment is: **"THANKS FOR NOTHING ... who died and made you God?"**

The Catholic Church teaches that homosexual acts are intrinsically evil because "they close the sexual act of the gift of life". In other words, they do not make little Catholic babies, and there's the rub. It is all about the propagation of the faith. How would religions survive if they condoned homosexuality? Their future is not assured if there is no guarantee of children to be born.

The Catholic Church will sanction that the homosexual person can be called to chastity and live a celibate life. If one chooses to live that way, it is their private concern. It might be of interest to point out that most homosexuals do not lead lives of irresponsible depravity and wanton promiscuity. There are many gay men who have actually fathered children in the context of a heterosexual relationship, to discover later that they are indeed homosexual and then embraced their homosexuality. It does happen, and often.

In the December 24, 2008 edition of The Montreal Gazette, I read the following remarks from Pope Benedict's Christmas Message. "Saving humanity from homosexuality or transsexual behaviour is as important as saving the rainforest." The Pope further described behaviour beyond traditional heterosexual relations as "a destruction of God's work." I was furious when I read these absurd remarks. These homophobic comments coming from a Pontiff only encourages disdain and further homophobia in a world where there is already too much hatred.

To my mind if you are gay, then be gay and get on it. Let other people mind their own affairs. Get on with your life and don't let them get you down. God created you to live your own life and not to be bullied by people who would disagree how you choose to live your life.

Organized religions are no different from any other authoritarian institution that for all intents and purposes are run as a business. They have their rules and rubrics which are steeped in tradition. If one can abide by them, then all is well. If one finds that they cannot abide by the rules, then seek other options which are more suitable to your spiritual needs.

I hold that all people are created in the image and likeness of God. And I ask, since when does God create second rate or defective creatures? The Eternal Spark resides within all. We are all of us, God's children, none greater or lesser in the eyes of The Eternal One. We are all part of the human family and we should not allow ourselves to be shamed because of our sexuality. Do not allow any organization or individual to tell you that you are not loved by The Creator based on their personal religious beliefs or moral code which transforms into intolerance, hatred and bigotry. Do not turn your back on God because of religious admonishments. Establish your own personal relationship with God and talk to Him directly. If need be find yourself a Church or a spiritually directed organization where you are made to feel welcome and which accepts you as you are. Every person has the right to live the life that God has given them in dignity and with pride. Do not let anyone put you down because of your sexual preference or whom you choose to love. Be who you are no matter what. Be true to your own nature. I have mentioned this in a previous chapter, but it bears repeating. **Being gay is not a choice.**

Individuals can have shades of Light and lavender and still be spiritually fulfilled. There is no conflict between the two. If you treat people the way they want to be treated and do no harm, then you are living in the Light.

The feelings of self-loathing and low regard in which I held myself because of my belief that I was not pleasing in the sight of God, was an extremely destructive force in my early life. This is my personal experience. In my life, my sexuality never came first, my humanity did. If people do not wish to befriend you because of your sexual preference, simply do not bother with them. You don't need them in your life and they are not worth the knowing.

2011 is a much different world than the one I grew up and came out in the late fifties and sixties. There have been great strides made in the area of gay rights but there is still a long way to go.

Lise Caron, a personal friend of many years and a well-known Montreal astrologer reminded me that she had recently listened to a tape recording of a reading I had given her in 1994. When the reading was finished, Lise and I apparently had a conversation which remained on the tape. During this conversation I expressed the desire to write about being gay and spiritual because I felt strongly about this issue. If I might spare only one individual from the anguish caused by the feeling of being separated from God, then I am happy. This is my reason for addressing this issue.

I believe God never gives us anything that we cannot handle. If The Lord closes one door perhaps it is because He has created a different door for you to enter.

For as God's own child you are a gift to earth, so rare
And whatever your path, know that God also walks there
As His eye is upon the sparrow, you are also in His view
Know that He accepts and unconditionally loves you
So accept yourself, and in your own heart be true
For this is what God wants of you.

-Joey Crinita

In my experience as a medium, I have come into contact with many and varied individuals. When I work with Spirit I am privileged to be able to see the Light within people. I see the beauty of a person's soul shining through their eyes.

I feel their energy and I believe that God the Creator of all does not judge us to make us wrong. The loving and healing energy of the Great Spirit is bestowed upon all of His children without exception. So if you happen to have a dash of lavender within you, be not troubled. God created you this way for His Divine Purpose and we all know that His way is not always revealed as we traverse this mortal plane. Be who you are and let your inner Light shine, and if it has a lavender hue, so be it.

You may just happen to be one of the 'enchanted' few.

CHAPTER VII
PEOPLE I'VE MET ALONG THE WAY

INTRODUCTION

In this lifetime, I've been most fortunate to have crossed paths with many exceptional people who at one time or another have made a big difference in my life. I believe that one is destined to meet certain individuals who leave an indelible mark on your heart.

The individuals mentioned herein have all taught me something and have left me a wiser being for having known them. For this I am truly grateful. There are others not mentioned here, but you know who you are.

Elizabeth and Bill McIntosh

Millie Gordon

Marie Perkins

Ben Henry Osborne

Isabel M. Hickey

Marjie Marquis

Christine Burnett-Smith

Elizabeth and Bill McIntosh

Elizabeth and Bill McIntosh have been Spiritualists and mediums for almost fifty years. Elizabeth was born and raised in Glasgow, Scotland. Her family were members of the Salvation Army. She knew nothing of Spiritualism until after her arrival in Montreal, Canada. Bill McIntosh, on the other hand was born into a Spiritualist family and raised in a tenant block in Glasgow. He recalls living on the first floor of the flats, his grandfather and grandmother lived above them and held Spiritualist home circles. Bill recalls when he was about seven years of age, before the Second World War, a séance was held at his great-grandmother's house. He was too young to be let in, but he would listen at the door through the letter box. He was told it was a materialization séance. The medium was one Mrs. Smith who was a deep trance healer. She went into deep trance and a materialized Spirit would give people healing. Bill thought this was normal as these things took place in his home environment.

His grandmother and a group of her lady friends would hold home circles. They always invited a female neighbour into the group who did not necessarily know much, (if anything) about Spiritualism. The neighbour agreed to be used as a battery. Spirit would take the energy from her, adding to the energy from the other women which enabled Spirit to move the trumpet in that circle. There was always a lot of physical phenomena that took place in these home circles. The practice of Spiritualism was quite common among Scottish folk, then and now.

Elizabeth did not become involved in Spiritualism until 1959. She was thirty-one years of age at the time. She had infrequently attended the First Spiritual Church in Montreal and did not fully comprehend Spiritualism, or what it was about. One evening, the pastor of the Church, the Reverend James Snook, (who was an excellent medium) gave Elizabeth a message from the platform. "I don't often say this, but you are a power center and you should be sitting to develop mediumship." After receiving this message from Reverend Snook, Elizabeth was invited to attend a development class in 1960, which was held in the Church and led by Reverend Snook. Out of mere curiosity, she accepted. There were about twelve people in the group sitting in circle formation in a dimly lit room. Elizabeth looked about the room and knew where all of the other sitters were seated. What she could not comprehend at the time was that they appeared to be different people. They were being transfigured by ethereal beings. These Spirit people appeared to be solid and their physical features were evident down to the twinkle in their eye as they overshadowed the people who were actually sitting in the chairs. Elizabeth started to describe all these different people she was seeing and asked, "I don't understand what is happening. Why am I seeing all these strange people?" The more experienced sitters in the room chuckled. They knew what was taking place. Reverend Snook assured her not to worry. Elizabeth though apprehensive, was interested and sat back to see what else would unfold. She said, "Towards the end of the evening, I realized that my breathing was becoming very definite and very noisy. I felt that I was drawing my breath all the way from my toes and it was getting long and very deep. I felt peculiar. My head had a swimming sensation and I thought it is all this breathing, but I had no way of controlling it. I couldn't cut it off and wondered to myself, what's happening? I realized that the power was being pulled from the back of me and I felt as if I were being drawn through the wall. I could feel myself getting taken in and I said... help me, help me – something is happening and there is somebody doing something to me. They are taking me some place and they are saying, "but you and I are one." I couldn't realize what they were speaking about. I must admit at the time because of my limited understanding, I was afraid; but I let go." I immediately went into trance and that was when 'Running Water' came through to me whilst I was in the trance condition. He told me his name was Running Water and that I had been his daughter in a previous lifetime and that 'Dancing Flower', who came with him, was my sister. I really did not know anything about reincarnation at that time. But it was real for me. I thought that it was right.

When I came out of the trance state, Reverend Snook turned to me and assured me that it was all right. "We are going to close you off. That means that you fold your arms across yourself and cross your legs. We'll just ask that the Guides stand back at this time since you are so new." Running Water has been with me since that time. He is my main Spirit Guide and helps me with clairvoyance, healing and many other things. Of that, I am sure.

"Two weeks later I returned to the circle and had my very first contact which was very definite. A beautiful English lady took me over and in a very Anglicized voice (Elizabeth has a broad Scottish accent), she told us her name was Mrs. Harickson, where she had come from in England, that she had been a school teacher and her favourite poem had been, 'I Saw a Cloud of Daffodils'. She repeated this and then she fumbled for a line and said, "My, it's been so long – somebody help me." From then on I had many wonderful contacts and without a doubt ample proof that Spirit is me and them and we're all one."

In keeping with that thought, a visiting medium from the United States, a Mr. Deeak gave Elizabeth a message concerning a Spiritualist Church in Glasgow, which did not mean anything to her at the time. But he said to "Ask your mother-in-law when you go back to Scotland to visit her about this and she will be able to confirm and tell you about what I am saying." When Elizabeth and Bill next visited Glasgow and spoke to Bill's mother, Mrs. Dorothy McIntosh (who was herself a gifted medium), she said, "Oh yes! That did happen. There was a split in the Spiritualist Church in Glasgow." That was true. This was great proof that Spirit does indeed know what is going on, and will do their utmost to prove it to us.

Bill McIntosh relates how Elizabeth and he came to be in Montreal and the part which Spirit played in this. "There was no reason on God's earth that we should come to Canada. We were contently living in Glasgow. This couple came to live next door to us. They had just come from Canada and that put the bug in my ear. We talked to them about living in Canada and in two years time we were here. We relocated to Toronto. Elizabeth got a job just like that. I on the other hand, could not find a job and I walked the streets of Toronto looking for work. I got an interview and I think this is quite important... we don't pay enough attention and listen to our thoughts. I was walking to an interview and walked past Molson Brewery. I saw the Employment Office and had time, so I walked in. Although they had no jobs, the guy gave me a form to fill out. I said that I had filled in hundreds of these things in the past couple of weeks. He said that being the case, I'll take a look. He took the form and looked at it. He then disappeared into the back office. He returned to ask if I could be there at half past two. I said I don't know, because I have a meeting with somebody down the road. He said if you can make it, come back. I get down there, the fellow I was to meet had missed his plane so I went back to Molson Brewery and said to the guy, "My appointment didn't work out." He said, "Good, we can interview you now because two engineers from Montreal are here for the day. I was interviewed and offered a job in Montreal. I said, "I don't want to go to Montreal, I prefer to remain in Toronto." A couple of days later I received a phone call from Montreal asking to please come down, we'd love to have you. Nothing was happening in Toronto so I came down and that is how it worked out. The mechanics of why and how these things happen are interesting. Had this fellow not missed his plane, I would not have gone into Molson's. I am of the opinion that Spirit knows things and did move things for me and this may have been a means to an end because when we got to Montreal, it was there that we discovered Elizabeth was a medium.

In 1990, after living in Canada for thirty-five years, Elizabeth and Bill moved to Perth, Scotland where they still reside. They continue to make a yearly trip to Montreal to keep in touch with their many friends. Through the years they have worked together travelling extensively in the United States and Canada conducting workshops and using their combined talents and experience as mediums, healers and spiritual teachers. I have had the privilege of their friendship and working with them for many years.

In April of 2010 on a recent visit to Montreal, we taped the following conversation:

Joey: How do you receive your Spirit messages? Do you hear them inside your head or outside of your head?

Elizabeth: Well, I send a thought for whomever I am going to be working for and I ask that the Guides come forth and that I be a channel for him. I ask Running Water to bring forward whoever needs to come and then I think no more about it. I open my mouth and I'm a ventriloquist. I just say what I get and I don't judge it because if I get into my head about it, I'll say, "Why am I feeling that?" And then I'll say to myself in my head, "I don't think that applied to him or her." So I keep out of it and I just repeat what

	I hear. It is mental mediumship. But it is not from me, it is from the Guide coming to me and through me. It is simply...from, through and out.
Joey:	You both have been mediums most of your lives. What does it add to your life? Does having this faculty make you feel any different?
Elizabeth:	I think it gives you a peace. It takes away fear, and because of all the things that have happened, you know there is a continuity of life. This life is one stage and you will go to another stage. I also think that just to have been of service is important. To me it is maybe a compensation for all the rotten things which happen in the world. It is definitely all about being of service.
Joey:	Do you think it is necessary for people to know their Guides?
Elizabeth:	I do not think it is necessary to know the name of your Guide. You just get out of the way and let it happen.
Bill:	I am not conscious of Guides or anything like that. When I am on the platform, I stand up, I get the impression to go this way and I start working and as I'm working with this person, then in the back of my head, there comes the face of the next person I am going to go to. I don't hear voices and that, I just get impressions to say things and sometimes I get a lot of emotional stuff. I know that I am picking up the emotions of the person I am going to. Then at times, I get pictures, like mind pictures. I might see somebody shoveling coal and I have to interpret the symbol.
Elizabeth:	It is not a disturbing feeling. There is a part of me that knows I am here to help somebody with what I receive from Spirit. For example, in a congregation of fifty people you cannot personally select an individual you wish to give a message to, you must go to the person you are directed to by Spirit I think that you go

where you are told to go and that is it. You just get this feeling, "Well, I've just got to talk to that person." I can give you an example just to show you how you don't know where to go. When we were in Glasgow in 1973, we went to Burrough Hall for a service and there was a blind woman giving the messages, doing the clairvoyance. Although she was born without eye sockets and was stone blind, she was an outstanding medium. She had to be led up to the platform. She'd go to the people in the congregation and identify them, saying... "The lady who has on a lavender scarf or the lady who has a flower on the side of her hat." She could give messages you wouldn't believe.

Bill: What impressed me about this woman was she would say... "I want to go four rows back, three seats in to the gentleman in the grey suit who has a red scarf."

Joey: What advice would you give to someone who wants to develop his or her mediumship?

Elizabeth: I think that they have to sit and meditate for awhile and ask if they can be used as a channel, that the power come to them. I think the prerequisite of any spiritual development is patience. To know that it is not instant soup! Seek out a group of dedicated people who are all willing and committed to be part of a development class. Whoever comes up as a medium, let it come. I think it has to be that type of thing.

Bill: I agree completely with one little proviso, and I have a thought. Generally in a group of like people, there is one individual who may stand out as having the ability. We all have psychic abilities, but one may be just a wee shade ahead. I think in order to help, if you wanted to develop one person in that group and have the one person concentrated on at each class, then I think the energy has to be focused. If you are leading the class, you have to be sensitive to the fact that someone may possess more psychic ability than another. To lead a development class, one must know about Spiritualism. A leader must not be selfish in terms that Spirit will work solely through them. Be observant of the group to see who amongst the sitters may have the gift more so than another and assist them to develop.

In terms of physical mediumship, get a group of dedicated people who are willing to sit for trumpet or materialization. Decide who is going to be the physical medium and who will have the trumpet beside them. Focus on physical mediumship alone. Messages will not be given. The only purpose is to sit and send power. In a sense, be a battery for the one who is developing the physical mediumship.

Joey: Do you think mediums are born with the gift?

Bill: I have always said that mediums are born. I am of the opinion that there are some unconscious mediums and if they get the opportunity to attend a group, then a confident and natural medium will help to pull it out of the individual. What does it do for me? I've not really given it much thought other than quite often I will say to myself, "I had that thought and totally ignored it and look where I am now."

Then again you see, you have to think practical. For example, when I'm doing a healing I begin to get feelings and sensations and begin to receive one or two little messages. However, in Britain when you are a healer you are not supposed to pick up things clairvoyantly when you give healing. This is something I disagree with. For example; if I am giving healing to someone and clairvoyantly pick up a bunion on their big toe, I tell them that because it is a fact. Where does that come from? Well, to me, that was a clairvoyant impression received while healing. That was the healing part of my work. Then I started to get into the clairvoyance. In my particular case it took twenty-five years. It

	was a long process. Thanks to Elizabeth, who would shout at me, "Don't get into your head about this stuff, just do it."
Elizabeth:	I can remember when I was young. I used to write poetry, all types of things and I would see people and I'd say, "Who was that?" and my mother would say, "Oh, get out of here." She was in the 'Sally Ann' and knew nothing of Spiritualism. My first real experience was at Reverend Snook's class. So you know, I think sometimes it is going into a group and just letting it happen.
Joey:	Elizabeth, in 1992 when you were sixty-four, you experienced a cerebral aneurysm. Were you conscious of Spirit during that time?
Elizabeth:	I don't know if you'd say I was semi-conscious but I knew the people were there. I was aware of the Guides being there and the other part of my consciousness asking them to help me through whatever was going on. I also asked to be full in the mind so that when I came back I would have my full faculties. And yes, I definitely think that I got a lot of help during the operation and after the operation. I remember my Chinese Doctor and Running Water were there. At the same time, I was aware of other Guides singing Christian hymns which had to do with heaven and God.

Also, I had another experience. I had a hysterectomy when I was forty-two. It was a period of convalescence and I did not do anything. I wasn't at Church for a while and then went back. I remember it was a Sunday afternoon. When I walked into the Church I was overwhelmed by the energy of the Guides. It was so strong that I thought I would pass out. I was being taken over. It was just the power of that. So I do think they are there and when you need them, they are there for you. I don't call in my Guides every day. I don't call on my Guides to say, "When will I get this dress"? or things like that. This is a lot of nonsense, they have better things to do. But I do think when you need something that has to do with a physical ailment or something, I am not saying they will give you the cure for it but I do think that they calm you down so that you can heal yourself a lot. I believe that there is a Spirit Healer. I believe that there are Spirit Doctors that do things. I also believe that you must pull yourself together, and use your own existing power. I do believe that they are on call and they are there when you need them. And the important thing I think is that they are on call for you when you are asking for healing for someone else via absent healing. I mean, it is not just talking to air. You are conscious of drawing Spirit in to you and ask that Spirit will direct the healing energy and thoughts you are sending to where it is needed.

Millie Gordon

Millie Gordon was psychic from birth. Although she had the sight, she did not think it to be anything extraordinary. A great faith in The Almighty came easily to her. Her father was a Rabbi and he taught his daughter from an early age that God always listened to our prayers... and pray she did. I met Millie through the kindness of Terry Martel and the connection was instant. I had never met a really 'spiritual' person prior to this meeting outside of my Roman Catholic experience. Learning that Millie was tuned in was great news to me. As I have mentioned in Chapter 4 of this book, Millie and I would have talks of things spiritual. She was born into the Jewish faith and was thus raised. When she was in her twenties, she had a vision of Baha'u llah, the founder of the Baha'i faith. It is interesting to note that his birthday was November 12, 1817 – Millie was born November 11, (a true Scorpio, the sign of the healer and the mysteries of life and death). Through her vision, Millie was inspired to follow this prophet and to live by his teachings. In the forties she travelled across Canada and into the United States to Georgia, Louisiana and Mississippi to share her beliefs as a Baha'i and was run out of a few Bible Belt towns. She adhered to the Baha'i teachings all of her life. She fully embraced the concept that "The earth is but one country and mankind its citizens." (Baha'u llah). There was an aura of gentleness about Millie and she had the bluest eyes that would often mist over when she was reading my palm. Millie subscribed to the Psychic News from the Spiritualist Association of Great Britain. This was my introduction to the psychic world. I loved my chats with Millie. I had so many questions to be answered, and there was so much to learn. Millie was a very giving soul and as kind as she was sensitive. That is what made her such a good intuitive. She certainly operated from a strong spiritual foundation, and that was most important to her.

Although she did attend the occasional Spiritualist service, just to see "what was going on", she knew little of Spirits and Spiritualism. She encouraged me to visit a Spiritualist Church. She sensed that was where I belonged. Millie had visions all of her life and would receive very strong and accurate premonitions which I have written about in The Medium Touch in Chapter 9. Millie worked in an office for a large shipping company in Montreal as a typist for many years. Her male bosses were always trying to get rid of her because she was older than many of the other women in the office. This caused her great distress. To remedy the situation, she wore a blonde wig and did not look her age. Millie was almost six feet tall and her presence reflected her inner serenity. She never felt comfortable at her workplace and she finally decided when she was sixty-five to resign, leave Montreal and move to Vancouver. She had a brother who lived there and the weather was much better. She moved in with me for a month before she relocated to start a new life at sixty-five. I admired her courage. I often visited Millie in Vancouver and stayed at her apartment. On one particular occasion I was working as a guest medium at the Vancouver Psychic Society where I acknowledged her from the platform, and she beamed. Millie lived well into her nineties and always retained her sweet disposition. Through her gifts she helped many souls including myself and I am proud to have known her. In my opinion, Millie was a woman of great faith who never lost sight of her spiritual purpose and the vision which helped to shape and change her life.

Like many of the conscious people who have crossed my path, Millie possessed a great sense of humour. An indication of Millie's sense of fun was the bright yellow stationery she used for her correspondence. Her personal cards were imprinted- a Dilly from Millie....

The following note is dated October 1980.

Dear Pal Joey

Your birthday will soon be nigh so I want to be on time to wish you the Best Ever. Have had you on my mind lately so expect its ESP. I've been laid up with a very bad cold but taking antibiotics is helping - plus sciatica, etc.... So what else is new? Anyway, maybe it is all contributing to OLD AGE creeping. Yea? How is your psychic ability? I am still an SOB (Sweet Old Believer). Am enclosing articles I found on St. Francis of Assisi, thought you would appreciate it. I'm playing piano and doing old time sing-along for Senior Lodges hereabouts. So sad, but glad to be of cheer as a volunteer.

So long for now, and have fun now that you are a year older.

Fondly always, Millie

In the thirties under the name of Rena Gordon, Millie trod the boards of Vaudeville as a comedienne with a Yiddish accent performing the same type of skits as the great Fanny Brice. She loved to entertain and always had a humourous song or one-liner ready. When I think of Millie, I think of paying it forward. If it were not for her guiding me when I truly needed spiritual direction, then I quite possibly may never have walked into my first Spiritualist Church. Millie empowered me and encouraged me on my spiritual journey. She helped me take my first steps. For this I am eternally grateful. She often referred to herself as "Mrs. Spook" and never took herself too seriously as far as her readings were concerned. She was always accurate and was an excellent reader.

Millie was aware of the maxim, "Serve or Suffer" and serve she did. Right up until the very end in true spiritual and Baha'i fashion. She walked the talk. She once told me that on her tombstone she wanted these words inscribed, "Not in Service" because she had seen this sign on a bus, and thought it hilarious.

Marie Perkins

I met Marie Perkins in 1970 whilst on my first trip to the Spiritualist Camp in Chesterfield, Indiana. I was accompanied by my friend Gloria Gari. On the day of our arrival, we attended an outdoor demonstration of clairvoyance. The medium bringing the Spirit messages was Marie. I did not know her. Part of her message to me was to bring a message from a Spirit who had never touched the earth plane. This was a male child who had been a miscarriage. She advised me that he was named in Spirit and his name is Paul. He had grown up in Spirit and he was very interested in my spiritual welfare. I was aware of him and knew that my mother had miscarried a male child in 1954. Had he lived, he would have been sixteen years of age at that time. I was aware that Spirits who never touch the earth plane grow up in the Spirit World. They, to my mind, become angels.

We did not speak to Marie after her message service. Gloria and I were both surprised when two evenings later we saw Marie again at James Tingley's materialization séance. Marie was Tingley's cabinet assistant which meant that she sat outside of the cabinet to ensure that all went well during the séance. It was for the protection of the medium, in case some over-enthusiastic individual tried to grab or touch the medium whilst they were in a state of trance. Gloria and I installed ourselves next to Marie to ensure we would have a clear view of the evenings' materializations. That evening my brother Paul materialized to me and gave me some information which I was able to have confirmed five years later from a medium in London, England, who had no idea of who I was. Paul had selected Marie to let me know his name, and for that I am pleased.

Marie Perkins was a very affable woman, always good natured and very well-spoken. She had been a nurse for many years and possessed a quality about her which many caretakers have. I believe that made her a very strong healer. She possessed physical mediumship, was a trumpet medium and also a very good clairvoyant and inspirational speaker. I enjoyed watching Marie work on the platform. She was always gracious and had a very pleasing public persona, combined with her obvious talent as a medium.

I met Marie and her then husband, Henry Curtain one day when they were out for a walk on the Campgrounds. Marie remembered me from the Tingley séance and invited me to her home for a cup of tea that afternoon. I accepted. It was the beginning of a lovely friendship. Marie was seventy-two when we met and Henry was seventy. I would tease her about marrying a younger man. Henry's last name was Curtain. The joke was that when Marie married Henry, it was curtains for her. I was to visit them in Camp Chesterfield a few times and also visited them at their home in Minneapolis, Minnesota where Marie was the Pastor of the Christian Ministry Church. Two years later in 1972, Marie Perkins ordained me as a Minister in the Universal Temple of Truth Foundation in Toledo, Ohio. At that time it was deemed necessary for one to be a Minister of Religion in order to practice mediumship in certain States due to some archaic legal requirement. I was thirty-two at the time and had been a Spiritualist for six years.

I always enjoyed my time with Marie and Henry, of whom I was very fond. I called him Uncle Henry. He was a small man, about five foot five with slicked-down black hair and a little waxed moustache. Henry was a Catholic and a Knight of Columbus. He was very proud of his regalia which consisted of a black cape lined in red, a black chapeau with white ostrich plume and a sword that he was always more than happy to show me. He loved Marie. They were like teenagers together. Neither had children, so I think I filled that gap. Henry was a heavy cigarette smoker and acquired emphysema, which would ultimately result in his death. I remember the last time I saw him in 1975. He had driven me to the airport in Minneapolis. There was a sadness in his good-bye and I sensed that we both knew this was a final farewell. It turned out to be so. Henry and I would talk about Spiritualism. He was not a Spiritualist and not too fond of some of the people in the Camp, but he never criticized or made any derogatory remarks. I must state that during my stays at Marie and Henry's home in Camp Chesterfield, I never felt there was anything unethical about her work. I say this because I was still leery about some of the workers in the Camp. My visits at that time were purely social, to visit with Marie and Henry.

Marie had studied her mediumship under Ethel Post Parish who was a very well-known accredited medium in her day. Marie's father was a Minister, so she was quite familiar with the Bible and was also a devout Christian.

She once told me this story; as a young girl she was watching a white horse perform at a fair. This horse could count to ten with its hoof. She decided then and there, there must be some great infinite intelligence behind all creatures, and that experience made her want to find out more.

Marie and I would talk about Spirit and Spiritualism, which she had devoted her life to. She impressed me with her simple and uncomplicated approach to Spiritualism. She had a large following and had given numerous consultations, was a pastor for many years, but always remained uncomplicated and humble in her service to others.

After Henry died, Marie moved to Scottsdale, Arizona. I visited her there and met her new husband, Joseph Tombs. I said to Marie, "After Curtains - now its Tombs. It is getting closer." We both laughed.

In 1976 Marie accepted my invitation to serve as a guest medium at the First Spiritual Church in Montreal. She was seventy-eight at the time and I appreciated the effort which she made on my behalf. Marie visited for a week. She served our Church on a Sunday and gave an inspiring and lovely talk followed by an excellent demonstration of clairvoyance in her usual kind and warm manner. She wrote me a note saying, "I shall always remember your kindness to me and the loveliness of your Church people and friends while I visited Montreal."

Marie retired in 1979 and moved to Prescott, Arizona. Marie graduated to the Higher Life on September 8, 1985. Well done Marie! See you on the other side.

Ben Henry Osborne

I first met Ben Osborne at a Life Spectrums Conference in the late seventies. I was introduced to Ben by his associate and friend, Shirley Chambers who ran the Karin Foundation along with Ben from their home in Jasper, Georgia. I have known Shirley Chambers from my early days when we met at a Spiritual Frontiers Fellowship in Poughkeepsie, New York. She had at that time told me of Ben and wanted us to meet, knowing we would get along. And we did. Ben was an Aries, born March 26 and had a quick-fire sense of humour and always ready to laugh. There was a playfulness in Ben which I found very entertaining. He was a devotee of Babaji and presented me with this simple prayer:

Prayer of Babaji

"Love – Truth – Simplicity - Serve all beings equally – everyone should consider himself a humble servant of the world."

I believe that Ben lived by these words. He travelled to India, Egypt, the Himalayas and Nepal. Ben loved the Eastern philosophies and he fully embraced the teachings which he gleaned from the many holy women and men whom he met on his sojourns. He was equally at home in both Western and Eastern mysticism and an excellent psychic and palmist.

Ben combined good common sense with a deep knowledge of things spiritual. He would speak with spiritual authority on such subjects as karma, universal law, the destiny of humanity and he believed and taught that the message for humanity was simply: "Know who you are, be who you are and go to your place." Ben and I frequently spoke about love, life and Spirit. One thing Ben did teach me was about Time, Place and Order. He taught in order for things to work out on any level of circumstance, these three things had to be in sync; the right Time, the right Place and the right Order. When these conditions are aligned in the Universe, then things unfold as they should.

Ben was a student of Isabel M. Hickey and of Ann Manser, two western spiritual teachers he held in high regard. He was the founder of the Foundation of Truth in Atlanta, Georgia and was also active in many other spiritually inclined groups. He frequently conducted and led tours to India to visit Babaji and other Spiritual Masters. He was truly a very eclectic metaphysical teacher who had much to teach to many.

One of my fondest memories of Ben: whilst on a visit to their home in Jasper, he and Shirley mounted me on a horse and we rode into the beautiful Blue Ridge Mountains of North Georgia. Well... Ben and Shirley (expert riders) rode while I clung on for dear life while being smacked in the face by what felt like every tree branch as we rode up and down again from the mountain. I was terrified and the horse knew it. It was two hours of misery for me and two hours of laughter for Ben and Shirley. As for the horse, I had my photo taken sitting astride him simply for the proof. That was my first and last time on a horse.

In response to life's problems, Ben would often laugh and say: "You can't put boxing gloves on and box with God, your arms are too short." Another of his favourite wisdoms: "Coincidence is God's way of making things happen."

On one occasion we visited the Georgia Guidestones, an unusual monument located in Elbert County, Georgia which I have written about in From Chains to Wings. It was a very uplifting experience for me and I was very impressed by the messages for humanity that are inscribed into the stone slabs.

Soon after meeting Ben, during one of my trips to Atlanta, he introduced me to his good friend, Sharon Hollis. It was instant friendship between Sharon and I. We have been closely connected ever since. As the years went by, Ben, Sharon and I were frequently in communication and we kept abreast of what was going on in one another's life.

In December of 1990, I was living in Bethlehem, Pennsylvania. In a telephone conversation, Sharon and I discussed our individual plans for the upcoming Christmas Holidays.

The following was related to me by Sharon: "On the morning of December 22, the day before I was to leave to spend Christmas with my family in Birmingham, Alabama, I had a telephone conversation with Ben and told him about a dream I had the night before, where I only heard a voice speak from a very bright white room, "Joey went to New York and when he returned, he had died, and then he cried." Ben seemed alarmed, thinking something was wrong with you, stating he thought you had been quite out of sorts lately. I told Ben that the dream was wrong because you had gone to Florida to visit friends for Christmas. Ben replied to me that you had changed your plans and had gone to New York. (I had indeed gone to New York to spend the Christmas Holidays with my friends Michael Wasula and Leo Cazares at their home.) As friends do and because he was concerned, Ben was going to try and telephone you to make sure you were okay. As it unfortunately happened, Ben was found dead two days later on Christmas Eve, December 24. I called you Joey and left a message to call me. The dream came to life just as it was spoken to me. When you returned from New York, Ben had died and I am sure we both cried." Sharon further states: "As I have actually written this, I remember this last conversation as though it were yesterday."

Those of us who have had the privilege of knowing Ben Henry Osborne will never forget him. He was a loving, charismatic, warm and true friend who left us too early in his life. I can still hear Ben with his very southern drawl saying: "Hi y'all." When he passed to the Higher Life on December 24, 1990 he did indeed surrender to the Will of God.

Isabel M. Hickey

Known as the Mother of Spiritual Astrology and often referred to as the Cosmic Mother, Issie as she liked to be called by her friends, authored Astrology: A Cosmic Science which is considered a classic in astrology. Issie also wrote two other books: It Is All Right, an inspirational book that has changed the lives of many people and Minerva Pluto a further book on astrology.

I was living at 222 Redfern Avenue in Westmount, Montreal in a classic red-stone building on the third floor. I remember welcoming Issie and her companion, Tom Jackson to my apartment. They had travelled up from Ottawa where Issie had conducted a workshop for the Canadian Federation of Astrologers. They were accompanied by Brian Clark who was the President of the Federation of Canadian Astrologers. I was President of the First Spiritual Church and had extended an invitation to Issie to come and address our congregation. I was delighted to be in the company of this renowned spiritual teacher. Issie and Tom got settled, after which we all had a cup of tea. One of the first things that one noticed about Issie was the twinkle in her blue eyes. She sat comfortably on the sofa, and with a glint in her eye said to me... "Tell my something about myself." I said the first thing that came into my head, which was, "I want to call you General." Upon hearing this statement both she and Tom rocked with laughter. Little did I know at that moment that Issie was often referred to as "General Hickey" by some of their closest friends who truly adored her, and I was later to learn that they sometimes called her 'King Kong'. It was all done out of love. The humour of this is Issie knew of the King Kong nickname, but she never let on she did.

Issie delivered a beautiful and inspiring address to the congregation at the First Spiritual Church. Being the highly evolved spiritual teacher that Issie was, she felt very comfortable addressing any spiritually inclined group. She knew that basically, all is one. Thus began an enduring friendship. I would frequently visit Issie at her home in Watertown, Massachusetts and through her I met some life-long friends, such as her daughter Helen and Marjie Marquis.

Issie loved to laugh and had a wonderful sense of humour. She often laughed at herself. She said, "A sense of humour is high on the tree of life." On November 7, 1979

Issie related the following to me in a hand-written letter. She wrote: "Did I ever tell you about a beautiful Spring day I asked a friend to drive me down to the Browning Drake factory to audition for a job. I wasn't too anxious to work with Spring coming on but thought I should. They gave me a letter to type and I wanted to show my speed. The first sentence was... "We make all kinds of parts in this factory." I began to type. On the left is ASDF, on the right UIOP. F is the left last finger and P, the right last finger. I went to pull the letter out and was horrified with what I had done. I struck the wrong little finger. (The letter read: we make all kinds of farts in the =actory). I gave the man the letter, literally ran out of the office, got in the car and said..."Don't ask any questions, just get going." We did. Needless to say I didn't get the job. Oh well! You can't have everything! I can visualize Issie laughing as she remembered and wrote this letter.

Issie claimed if you went toward a spiritual group and everyone was very serious, and the group was very heavy, it probably was not very spiritual, because the light touch meant that there was Light within the group itself. Issie had a clear vision of who she was and why she was here on the planet. She never lost sight of the fact that as a spiritual teacher and counsellor, her life's work was to serve or suffer and even though she was aware of this, many people saw Issie as a spiritual Master. She never accepted it, or wanted to be known as such. She felt that you should not believe your own press clippings, or thrive on accolades. There was a spiritual trap, and a person could really get caught up on the personality and ego level. She believed that you had to die to your ego, or you could not evolve on the spiritual level. She did not encourage people to follow her, and never placed herself on a pedestal. Sometimes she did not always want to be the teacher; she loved to meet people socially, laugh and have fun. She always kept her ego in check.

As a teacher she would never speak about anything which she had not experienced herself. From Issie I learned the concept of a double-check and she was famous for them. She always had to be sure. She taught that if you were trying to receive psychic impressions from the Higher Self during meditation, you might get what you wanted to hear. You could interpret it the way you wanted to interpret it; it is really a delicate issue. For example, you may have a dream which you might interpret to go along with what you wish or need to hear or take psychic impressions in the same way. When she received a strong impression, she would not use it or credit it until she had a double-check on the physical level. It would be like saying, "God, how do we refine this? Has this come down through my Higher Self?" And she would wait until she received her second confirmation or double-check. There was an honesty about Issie. She never tried to make anyone like her, and she did not have to. You never had to wonder what her opinions were. There was a directness about her and she always said what she felt. She valued honesty in others and respected peoples' opinions, even if she did not concur with them. The people she felt strongest about were the ones who did not always agree with her. She did not have time for yes people. It was not a judgement on them; she just did not have the time.

In a letter to me, Isabel's daughter Helen Hickey related the following anecdotes concerning Issie in her words:

"I would kid Issie and say yup, I came at eight months because you did not want to carry me any more... you pushed me out." She always replied, "No, you chose the time you came, you were too nosy and wanted to get out to see what was going on here."

When I found out in neurology class in physical therapy school why I had been a klutz all my life, I called Issie up all excited to share with her the reason for my awkwardness all my young life. I used to fall all the time, even up the stairs. My father used to say if I was walking across the Sahara Desert and there was a pebble, I would stumble over it! Anyway, when I finished telling her all about vestibular stimulation, etc..., she said, "Well that's interesting. Now that you know that, will you be less of a klutz?" I responded, "Only a mother could make a remark like that!"

Helen Hickey passed to the Higher Life on March 16, 2005 at the age of 82.

Issie received her calling to be an astrologer through her meditation. She said that she was impressed to study and that she agreed to pursue her impression on the two following conditions: she would never look for a student or client, and whoever was drawn to her must be drawn in by love. If she could not draw people in by love, then she would discontinue her work. She believed that astrology without a spiritual connection was hollow. You had to love the person you were reading a chart for. She felt the astrological chart was like a road map that people could use, but it was necessary to see the spiritual principles that were underlying it. She once stated during a conversation that if you kept looking down at the chart and not into the person's eyes, you were probably not a good astrologer. It was necessary to operate from a caring and loving space in order to be effective when dealing with peoples' lives. She said, "The true purpose of astrology is to help us find our way out of dependence on external influences. So we can be a free soul guided only by the Light and love of our own being."

She believed that astrologers should be healers, and referred to astrology as God's fish hook. She loved her astrology, political astrology and personal astrology. She would also use her astrology for delving into history. There was not a subject that she did not know about or converse on. Her meditations however, were far more important to her than her astrology. Issie was very aware of her responsibility as a teacher and she felt her role was more spiritual than astrological. Issie believed firmly in spiritual healing. She felt that LOVE was the healer. Sometimes her lovingness would come in a hard critical form to people. If she felt that people were creating their own problems in their lives, she was quick to draw the matter to their attention. With some people she was hard. She said, "There are people that need to be hit over the head; that is how you reach them. Lovingness is not always soft words, and it is not always saying yes. Lovingness is sometimes very hard, and it sounds critical, but when I get that impression with people, that is how I deal with them." Helen stated, "Even when Issie was difficult, it usually was because Issie wanted you to be better (according to her standards) so you can't fault her for that. And she worked so hard on herself, knowing that she had warts, barbs and barnacles. The message that comes through over and over again in the letters from folks saying thanks for her books, is that they are helpful, practical and useful." Issie was very aware of the need to give back to the Universe and she believed in working for God, and periodically while doing charts she would get a feeling that she did not want to take money. So on that day she worked for God and took no payment for her work. She was using the principle of the law of supply by the giving she received. She remarked that on the days she worked for God, she either got people for whom it had been very difficult to come up with the money, or the people who came on those days had reached a point in their lives where they felt that no one would give anything for free. They would see her that day, and quite often the reading was not dramatic, but the important point was that here was someone who said, "No, it is free, I am working for God today." That was the ingredient they needed in their lives to begin to trust again.

Issie believed in reincarnation and she felt that she was Reverend Parker of Charlestown, Massachusetts in a past life. I found this very interesting because my paternal grandmother, Catherine Ryan was born and raised in Charlestown which is only one square mile, not very big.

Issie always had sage advice to impart. She said, "Turn our minds within and win the battle there – it is the only battle we need to win. It is the only battle for which we are responsible. It is an inside job. Do not fight our enemies deep within. We give them more power if we do." She would use the expression: "Never Mind – Always Heart", which meant that we needed to get out of our minds (heads) and into our hearts when walking the spiritual path.

One of my favourite Issie stories is this one related by Marjie Marquis.

"Issie, Tom Jackson and I motored to New York City to attend a Conference. It had been a hectic trip from Boston and we were fatigued. We arrived late at the Americana Hotel, got settled late, and woke up still weary. The three of us went down to the hotel restaurant for breakfast. We seated ourselves at a table and along came a waitress. It was like a movie; she was awful. She was slamming water on the table and was rude, and I thought, "Oh, we really need this, this morning, this vibration to start the day." The waitress left and Issie said, "Here is a good chance for us to watch how this stuff works. Want to turn her around?" We agreed. She said, "OK, everybody pray for her quietly, and each time she comes back, send her every bit of love you can." I thought, "7 o'clock in the morning, I want my coffee." We prayed and the next thing was that she put Issie's coffee down and she looked at her and said, "What a day I had." She must have told her every trouble she had, all the things that had gone on in her life, about the pain in her legs from arthritis, and so on. By the time we finished, she was bringing us extra coffee; she had even brought muffins and pastry. That for me was so important because it was real. Issie was about to lecture, and Issie was shy. I do not think anybody ever saw how shy Issie was, and right before she had to speak she was tense. Once she got into it, something else took over. However, on that morning, with her due to speak, having travelled most of the night and needing breakfast, she could easily have forgotten her own beliefs, and the waitress could have been a problem. Watching her turn it around was beautiful."

Issie believed in karma, it was important to her. She believed that we didn't come into this lifetime with a clear slate; we had debts we owed, and we had things we would get back in the form of gifts that we had given out. It was not so much that you had to pay for it; you had to understand it. Let us say you chose to come in for a lifetime of service. Issie would say, serve or suffer, by that she meant you should take joy in serving. But it was your free choice, and if you chose not to serve, that also was your prerogative. She stated that, "We all have a spiritual bank book and some people had more in their account than others." Today is all we have. Fill it with living and loving and the future is assured. Love comes, many times love goes, but love never leaves. Love is an energy. Use it or abuse it, the choice is always ours. Growth comes from being loving, not from being loved."

No story of Issie would be complete without the mention of Harmony Hill in Nottingham, New Hampshire. That was her Summer retreat, and she loved the place very much because it was in touch with nature. Her favourite time up at the Hill was between 6:30 pm and 7:30 pm in the early evening. She would refer to that time as the hour of the changing of the guard. Marjie Marquis recalled, "We would sit on the porch and as that time came, she would say, "Listen!" And you would hear the noises of nature, especially at Harmony Hill. The wind was magnificent. It almost sang in circles. Then everything would get quiet and you would feel this stillness. Issie would say the night devas were coming out, but there was a changing of the guard, where everything went still at that point, and she always tried to get quiet at that point to feel it. I do not think I would have noticed it if she did not say, "Listen" – and you could feel it, it would change."

In a letter from Issie postmarked April 28, 1980 she wrote: "Last night Harmony Hill was wrapped up in a cloak of mist and fog – and above an anemic looking moon. It was weird and beautiful. Made me think of the Hounds of the Baskervilles – only there were no hounds! This is the quietest place in the world when there isn't a great deal of company."

I have fond memories of Harmony Hill and of my visits to the Hill with Issie. I would fly into Boston and Issie and I would drive up to Nottingham, New Hampshire. I do not drive a car, and Issie would be at the wheel of her "big boat", a Cadillac I believe. My job was to sing along with her. Two of her favourite songs were, "Let the Rest of the World Go By" and the song to The Blessed Mother, "Dear Lady of Fatima". She would request that I sing the latter repeatedly, because of her great love of the Mother Mary, not because of my voice I am sure. Although not a Roman Catholic, Issie took the name Mary as her second name, in honour of The Blessed Mother.

I feel very blessed and privileged to have known Issie. I am grateful I had plenty of alone time with her. We would laugh and enjoy each other's company. Meditate, and talk of Spirit, to whom she referred to as "The Invisables" – she had a great faith in Spirit. It was always a special treat when Marjie would join us as they were two of my favourite people on the planet.

Issie slipped away quietly during her sleep on Tuesday, June 7, 1980 at her home at Harmony Hill. She was buried there on the Friday. She is buried in a tiny graveyard which contains the remains of two Generals dating back to the time of the American Civil War. So it is a fitting final resting place for General Isabel M. Hickey. There is no need to ask who is in charge.

I learned much from this wise woman. She wrote in my copy of her book, It Is All Right, To Joe – my cosmic Son who I've adopted whether he wants to be or not.

In her last letter to me on April 28, 1980, two months before she passed, she ended with,

Always and forever,

ME

I say – back at you Issie!

Marjie Marquis

I met Marjie at the same time I met Issie. Marjie was a past president of the Star Rovers, a well-known astrological group in the Boston area. She was also part of Issie's intimate circle of friends, and knew Issie extremely well. Born on July 30, Marjie was a strong and extremely serene Leo woman who committed her life to serving others. In May 1979 I gave a reading to Marjie at Harmony Hill, which was Issie's Summer retreat. During this reading, Marjie's nephew Phillip who was killed in a car accident in February 1979 at twenty years of age came through loud and clear for his favourite aunt. In another sad turn of events, Phillip's older brother Michael tragically passed on January 4, 1981. The two brothers were very close, and their untimely passing was extremely hard on Marjie and her family. The story of Phillip is related in The Medium Touch; Chapter 3 on The Experiences of Mediumship.

This particular reading further established the strong bond between Marjie and myself. Our hearts spoke and we connected with an energy that defies words. Marjie became my spiritual counsellor and we had many lengthy telephone conversations as well as in-person visits through the years to follow. I had such respect for Marjie's advice and guidance. She was a tower of strength for me during difficult times. She always had a simple, sincere and logical response to questions. We would discuss books, spiritual matters, world events and life in general for hours on end. Marjie was a loving, sensitive and oh! so wise individual. Her innate kindness was evident to all who met her. She kept a copy of my astrological chart in a frame on her desk and she always knew what astrological aspects that I should be aware of. She would telephone me and say, "Joe, I notice that you have a strong Jupiter aspect on now" and then proceed to advise me in astrological terms what it meant. In turn, I would translate this information into my own words. I am not an astrologer but I could always understand the essence of the message and I would say, "You mean this Marjie" – and she would laugh and say, "That's it exactly Joe." Marjie was so patient and very good at explaining astrological aspects to me, and she really got a kick of how I could tune into the interpretations intuitively.

I can still hear her voice and her gentle laugh in my head. I will never forget her. Marjie always encouraged me not to be too hard on myself. Because she knew me, I think better than anyone on the planet. She would send me clippings from newspapers or copies of poems or things that she thought I would like to read. She was really a guiding light to me and I do miss her terribly. Although I know that she is around in Spirit, I smile when I open a book and unexpectedly find a picture or a little note from Marjie is there. I gave her an icon of Michael the Archangel which I had purchased for her here in Montreal. She kept this in the office on her desk next to my chart. After her death, her daughter-in-law, Gina forwarded the icon to me because she felt that Marjie would want me to have it. I keep it in an honoured spot in my home, next to the relic of St. Francis of Assisi.

One of my favourite memories of Marjie was from a visit on a Sunday morning at her home in Cambridge, Massachusetts. Marjie prepared for me a breakfast of bacon, eggs and fried apples, which I had never tasted or previously heard of. She told me that her grandfather would make them for her when she was a child. Marjie loved her family: her wonderful son Dan and daughter-in-law Gina: her grandchildren, Matthew, Kristopher and Dawn were very close to her heart. They are lucky to have had such a one as Marjie in their midst as were her friends, students and all who knew her. When I visited Boston, Marjie would take me to Charlestown and up to Bunker Hill where my grandmother had come from and she also looked up family records for me.

Marjie's illness came on quite suddenly. During the Christmas period I had spoken to her and she advised me that she was going into the hospital, nothing serious, not to worry and we'd speak again soon. I was living in Toronto at the time. On Saturday, January 10, 1998 I went to a film at the Varsity Theatre which was near my home in downtown Toronto. The film was The Boxer, with Daniel Day Lewis. I was looking forward to seeing it. I went to an early afternoon screening and as I watched the film, a feeling of pathos and sadness came over me. I could really not concentrate on the movie and I knew within my heart that something was not right. I kept on thinking about Marjie and there was a sinking feeling in my gut. Something was not right, and as I hurried home on that cold January day, I intended to call Marjie or Gina to see what was up. I was not home long when I got the call from Gina. Marjie had passed. This was not expected. I had no idea how ill Marjie had been. She was diagnosed with lung cancer and I never knew or had any intuitive feelings about it. To make matters worse, I was not able to attend her funeral due to my business obligations in Toronto. I was in the middle of training sessions and could not get to Cambridge in time.

I lost one of my best friends whom I dearly loved. This was a tough one to take. I do feel Marjie around and I know that she guides me still. Her graduation to Spirit at sixty-two years of age left a huge void in my life. In a letter addressed to me, dated January 15, 1998, Helen Hickey was kind enough to share the following: "There were many, many friends at the wake and the funeral. Folks from the Star Rovers, from the Friday Nite Fix and of course, lots of Marjie's clients and students were there also. The presence of folks from the past brought in so many memories of Issie and her classes. Gatherings at Harmony Hill where we used to sing hymns sitting on the porch while Issie played the organ or the piano; our retreats in Rhode Island and a couple here in this area; and the role Marjie always played in helping others I directed to her, either to study with her, or to be counseled by her. The place was loaded with memories – so rich, so wonderful to remember, etc. At the funeral service we entered the church singing Amazing Grace; during the service the soloist sang Ave Maria, and Here I Am Lord. Then, as we were exiting, the organist played Kumbaya, My Lord. Oh, did the tears flow then. Because of not driving and transportation difficulties, etc, I did not go to the cemetery for the graveside service or to the Irish-American Club where the family had a reception following the burial.

Because of her great sensitivity, Marjie wrote beautiful poetry. The following poem which she wrote about her garden that she loved so much, was displayed at her wake.

The Garden

Come into my garden and take off your shoes.
And enter a chapel with no wooden pews.
Breathe in the fragrance and eat with your eyes.
Hear the sweet sound of the daffodil sighs.
Talk with the daisies in friendly array
Bow to the roses majestic display.
Be kissed by the lilacs that brush by your face.
And kneel before carpets of heavenly grace.
Touch the wild cosmos that reach for the Sun.
Pick the bright pansies, who laugh at the fun.

Each flower needs a different soil, a different kind of care.
Some are common, strong and hearty, some are delicate and rare.
One needs lots of sunlight. One hides in the shade.
The water lily loves the wet which makes the cactus fade.

As I ponder on what I would be, in this symphony,
A tulip tall, a sweet pea small, a fragrant peony,
An orchid with its mystery, a lily, strong and fair,
I spy a tiny, glowing light, growing everywhere.
A humble little beauty, which holds the juice of wine,
I choose to be, in the garden, the lovely dandelion.

-Marjie

Marjie and I were fated to meet and I look forward to our reunion someday in the great beyond. Until then, she lives within my memory, and always in my heart.

A final word of advice from Marjie taken from one of her notes:

"Be sure to ask for guidance in your decisions"
Love, Marjie

Christine Burnett-Smith

Christine Burnett-Smith was born in the town of Buckie, approximately fifty miles north of Aberdeen, Scotland. When she was a young child, the family moved to their hometown, Aberdeen. They lived in The Woodside area of the city. Christine was very proud of being a thoroughbred Aberdonian. Both of her parents were psychic so it was not unusual for the young Christine to follow in their footsteps. When she was eleven, she was stricken with polio and for five years was forced to lie down a great deal. As a result of this illness, she walked with a gait for the rest of her life and had severe back problems for many years. Christine related that "when you lie quietly you begin to discover the creative world about you. It is very important to stand and stare – to see the shimmer on a lake, listen to the sound of the wind, see the poetry of motion. This awareness is vital to a sensitive. Through it comes that extra-sensory perception of the power that permeates the Universe."

Although aware of her psychic abilities, she chose to ignore them, until one day during the Second World War, as she tells it: "I was working in the Foreign Office as a proof-reader with top-secret information. I was doing the late-night shift with a colleague in a room with no outside windows, so there was no draught of any kind, when suddenly like a flock of birds a pile of papers rose from my desk and went flying about in the air. It was most astonishing and I couldn't make it out, but my fellow-worker looked at me accusingly. "This is all your fault, Christine," she said. "What on earth do you mean?" I asked. "It's you and your psychic aura. Don't think I haven't noticed it. I can see it all round you. Now you'd better get those papers down somehow, and fast because we haven't much time left. What would the editor say!" So I concentrated on those papers, and they came quietly down and settled into a neat stack on my desk, all in perfect order again. "When we've finished this shift," said my colleague, "You're coming with me. I'm going to take you to see the finest psychic I know." "Well, if I come with you, there must be no collusion," I said. "From now until we get there I'm going to stick to you like a leech. You'll make no private phone calls." In the East End of London my friend knocked on a door that was opened by a little man who looked at me and immediately described the whole scene that had taken place.

He advised me about my psychic abilities and told me Spirit had done this to attract my attention and that, they did.

My back often troubled me a great deal, the aftermath of my polio, and a neurologist painted a bleak picture. One night as I lay in bed in great pain, very depressed, suddenly I saw a tall figure in a long brown robe crossing the room towards me. I wasn't a bit frightened because he exuded love and compassion. He came to my bedside and I could see the sandals on his feet. He made me turn over with my back to him and my knees drawn up. "From tonight," he said, "because you have the faith of a Trojan you will be healed. Tomorrow you must go to 42 Russell Square." He made me repeat the address. "Don't disobey me." I must have fallen into an instant deep sleep then because when I turned over it was morning. "What an amazing dream," I thought. Suddenly I heard a man's voice from the other side of the empty room. "Do you remember the address?" "Yes," I said. "Forty-two Russell Square." "Go now," said the voice. The place was a large house in an area unfamiliar to me with about sixty people waiting. A man's voice from behind a screen said: "Send the little lady in next, please." In I went to find a woman washing her hands at a basin. She made me sit with my back to her and ran her hands down my spine and all over my back. "From today you will begin to get well," she said in the same deep voice that I had heard earlier. "You are to join my developing circle and sit on my right side and all your gifts will be unfolded. A weed can spring up overnight, but an orchid requires care." For eleven years, every week I sat on the right hand side of Nan MacKenzie in her developing circle – a regular gathering of psychic people expanding their sensitivity. Nan was one of the most well-known mediums in London. I was never a chatty person, and it was only after three years that Nan MacKenzie asked me how I came to be there. She was quite astonished when I told her. She had absolutely no idea because when we first met she was in deep trance, and it was not she but a controlling Spirit entity who had invited me. Nan trained me, taught me how to use colour therapy and musical vibrations in my healing work, and how to diagnose certain physical conditions by smell. A wonderful, wonderful teacher.

There is an amusing anecdote about the class. One evening a tiny Cockney woman came in for healing to see Nan, who of course worked in deep trance with her eyes closed. The Guide in his deep voice said to the woman; "Madam you have FLATULENCE." The little lady became very indignant and replied, "Here, I know you're a blind old man and all but you are wrong. I ain't got NO FLATS TO LET, you made a mistake."

    I first heard about Christine from a friend of hers from London who was visiting Montreal. Margaret Wilson was the Secretary of the International Spiritualist Federation and President of the National Federation of Spiritual Healers. Margaret came to speak at the First Spiritual Church. Margaret was quite charming and a very good public speaker. She sang the praises of Christine Burnett-Smith and suggested we invite her to work at the Church. An invitation was extended and accepted. I agreed to host Christine at my apartment at 222 Redfern Avenue in Westmount. In October 1974 Christine arrived. I remember her walking up the stairs to my apartment. I had opened the door as she was coming up the stairs and she greeted me with, "Hello Joe." I was impressed by her speaking voice. Christine had the most beautiful Scottish accent I had heard in a long time. I said to her, "Oh my! You speak just like Jean Brodie", as I welcomed her into my home. Well! That did it! We became fast friends that instant. Christine informed me that her mother's maiden name was Brodie. So I was not far from wrong. She took to the name of Jean Brodie and from then on I always referred to her as "Miss Brodie" when we were alone and she would sometimes sign her letters Jean Brodie.

    Christine served our Church for the first time at the service on the Sunday after her arrival. I introduced her at service and then took a seat on the platform behind Christine. Her inspirational discourse was brilliant. Sitting behind her as she stood at the dais and spoke, I was able to witness her aura as she addressed the congregation. To my amazement her back was completely transformed and encased in a deep purple colour as she spoke. I have seen auras but never anything like this before. I could tell by the brilliant content of her address that we were in the presence of a very highly evolved soul. At a later time when we were in private, Christine informed me that one of her Spirit Guides was William Stainton Moses who was an ordained clergyman of the Church of England. He was a trance medium who had written the well-known book, Spirit Teachings in 1883. I was not surprised Christine had attracted a Guide of such a high calibre. She was well-educated and an erudite person. After the address, Christine gave a brilliant demonstration of clairvoyance selecting people at random from those assembled. She was entertaining, warm and accurate as she touched many people with the Spirit messages. Her humour was never far from the surface. She addressed one woman in particular who appeared to be a little slow in her responses to Christine's comments to her. At one point, Christine mentioned to the woman that she had problems with her eyes, but all would be well once they were attended to. She then proceeded to tell Christine (and for that matter, the entire Church) how unhappy she was because of her eyes, et cetera. She went on for quite a bit. Christine was a quick medium and when she gave messages she needed to move on quickly – because the messages flowed quickly. So Christine replied to the woman, "Well, you can't be optimistic with a misty optic," and then moved on to her next message. That quick humour made me smile. To my mind, here was 'Jean Brodie' indeed with no time to waste and in her prime.

The congregation was very impressed with Christine's platform demonstration and many people requested private consultations with Christine. At this time, I was a board member of the Church and had access to letters written to the board. The following one such letter concurring Christine's platform demonstration at our Church written by Eddie Barr, a medium himself who had sat in my development classes.

Dear Board Members,

Recently, we have been blessed by having had the pleasure of witnessing a most interesting medium at work in the person of Miss Christine Burnett-Smith from England.

Not only does she deliver very educational discourses but displayed a special skill in her messages work in my mind, indicates that she knows where it's all at, so to speak.

I was very impressed by the disciplinary and sincere manner in which she conducts herself while delivering her messages, so much so that I really felt I was at a Church and not at a circus.

Admittedly, being a bit of a skeptic, she did wonders for me in that of all the mediums that I have witnessed, she appeared to be the most genuine and convincing of all and I would certainly hope to see her back again in the not too distant future.

Sincerely, Eddie Barr

On this, the first of her many future visits to Montreal, Christine was my house guest for a month. She paid her own airfare from London, hence it was worth the stay when one had travelled so far. Whenever she visited in the future, she stayed for sixty days.

We soon settled in and I would go to my daily job at Eastern Airlines and the evenings were free. Someone had given me a bottle of liqueur called, Parfait d'Amour. The liqueur was purple. Christine and I would have a wee glass of our purple drink in the evening. It had a terrible taste; but we loved the colour and we'd get a big kick out of it, (not the drink, the colour). We would joke for years about this one. Needless to say, when the bottle was depleted, it was replaced with Harveys Bristol Cream which is a proper sherry for a Scots Lady.

Christine, who henceforth shall be occasionally referred to as Miss Brodie possessed a brilliant wit. She was quick and sharp. Her voice was rather soft and low. I would listen enthralled by her words. She had been a medium for over fifty years and had much to share. We would talk for hours and as the shadows began to fall in the apartment, there often was a feeling of magic in the air. When she spoke it was pure poetry. At times we would fall silent and just sit quietly enfolded in sacred space. Christine was a Christian Spiritualist and we frequently spoke of Jesus. She often referred to him as a Man of Sorrows much acquainted with grief. She liked to speak of His humanity and of His love of people. We thoroughly enjoyed each other's company. I was eager to learn from this charming old soul. At evenings end prior to retiring Christine would announce that she was off "Into the arms of Morpheus" and with that she would toddle off to bed. In the morning she requested, prior to my leaving the apartment for work, I was to "place a tray with a pot of hot tea and buttered toast outside of Miss Brodie's bedroom door". This I always did with genuine pleasure. Miss Brodie related this experience of how Spirit works.

"I once had a phone call from Scotland rather late at night from a woman asking for an appointment with me. "Come at 2:30 tomorrow," I said. "I see you're coming to London tomorrow." The woman was very surprised that I knew her plans. Next day I found it impossible to keep the appointment so I sat down and concentrated on how to find Mrs. Thompson. After five or ten seconds I saw, as if in neon lighting, "SLO" followed by a telephone number. I went to the phone, dialed the Sloane Square number and asked for her. "There's no Mrs. Thompson here." "Well, will you page her please? Especially on the top landing." A rather doubtful voice came over the line. It was the woman I was seeking. "My God!" she said. "Now I believe anything you tell me."

Miss Brodie believed that the gift of prophecy was a very precious talent and was to be used carefully and wisely. Mediums were not fortune-tellers; a medium's job is to help, comfort, heal and uplift. People who came to see her got what they needed, not what they wanted. Christine always gave exactly what she received from Spirit as she relates in the following:

"Whilst in London, a young man from Germany came for a reading and I told him: "A week from today your sister will catch her thumb on a rusty nail. "Don't put a dressing on it, but get her to a hospital at once." He returned to Germany and two months later wrote to say that eight days after our conversation his twenty-eight year old sister, bringing the cows in, caught her thumb on a rusty barbed-wire fence. He didn't heed my warning but put a dressing on the wound. Next day her arm was painful and badly swollen, so he took her to the hospital, but it was too late. Her arm had to be amputated at the shoulder.

In her experiences, Christine travelled to Holland, Germany, South Africa, The United States and Canada. She was the resident medium at the Greater World Association which was housed in two buildings: Number 3 and Number 5 Lansdowne Road in Holland Park, London. This building also had flats for the staff and the resident medium. She also did readings at the Society for Psychical Research, a well-known Spiritualist Centre which was founded in 1882.

In a letter dated August 13, 1987, Christine wrote: "The Greater World is no more. Sunk without a trace – weeds, dirty windows are all that visitors can see when they make their annual call to see and ask about old friends. No card in the window or notice on the door. NOTHING. The asking price for each house was 1.5 million pounds. And when I called to have a look three weeks ago, I saw the SOLD for Development board." This must have broken Miss Brodie's heart, 5 Lansdowne Road had been her home for over thirty years. She had relocated to 42 St. James Gardens. This was her last known address.

During the course of our friendship, Miss Brodie would share some of her favourite expressions with me.

"Hearts are never broken, they are only chipped" or "Never give your heart to a dog to tear." And lastly, "Here on earth we are governed by the three C's: Calendars, Clocks and Currency."

She was never at a loss for words. I was working on Saturday, August 30, 1975 sharing the platform with Christine at the Service at the Greater World in London. I had been invited to speak and give a demonstration of clairvoyance. Christine and I both gave Spirit messages that day. Of course it was an honour for me to share the platform with Miss Brodie, in her home Church. During her demonstration, Christine addressed a woman in the congregation. In her message, she brought Spirit greetings from the woman's father who had recently passed. Christine gave evidence to the woman of how the gentleman had passed, of his personality and even mentioned that the Spirit in question had a fondness for bananas when he was alive. All the while, the woman is saying, yes, yes that's true. Then she said to Miss Brodie, "But he is dead." I thought that I would fall from my chair. Christine looked at her and without missing a beat said, "Well, nobody lives forever." She quickly moved on to the next message, and that as they say, was that. My question to Christine later was: "Did this woman know she was in a Spiritualist Church?"

Christine was very devoted to her beloved sister Ann, who was a gracious and charming person. When I visited Christine in London, I often stayed in Ann's apartment which was next to Christine's because she had a spare room in her flat. I recall gentle Ann quietly knocking on the door with a cup of tea in hand for me to welcome the day. I was very fond of Ann and both sisters always spoiled me when I stayed with them.

On the morning of October 30, 1975, I was awakened from my sleep about 6:00 am. Flashing before my eyes, I saw an obituary column that read: "Ann Noble passed October 30, 1975". Christine was by her sister's bedside when she passed that day. She was her sister's best pal as Christine would say. Ann would refer to Christine as her little man. It was a sad occasion indeed. Christine telephoned from London later that day to tell me what Spirit had already let me know.

On the 21st of September 1977, a tragedy befell our family. My sister Susan gave birth to my nephew Nicholas, who was born with a life threatening condition. He lived for thirty days and passed to Spirit, October 22. Christine was staying with me during this time and she would frequently accompany me to St. Mary's Hospital when I went to visit Nicholas. She was a great support to my family and me during these sad days. Christine would often say: "When sorrowing bereaved people come to me for help, and I see and hear the ones they love who have died, it's the little things that count – the intimate, heart-warming evidence which really establishes the reality of the contact. Sharing a familiar old family joke, reference to a watch that's five minutes slow, using a fond nickname: these things are immensely valuable. Pompous sermons which might come from anyone's lips will never prove that it's really granddad or Aunt Maud who's coming across."

I still read Christine's letters and I have a good laugh. She often said that laughter was so important. A day without laughter is a day wasted. In that vein, I offer excerpts from a letter written by Miss Brodie which she penned on August 8, 1975 during a strike by the Royal Mail. She was obviously frustrated at not being able to send mail by the post – so she thought of another alternative. This was long before J.K. Rowling and Harry Potter came on the scene in 1997.

Dear Joe,

Blame the P.O. for holding up the mail. Well, all the more reason for getting down to business and learning Broomstick drill. Classes commence at midnight on November 18 (Full Moon) - interested parties should forward documentary evidence that their Broom handles are made of ivory – bristles of porcupine quills coloured green; these precautions are for the protection of students – during Full Moon the student must be invisible owing to the malevolent influences abounding in the ether. A fast for one month previous to take-off will ensure safety for the student as he undergoes training; during the lectures all members of the class, owing to dehydration etc, will be unable to stand or sit – space will be provided on the hard gravel drive and members will lie two feet apart after attaching the suction pads to their under parts which will ensure that each person remains earth-bound until the whistle blows for take-off. In the unlikely event of any student turning chicken or, in cases of panic, (everybody can be weak at times) patrols (life members of Cloud Cuckooland, average age 85) will be at hand to smack the face briskly with a holly twig (holly tree in Garden will be in full bloom). Before enrolling, students would be wise to consider carefully their stamina and courage. It is the duty of every world citizen to join up and train to beat the Post Office who are now planning to cut people off entirely from communicating with one another. The End.

I personally think that this missive was Miss Brodie's masterpiece and therefore could not pass it by. Christine believed that: "When you reach an understanding of what living and dying are all about, and when you know for certain as I do that death is not an end but a lovely beginning, then there's no need to be anything else but content with what this life holds and if you are given a talent, you must use it."

Christine was truly an exceptionally gifted and talented medium who taught me so much and frequently made me laugh. On January 13, 1990, Christine was scheduled for retina eye surgery on both eyes. She graduated into the Higher Life soon after.

In one of her last epistles to me, as always Miss Brodie gave sage advice: *"Love many, trust few and paddle your own canoe.*

The Crinita Family: (from left) Uncle Frank, Grandma Catherine, Grandpa Nicola, Aunt Victoria, and Daddy.

Aunt Victoria and Grandma Catherine Crinita.

Grandma Maude and Grandpa Joseph Bowker.

(Clockwise, from top left) Joey (me), Shirley Mallette, sister Kay, sister Sally, cousin Eileen, brother Frankie, and sister Emily outside our home on Barre Street in Griffintown. 1945

(Clockwise, from top left) Belinda, sister Irene holding doll, sister Gloria and sister Susie on steps.

Above: Family and friends outside our Barre street flat enjoying a February day in the sunshine.

Left: (From left) My sister Linda, brother Frankie, cousin Brian, my sister Irene, cousin Geraldine, my sister Emily.

Left: (standing) My mom Emma, and her sister Aunt Geraldine.

Grandma Maude Bowker
Approx: 1962

Above: The bingo gals - cousin Shirley, Aunt Geraldine, cousin Doreen, Aunt Cecile (Diddles) and my mom Emma.

(right) My Grandmother Maude Bowker at 203 G Murray Street in Griffintown.

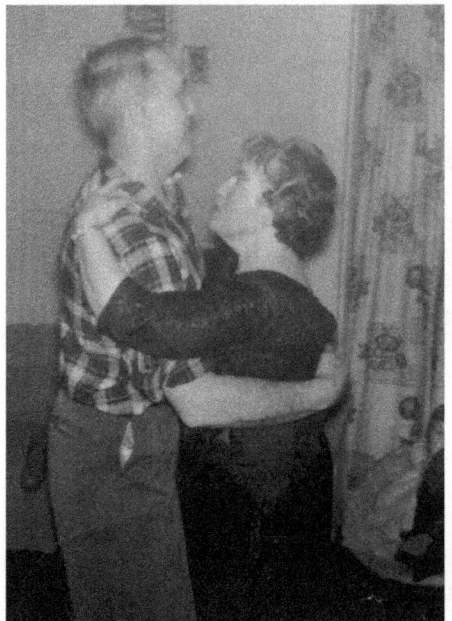

(Left) My mother Emma and father Joe. Approx: 1967

(from left) me, my mother Emma, father Joe, and sister Kay.

(Above) Gloria, age 3 and myself. Feb 1956

(from left) My sisters Susie, Sally, and Gloria all dressed up and out for the day. Approx: 1960

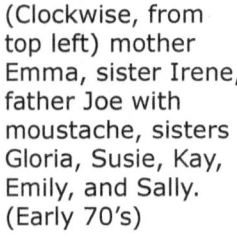

(Clockwise, from top left) mother Emma, sister Irene, father Joe with moustache, sisters Gloria, Susie, Kay, Emily, and Sally. (Early 70's)

(Below) Shrine of Our Mother of Perpetual Help.

(Above) St Ann's Church, Griffintown Montreal. Built 1854 - 1970

(Below) Main Altar - St Ann's.

Reverend FRANCIS KEARNEY, C.Ss.R.
Redemptorist

My mother, Father Kearney, Susie, Kay, Gloria

(below: from left) Francis Ivess, myself and David McAleer in Mary Bennett's seamstress room at St Ann's Church, 1957

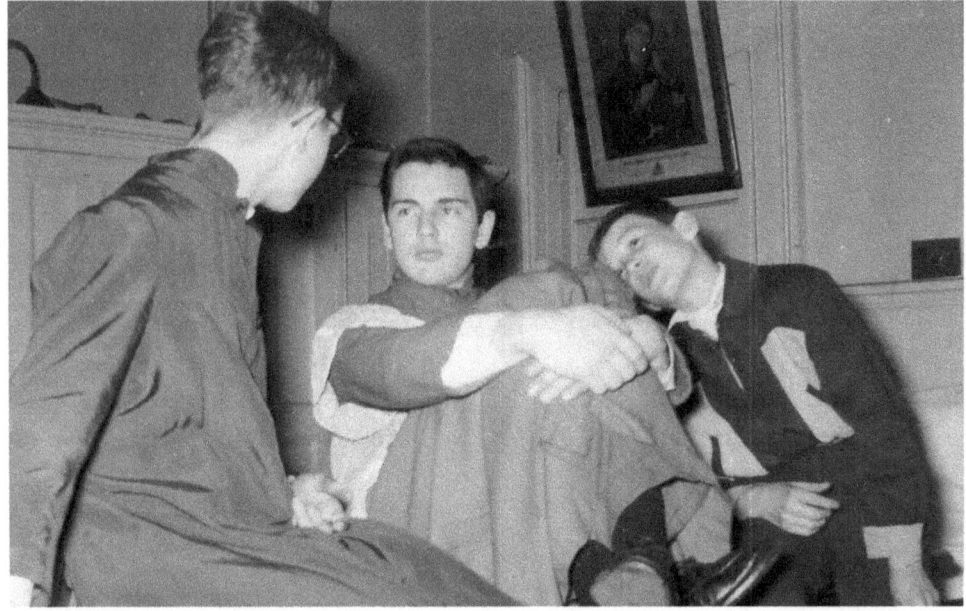

1954 Centenary of St Ann's Church in Griffintown with Bishop Whelan and we altar boys. I'm second from the left with the spiked hair.

High Mass celebrated by Paul-Emile Cardinal Leger.

At the altar of the Infant Jesus of Prague, 1953 with Brother Andrew.

Again in 1957 with Brother Gabriel.

Me at 20 (1960)

(left)
Carol Tucker
Feb 1975

(right)
Alvin Cohen

(left)
Me, Carl Cormier, and Liz Bruni at Eastern Airlines Reservations in Westmount Square, Montreal.
Feb 1985

My first spiritual teacher Millie Gordon and me. Approx 1975

My close friend Gloria Gari and me. Oct 1990

(above) Millie Gordon, Vaudeville 1932

(above) My dear friend Andree Duquette and me in Paris, France.

(above) Noella Martinez and Jim Almer at Eastern Airlines.

(right) (L-R) Jean St. Pierre, Elizabeth Bruni, myself, and Gloria Gari on a night out.

Some of my development class (from left) Gwen, Louise, Mary, Noella and the back of Gloria Gari.

(Top row: from left) Mary, me, Eddie, and Andrea
(Bottom row: from left) Shirley, Janie, Peggy, and Patricia.

(Top) Peggy Eaton and me at Life Spectrums conference at Elizabethtown, PA. Approx Early 80's.

(Right) Margaret Wilson of London UK, and me at my 35th birthday in Montreal. Oct 29th, 1975

Both of my heroes through the years, Joni James (below) and Susan Hayward (right)

Joni James holding her son Michael with me. Wildwood Manor, Wildwood NJ July 1963

Elizabeth and Bill McIntosh and me. 1992

Isabel M Hickey, Tom Jackson, Marjie Marquis and me at Harmony Hill, NH

Christine Burnett-Smith aka Miss Brodie, Holland Park, London, England

(left) Marie Perkins and her husband Henry Curtain Chesterfield IN 1970

(right) My cherished and dear friend. Marjie Marquis

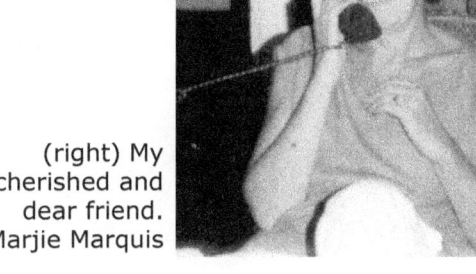

Isabel M. Hickey

Ben Henry Osborne

(above) Me on the horse, Jasper, GA   June 1984

(left) Ben Osborne and me at the Georgia Guidestones, Elbert County, GA   June 1984

Don Galloway and me. 1982

Peggy, me, and Miss Brodie in Ottawa, Ontario

Workshop Jasper GA, 1981

Patricia Spells Palmer and me.

Photo by (Gaby) Desmarais

Eddie Barr

My nephew Justin and my mother Emma.

(below) (L-R) Me, Carl Cormier, and Elizabeth Bruni.

Dr Marvin and Dee Lois Sward

(right) Bill and Elizabeth McIntosh, Bethlehem, PA 1993

Monsignor Michael Regan, Pastor of Our Lady Of Perpetual Help Church in Carrollton, GA singing Danny Boy.

(left) Monsignor Regan, me, and his Irish Wolfhounds.

Our Lady Of Perpetual Help Church in Carrollton, GA.

Final resting place of Susan Hayward Chalkley and her husband Eaton Chalkley at Our Lady Of Perpetual Help Church in Carrollton, GA.

Me at the side altar in Our Lady of Perpetual Help Church which Susan Hayward had decorated. The golden crucifix she brought from Rome is visible.

Monsignor and myself talking in front of Susan Hayward's final resting place.

Portiuncula in the Basilica di Santa Maria degli Angeli, Assisi.

(above) Plaque above the entrance to the home of Bernardo di Quintavalle.

(left) Home of Bernardo di Quintavalle.

Assisi, Italy October 1976

Robert Negro, Noella Martinez, and myself. Assisi, Italy May 1985

The Sisters at St Anthony's Convent, Assisi, Italy.

(from left) sisters Linda, Sally, Susie, Gloria, mother Emma, Joey (me), sisters Irene and Kay. (Early 90's)

(left) Cheers from my mother Emma.

(below) My good pal Gillian Payne.

(left) Borja Puentes Sanchez, me, and Andree Duquette. Montreal July 2001.

Joni James, Wildwood, NJ 1963

Joni James and me
Syracuse, NY 1995

My sister Irene, me, and Joni James. Los Angeles, 2002

Shawn Asling

My stalwart wingman and friend Jean Sexton

For Purpose On Time Community Conference Sharing Sacred Space. October 2006 Virginia Beach VA.

My 70th birthday in Los Angeles. (L-R) My sister Susie, Ron Sexton, me, and my sister Irene.

CHAPTER VIII
SPIRIT WORKER

I am a Spirit Worker. As a medium, I work hand-in-hand with Spirit. My mediumship is my life's work. It is a choice that I have made to serve. Prior to sharing how I function as a medium, these are some points I wish to cover:

One does not become a medium in the twinkling of an eye. You must possess the faculty to begin with. I hold that mediums are born and not made. Mediums possess a heightened sensitivity which allows one to tune into the higher frequencies of the Spirit World. It is not something that can be turned on and off like a tap. The faculty must be honed and worked upon in a deliberate and consistent fashion framed by prayer, meditation and a keen sense of responsibility. Part of a medium's responsibility is to bring the Light. In order for this to occur, the individual must therefore be of the Light and be as a beacon for the Invisibles who are of the Light. The Law of Spirit is the Law of Attraction – there is no other way around it. The adept must look deep within his inner being and therein touch into the highest part of his nature which is willing to serve solely for the joy of serving.

To begin with, if you choose to work for Spirit on this level, then you are entitled to demand that you receive only the highest and best of what Spirit has to offer. It is a working relationship based on cooperation and mutual respect, between the medium and the Spirit Associates who guide, guard and protect. One of the prime requisites of a good medium is that he or she possesses incredible sensitivity and compassion to his or her environment. This combined with an alertness and attunement to Spirit fosters the medium's true nature. At all times, the thought that we are Spirits with a body having a human experience can never be far from your consciousness.

People often ask me about the distinction between being psychic and being a medium. This is my opinion:

The gift of seeing is nothing new. People have possessed this faculty for centuries. There is nothing supernatural about being psychic. Many people use their sixth sense or their psychic impressions, (often referred to as a hunch) in their everyday lives without giving it too much thought. We are creatures of instinct and we are divinely programmed for survival. For some, to discover that they have been blessed with the gift of "second sight" may come as quite a revelation as they come to grips with the fact they are in some way different from other people who do not possess their keener sense of perception. They may attribute their "feelings" or intuitions to their being overly sensitive or in some cases, more sentimental than most. The individual will choose to heed the inner stirrings or to ignore them. Although in many cases of the naturally gifted psychic, their second sight becomes too reliable for them to ignore and disregard their inner promptings. The sixth sense is not something far away, in some other dimension of the self. It is part of the self, it is vital and living. It is real. The challenge is for you to accept the gift and the responsibility which goes with it. Our sixth sense or inner voice is a mechanism for survival. Individuals who believe that they do not have an inner beat on things in their lives, perhaps live in a cocoon of their own making, because they have not learned to listen or pay attention to their inner guidance. It is possible to follow your intuition or gut feeling for wont of a better word, without actually putting a name to it.

There is a vast difference between being a conscious or unconscious individual. Many people have psychic abilities. Some may possess mediumistic abilities without being aware of it. When people have this faculty, they usually become cognizant of it as they progress through life. Things occur which capture their attention. For example: you make a prediction; you get a feeling about something or comment on an event of which you have no prior knowledge. There are spontaneous psychic experiences which do occur only once in a lifetime. For others gifted with the sight, it becomes a more frequent occurrence. It is what you do or don't do with this faculty that really matters. It is a question of personal choice either to develop the gift or not.

Are mediums psychic? The answer is yes. Conversely, are all psychic people mediums? The answer is no, they are not. The difference lies within the capabilities of the individual. The psychic individual may not give much thought nor are they concerned as to where the faculty comes from. A psychic individual may not see or sense Spirit nor have any interest in doing so. My first teacher, Millie Gordon read cards, palms and tea leaves. Millie considered herself a psychic with ESP, but not a medium.

Mediums possess an inherent and natural faculty to perceive Spirit, and many mediums will tell you they have seen Spirits since they were children. Others develop their mediumship under the tutelage of a trained medium. They attend a development class week after week and in some cases, year after year with a qualified teacher who is able to guide and instruct them on the laws of contacting Spirit and how to protect themselves as they set-out to cross the threshold of the two worlds. Mediumship is not a desirable stopping place for the dabbler or persons ignorant of the rules and responsibilities of authentic mediumship. A good medium requires proper training to open him or herself for contact. When one enters into communication with Spirit, you need to be spiritually, emotionally, intellectually and physically prepared. Spirits are not to be tampered with. You must comprehend the seriousness of attempting to contact those on the other side of life. Seeking contact with Spirit is not a parlour game, and a shiver up your back does not a medium make. Your spiritual sense must be garnished with a large dose of common sense.

A medium's life is no different from anyone else's other than the mediumistic individual is able to perceive Spirits clairvoyantly. Spirit can be seen as flashes of light which appear out of the blue, as it were. You do not necessarily have to be a medium or psychic to see them. Since we are Spirits with a body, it is not unusual that a loved one who has passed will appear in this form hoping to gain our attention. These Spirit lights as they are known are bright and appear as white, blue or silver in colour. Under certain conditions, the sensitive individual is aware of things which remain unseen and unperceived to other people occupying the same space. Mediums are not saints nor are they angels. They are ordinary human beings who possess an extra-ordinary faculty which enables them to perceive the vibrations of Spirits through sight, sound, sense or smell. The Spirit transmits and the medium receives. Mediums like everyone else, come in all sizes, shapes, colour, male and female. The more sensitive or in-tune the individual, the better medium they make.

Working as a medium requires commitment and dedication. When an individual is properly trained and developed, meaning they have attended a development class over a reasonable period of time, they are then prepared to do the work. The development of mediumship does not consist of attending workshops or seminars every few months to glean information or watching psychic television programs. This means the individual has come through the ranks of a spiritual development class under a trained and qualified teacher who is capable of discerning Spirit. The development class is the training ground for both the budding medium and the Spirits who will work through and with them. It provides the space for the Spirit and medium to become attuned to each other's vibration. It is in the development class that one learns the proper method on how to make contact with Spirit and a link is forged. The neophyte learns how to receive psychic impressions, how to interpret what they receive and how and when to use the faculty. The leader of the class will ensure the student is properly instructed in the area of self-control and how and when to give Spirit messages. A spiritual development class is not a competition between individuals to determine who is more psychic. The other participants in a class will occasionally be used as batteries for energy. More often however, they will be used to help one another during the allotted concentration period and the receiving of messages. It is about empowering the potential medium. When Spirit is ready to work through the medium, they will be the first to know.

A medium is not tuned in twenty-four hours a day, seven days a week. Spirit is not interested in taking over a person's life. People who claim their Guides are always with them as if micro-managing their daily activities are self-deluded because there are agreements and rules for Spirit as well. Spirit is always available when the medium needs to work, give Spirit messages or do a private consultation – you must use common sense. Do not expect Spirit to advise you when you want to purchase a new pair of shoes. As a human being, medium or not, you are solely responsible for your daily living on the planet. It is not necessary to 'consult the Guides' for every breath you take or every action you perform. Working with Spirit is a mutual agreement not an indentured lifetime contract.

The sensitive knows when his Spirit Guide is around and when it is time to tune in and receive. You become very acquainted with the vibration and when sincerely needed, Spirit will never let you down. As in any spiritually related activity, the medium also needs to focus on his personal inner development and keep the ego in check. Mediumship is hard work, though gratifying, it is not razzle dazzle. Mediums, like all people, have their unique personalities and may differ in the manner in which they obtain their psychic impressions and deliver the same to the recipient of the message.

Mediumship is a calling in the sense that it is a quality of the Spirit. The mediumistic individual is extremely sensitive to the vibrations around him. Serve or suffer is a reality and a fact of life for the medium who chooses to follow on the path of spiritual service and awareness. The medium then acts as a bridge between the two worlds. This principle never alters for those who serve and give to others, because in the giving to others we receive and are made richer by the giving. It is believed mediums retain the gift after death and continue to use the faculty after their current lifetime. If one holds to the theory of reincarnation, then the medium of today quite possibly was a seer in a former life. As previously stated concerning mediumship, either you are or you are not. There is no in-between. If you do not initially possess the ability, then more than likely, (no matter how you may try), you will not be able to pierce the veil that separates the two worlds.

I am a public demonstration medium and on occasion I do private, individual consultations. A medium in any circumstance is never aware of what impressions they will receive from Spirit. The medium cannot guarantee if a particular Spirit entity will come through or bring a message. Every sitting is an experiment in the sense that you never know what you are going to receive.

Prior to any demonstration of public clairvoyance, I always prepare myself and meditate for quite some time before working. I prefer not to engage in conversation prior to working. I require a quiet moment in order to attune to my Spirit Guide Wana, who is my Message Bearer. I enjoy working with a group in public and I do like to have some fun. When delivering Spirit messages, the audience or congregation help to create the atmosphere. If you are working with a lively (preferably spiritually aware) group of individuals, you can have a very joyful experience. I work on a very quick vibration. My Guide provides the information in a very quick manner. As a medium one must be sensitive to the vibration of the group, as well as tuning into the information they are receiving from their Spirit contact. Some groups have a high vibration and are very lively and fun. On other occasions, you may find yourself in the midst of a very somber group. This can be a challenge because you, as the medium, are the focus of attention and must hold people's interest by your delivery. This is where your training comes in and it is up to you to try and raise the vibration (level of energy) of the group. In a public demonstration of clairvoyance, the message you bring may be meaningful to more than one person in the room. This can occur when the medium offers words of encouragement to one individual, which may be of benefit to someone else in the room who may not necessarily have received a message. When I give clairvoyance, I never know what is coming through as the content can be purely psychic messages for one person and at other times, the messages are solely regarding people who have passed into Spirit. They are often a combination of both, I never know. I have full confidence in my Guide and whether in public or private, I give people what I get for them. Sometimes it is what they need and not what they want. Spirit decides that, I do not. My job is to deliver the message and bring the Light.

Many mediums work in symbols – and often what we receive makes little or no sense to us. Our job is to give what we get and not perform an autopsy on what comes through. Frequently the simplest or smallest word, or symbol, may have great significance to the person receiving the message. This is why a good medium will ask the recipient, "Is that clear?" or "Do you understand?" Or, often they will ask the person, "To please hold that" – if the individual cannot place something at that precise moment. The medium's Spirit Guide knows what they are doing and the medium must learn how to trust what they are given. At times in a public demonstration of clairvoyance, the person receiving a message is reluctant to acknowledge it because they are not inclined to have other people know their personal affairs. Some people freeze up when spoken to in public because of shyness. One should bear in mind that the well-trained medium is a compassionate and sensitive individual who endeavours not to cause pain or embarrassment to anyone in public. Some information one receives can be very personal and the communicating Spirit Messenger would not give public information that is inappropriate or may cause embarrassment. In cases where this would occur, it is the medium who is at fault and not Spirit.

A sense of humour is a great asset to a medium. Humour is a healing force and an amusing remark can ease the tension in a room and make for an enjoyable experience for all present. Some advice for people attending public demonstrations of clairvoyance; please respond to the medium when addressed. This is helpful to the medium because he or she will know that you comprehend what they are saying and if the information is correct. It also serves the other people present and holds their attention. It can be rather tedious to listen to messages that no one responds to. A simple yes or no will suffice. The medium is not going to divulge your life story for all and sundry to hear in public.

I reiterate that mediumship is not something that one turns off and on like a spigot. When I agree to do a private consultation, I always enquire if the person is spiritually aware on some level and that they understand I am not a fortune-teller. I do not read for everyone who requests a reading.

Before a reading, you must prepare prior to knocking on the portals of the Spirit World. This is done by meditation and entering into silence and you pray to receive what this person needs. At the same time you request their loved ones in Spirit gather near at the time of the reading and if they choose, are able to communicate through you, the medium. The authentic medium has no input or control over who will manifest, or what is forthcoming during any given reading.

As a rule however, it is the Message Bearer of the medium who transmits the information to the person receiving the reading. In most cases where there is Spirit contact, there are four individuals involved in a reading:

1. The communicating Spirit
2. The Message Bearer of the medium
3. The medium
4. The person receiving the reading

Your Spirit Control – (Door Keeper) will decide when it is appropriate to allow a Spirit entity to draw very close within the auric field of the medium during a reading. I say this because at times, the communicating Spirit is permitted to do so. This occurs when the Spirit entity possesses a very strong vibration and is a powerful communicator.

Spirit entities are easily recognizable by certain familiar phrases, intimate memories or associations known only to them and their loved ones. In some instances, the medium will assume identifiable physical characteristics or exhibit personality traits that the communicating Spirit may have possessed. They might wave their hands a certain way or hold themselves in a manner which was indicative of the deceased individual.

Each reading is different in the same sense that each person is unique and different. You bring your own particular essence and energy to your reading. In my experience, I have determined that the more spiritually evolved or aware an individual, the more flowing the message. Some people possess more spiritual grace than others, and it shines through. That is a fact. I believe people make their own reading – the stronger and clearer your energy, the better the reading. For example: if an individual lives a bland and uninteresting life, then their reading will reflect that. One brings a personal flow of energy to the process, some people possess more of a vital life force than others. You cannot read an empty page.

When I am working, I rely totally on my Guide, Wana. I generally start a reading with a symbol which I will interpret. It can be an actual symbol, but more often than not, it is a song title that I hear, which indicates something about the person or is a reflection of their personality, or their outlook on life. It all depends... I never know what I will get.

During a reading I might receive a combination of things, meaning loved ones who have passed on in Spirit. (Sometimes they come at the beginning of a reading, other times in the middle of the reading, occasionally at the end. Some stay the duration of the allotted time and comment at different intervals during a reading. I never know). I may get impressions of what is currently going on in a person's life. I may start with the past, then the present or future happenings. Things do not necessarily follow in any particular sequence. I move quickly from one thought to another. On occasion, I might receive insight on the karmic ties in one's life and how they relate to a person's current experiences and situations they are now living. During a reading, I will often check for understanding by asking: "Do you understand?" or "Is that clear?" I need to be sure I am on the right track. Sometimes my job is to give people a double-check, which is akin to a spiritual check-up. Recently, an individual who is very familiar with the process described her reading with me as coming in to see a Doctor for a spiritual check-up. (I quite liked the analogy).

When I read for some individuals, my Guide Wana provides me with insight into their inner being. It is similar to holding up a mirror before someone and informing them, this is what is going on in your life. In other words... a reflection of their spiritual essence.

During the course of a reading, at times I repeat the same thing in a different way. I believe that when Spirit really desires to make a point – they want to ensure their loved one receives the message loud and clear. Where a loved one is involved, emotions are bound to be close to the surface and people can be overwhelmed by the information coming through. The thoughts and impressions do come very quickly, often with split second consistency and accuracy. People do not listen to what is being said – understandably because of the emotions involved, one simply does not hear. There are times when I do not finish one thought and I am already on to another one. My Guide Wana is very quick. Her energy is very mercurial and she is aware that time is of the essence when Spirit is communicating. The energy used in the process lasts for only so long. I am a quick medium by nature and not very patient. I like to receive my information at a rapid-fire pace. That way, I just give what I get quickly. There is little time to dilly dally and analyze what you are being given by Spirit – who are very anxious to get their message through to the sitter.

I hold that the communicating Spirits seek to constantly reassure their loved ones that they are indeed aware of what is going on in their lives. As Spirits they are cognizant of the constraints placed by time. Time has little effect on them but certainly is important to the medium and their Guides who facilitate and manage the process of communication between medium, the communicating Spirit and the recipient of the message.

Sometimes when I read for an individual, there is no Spirit contact whatsoever. The reading simply consists of what I receive for the person involved which relates to different aspects of their life. **No medium can guarantee to contact any specific person in the Spirit World.**

There could be a myriad of reasons why Spirit may not show up during a reading. The simplest is that the Spirit may not be ready to communicate or more often, not aware that they can communicate because they may not realize that they have passed. This occurs if a person has died in a traumatic or unexpected manner – either by murder, accident, war or had little or no spiritual awareness. The individual, in his lifetime on earth may have been totally unconscious of the Light and therefore, finds himself in a dark void on the other side of the veil. They can be helped however by prayer from this side. This is why it is a helpful spiritual practice to pray for the dead. The mind and personality lives on after the change called death. How a person thinks whilst in the body, is how they will think in the Spirit World. It is as simple as that. The consciousness lives on.

Since I do work with symbols, I find it most interesting that if a person is aware of his or her astrological chart, then I can frequently tune into the aspects of their chart and describe what I feel in my own words. Since I am not an astrologer, I do believe that my astrological friends in Spirit, Isabel M. Hickey and Marjie Marquis do help me on this level as they did when they were here on the earth plane. If a person has a personal astrologer, I ask them to double-check the information to ensure it is correct. I presently enjoy a similar process with astrologer friends Lise Caron and Gillian Payne. Both gifted astrologers, who on occasion look at my personal chart. They give me astrological aspects which I then interpret with my own words, much in the same manner I did with Marjie Marquis.

On occasion in a reading, Spirit Guides or Guardian Angels will make themselves known. I never know. Each reading is an experiment. My purpose in a reading is to give comfort to the bereaved, touch the human soul whilst striving to bring Light into a person's life. Hopefully, this will empower people to get in touch with their own potential, foster an awareness of Spirit, and leave them with food for thought.

In the late seventies, I was visiting a friend in Los Angeles who as a favour asked if I would read for an acquaintance. I agreed. During the course of the reading, I brought up the fact that this woman and her mother did not get along and it was important for her to make peace with her mother who was not in good health. The reading concluded. Later my friend informed me the woman was not happy with what she was given. It seemed I did not tell her what she wanted to hear. I did not say she would meet and marry a wealthy man. That was all she was interested in and nothing more. What I gave her was correct, her mother was ill and she disliked her intensely. She was not happy to have the reading focused on her mother instead of her romantic aspirations. Be that as it may, I did not get a man for her in her life, rich or otherwise. In passing a few years later, I asked after her and was informed she remained single and unhappy. As a medium, you never know what people expect from you. I am not a mind-reader or a match-maker.

In the seventies I was invited to a private residence in Rosedale, Toronto. As a personal favour to a friend, I agreed to give several readings. One in particular comes to mind: towards the end of the reading for a very charming British woman, I remarked she reminded me very much of the famed actress Vivien Leigh and that I felt her presence here in the room. The woman smiled and said, "Oh yes, she was my best friend."

In January 2009, whilst in Los Angeles, an older gentleman came to see me for a reading. His wife had recently died. He was very aware spiritually and had studied metaphysics for years. At the end of the reading, he asked me a question, "I want to die. When am I going to die?" I was taken aback for a few seconds. I then responded I could not tell him that because I did not receive the information.

One can sense death on occasion. I remember being in Atlanta, Georgia at the Foundation of Truth speaking with Ben Osborne after a workshop. There was a tall, tanned and handsome man present. Ben knew him and greeted him. As I looked at this person, I saw his pallor turn gray for an instant. I quietly remarked to Ben that I did not think he would be around much longer and that he would die. Approximately one year later Ben informed me that this person had indeed passed quite suddenly and no one had expected his death. I was not surprised.

In July 2010, a woman came to see me for a reading at my home in Montreal. Whilst she was very pleased with the reading, before leaving my home, in casual conversation she expressed she had been hopeful her grandmother whom she deeply loved, would have come to say hello. Naturally, I understood her disappointment. However, I explained whoever comes through from Spirit has nothing to do with me as the medium. Spirit makes the choice of who comes through. Perhaps her grandmother knew how important this reading was for her. (Since she did have many personal problems in her life and that was at the forefront of her reading.) I personally do not know why the grandmother did not communicate. I do believe that the message which does come through for people is the message that is meant for them. Again, the emphasis is: the medium is the conduit and can only deliver what they receive from Spirit.

I would suggest that people who wish to seek out a medium be prepared before they go for a consultation and keep in mind that an authentic medium will give what he or she gets, nothing more or nothing less. Mediums cannot compel Spirits to manifest or to communicate at whim.

In the following Chapter, 'Spirit Talks', there are excerpts from several individual readings which I have given over the years as a Spirit Worker, which may provide further enlightenment as to how Spirit works through a medium.

CHAPTER IX
SPIRIT TALKS

I Wonder

I wonder how it will be when I get to the other side

Who will be waiting there for me to welcome me inside?

Will it be my guardian angel who has watched over me all of my days?

What of my family and friends who have gone before me on their way?

I wonder how they will appear in splendour of Spirit robes refined

Will they have a luminous glow and deep within their eyes a shine?

Theirs is not a physical body now; this is a world of mind

They come and go at their own whim without constraints of time

Have they now found each their own truth?

Those who passed at ripe old age and those who crossed in youth?

I wonder how a parent feels when they meet the child taken by war

Or a life cut short by tragic death that never saw three score?

Oh, what joy there must be on that glorious morn!

When souls whom we thought of as lost have in Spirit been reborn.

I wonder how the angels sound as they sing to God in adoration

How all souls converge as one, free from colour, gender and of nation?

What delight it must be and such a time of bliss

when we encounter once again those whom we truly have missed

Will they tell us of times when they wafted through the mists

and in the quiet of the night, upon our brow, did place a silent kiss?

I wonder how I will react when I see for myself

All the fragments of my life woven into my soul's tapestry of wealth

Will I be duly grateful for all the blessings which on me God hath bestowed?

And be more than thankful for all the people whom I have met along life's road?

I wonder.

-Joey Crinita

INTRODUCTION

The contents of this chapter are unabridged and actual accounts of tape recorded consultations. I do not retain personal records of consultations. Hence, I must rely on the willingness and kindness of people to share their intimate and very personal remembrance of a reading or other personal experiences in which I, as the medium had a part. It bears repeating at this point that a medium cannot guarantee the outcome of any communication with Spirit. In the following individual recounting of various consultations, the style and content varies from person to person, the wording of the recipients has not been altered. These are messages of hope coming from Spirit loved ones who will be waiting to greet and be reunited – one with the other in the great hereafter. I believe that the personality survives the change called death, and this is apparent in the content of these readings. I offer these instances of Spirit contact to honour the memory of the named loved ones who have crossed over into the realm of Spirit and onto the Light.

Jose Martinez

Sarah Preston Worrell

Helena Reath

Shawn Asling

Linda Zaccardelli Borsi

Jack Gray

For my part, I am honoured to have served as a link for these communicating entities. I thank the Spirit Guides who make this process possible.

JOSE MARTINEZ

The following narrative is related by long-time spiritual healer Noella Martinez and pertains to her late husband Jose:

I met Joey and Gloria Gari in 1967 when I started to work at Eastern Airlines Reservations in Montreal. We three have been steadfast friends from that time on. In 1968 Joey invited Gloria and I, along with some other people to attend his spiritual development classes, which he held weekly at his apartment, and we met as a group for at least ten years. On July 26, 1975 my beloved husband, Jose passed away after a brief illness.

In the months following Jose's death, unimaginable sorrow overtook me and I became extremely depressed. On a solitary Sunday afternoon in November, so overcome with anguish, I tried to take my own life. This was not a calculated act or something which I had given any thought to, but on that day, so great was my pain that life seemed unbearable. I attempted to slash my throat with a nail file... crazy I know.

In emotional turmoil I decided to telephone Joey and although I did not know his phone number by heart, (and normally I would have consulted my personal phone book for his number) I dialed it automatically. I have always had very poor eyesight since childhood and could never dial a phone number without my glasses, but that time I did. Joey usually would be at the Spiritualist Church on Sunday afternoons, this time he was at home and he picked up the telephone.

When he answered the phone I was crying so hysterically on the other end of the line that I could not speak. He guessed immediately who it was and realized my state of mind. He tried to comfort me and said, "I will be right over, let me call Gloria." He called Gloria and by coincidence she was home.

I do not live in the City of Montreal but in the suburb of Brossard about thirty minutes away. Joey does not drive and Gloria was willing and able to drive Joey to my rescue. I waited for them outside of my house because I feared that if I remained inside I might do something foolish again, as I was still in a highly emotional state. When they arrived we stood in the living-room together as they spoke words of comfort to me and proposed that we pray together.

I suggested that we talk in the basement playroom, it was quiet there and I had earlier started a fire in the fireplace so it was nice and warm on this chilly November day. I sat with Joey and Gloria facing me on either side. We began to talk and to pray, and a strong fire was burning brightly in the fireplace. Quite suddenly and much to our surprise, we watched as the flames lowered as if someone or something was blowing on them. Not realizing what was happening, I poked life into the fire to rekindle it. It burned for a few moments and then the flames were once again totally extinguished until there was no fire in the fireplace. It then occurred to us that someone or something was trying to get our attention and it became obvious by the shift of energy in the room that Spirit was present, which was something that we were aware of based on our experiences in our weekly classes.

A few moments later Joey clairvoyantly saw my husband and said, "We have a visitor and he has a little girl by the hand." I immediately recognized my husband's vibration although I could not see him. The little girl with him was his first-born child from another marriage. A fact that neither Joey nor Gloria were privy to, as this was a private family matter and never spoken of but I knew exactly what Jose was showing Joey. Joey saw my husband Jose standing behind me caressing my undone long hair. No one knew about this, as it was part of our private life between husband and wife, something that Jose loved to do in intimate moments when we were alone.

In another instance Jose stood in front of Joey and held up a beautiful Cashmere jacket on a hanger. Joey related what he was seeing. This was a jacket which Jose had wanted to buy only two months before he died. How could Joey know about that?

What happened next as final proof was a little strange to Joey but very conclusive for me. With a smile on his face my husband proudly and with great pleasure showed Joey his bare feet. Naturally, Joey did not understand the gesture, but I did.

In the hospital room on the day before he died, Jose was aware that the skin on the soles of his feet was peeling off. He had been bedridden for three weeks and I remember telling him this made his feet look brand new and I distinctly recall telling him that his feet were beautiful. There was more to this as well because Jose was always concerned that his feet were not as attractive as he would have them, so in a manner of speaking, he let me know that he was now quite proud of his Spirit feet. That afternoon Jose made his presence felt very strongly at a time when I really need hope and reassurance. We felt the presence of Spirit very strongly and I knew in my heart that Jose was still around and always would be.

SARAH PRESTON WORRELL

Sharon Davidson shares the following experience:

I had heard about Joey Crinita from Stase Michaels who is a very good friend of mine and also an intuitive astrologer.

On Thanksgiving morning in November 1989, I had a very telling dream. In the dream it was night time and I was on a river in a big boat somewhat like Noah's Ark. Also in this boat were other people whom I cared about. There was some type of disturbance in the river, and I was the one who moved everyone off this big boat onto smaller rowboats for them to get to land and to safety. Finally, I managed to get off this boat, and out of nowhere I noticed a shark scaling the dark water and I hurried rowing to land. However, once I reached land, this shark seemed to be chasing me and slid up onto shore. I was petrified! As I ran from this shark, I noticed an opening in the woods that seemed like the doorway to a cave. From out of this doorway came the brightest white light, like the whitest light within a flame.

Coming out of this brilliant white light appeared a man who was wrapped in some type of golden garment, like a mummy, and as he approached me, he beckoned to follow him. At first I followed him and for some reason I stopped to look back and decided not to go further. It was then that I woke up from this dream feeling strange and sort of panicked, like there was a message or something important that I needed to know. So I telephoned Nana, my grandmother who lived in Birdsnest, Virginia, because she knew all about dreams. I called her to find out what my dream meant. I relied on my grandmother because she gave and taught me what faith was about. She taught me that I could count on Jesus for everything. I always hoped that one day I would be able to take her to Bethlehem at Christmas and that way we could celebrate His birth-date together, Nana, me and Jesus.

As I was dialing her number another call came in from my cousin Chris, and so I stopped dialing my grandmother's phone number to speak with him. After telling Chris about my dream, I had to hurry and leave for work and never did get to call my grandmother about my dream. Little did I know, that at the same time I dialed my grandmother's number, she was having what turned out to be a fatal heart attack.

My family drove from Montreal to Birdsnest, Virginia and within two days of our arriving in Virginia, my grandmother whom I loved so dearly, passed away right in front of me. Nana was the first person whom I had ever seen pass away, I was alone with her. Because I adored and loved her so dearly, I had many months of great difficulty absorbing and dealing with her death and the loss. For months on end, Stase had tried to help me cope with her passing and interpreted my dream as a spiritual warning of my Nana's death. It was during this time of Stase helping me she mentioned that she had decided to move from Montreal to Norfolk, Virginia.

Stase decided to move by driving to Virginia in June 1990, and I accompanied her since I also had to go to Virginia to help my mother clear my grandmother's belongings. Stase also mentioned she felt that her friend Joey could help me because he was a medium and who ironically, had originally lived in Montreal. On the way to Virginia we stopped in Bethlehem, Pennsylvania where Joey was living at that time. I had never seen a medium or had a reading from one and was not sure what to expect when meeting with Joey, but I felt safe with Stase and since I was so distraught, I was grateful that he agreed to do a reading for me.

We arrived at Joey's place and it was so unique and just gorgeous. I remarked on his lovely artwork and the layout of his house. Joey got busy showing us around and to our rooms since we were staying over for one night. The following is an account of my taped consultation which took place at Joey's home at 214 W. Broad Street in Bethlehem, Pennsylvania in late June 1990.

Joey opened with a prayer asking that he (Joey) receive (for me, Sharon) the highest and the best of Spirit and that I receive what I needed from this reading.

Joey started the reading by saying, "I usually start with a symbol but what I got today is a pain in my back and it has nothing to do with you. Do you know someone who has passed away that had pains in her back before she died? Her back had to be rubbed and taken care of."

Joey stood up at this point to emphasize the hand on his hip and slightly leaning over.

Joey. Look at the position I am taking. I am older and my hip would have been sore. Do you understand? Do you recognize this person?

Sharon. Yes. (I could not say much as I was in awe of being with Joey... the medium, and I really did not know what would happen next or if my grandmother showed up in Spirit, if I could handle it. I was open to the experience but I really had no idea of what to expect next.)

Joey. The energy that I feel is someone who has told you off occasionally, who said exactly what was on her mind. However, you Sharon, always understood because you were always very gentle and very loving. I feel very expansive, a large personality. I want to sing songs, I want to sing "Nearer My God To Thee" and "What A Friend We Have In Jesus" and all of this stuff. I feel that this is a very religious vibration. In addition, there is energy around the top of my head so I feel the energy of a grandmother. She was very particular about her hair; she was concerned because appearances were very important to her, only because one had to always be proper. I am looking at her and she is holding her hands like this... Joey stood up and held his hands folded with the fingers intertwined in front of his solar plexus, as my grandmother did when she spoke, to demonstrate what he was conveying.

No matter what you said you had to have dignity, for this lady, dignity was important. As I am talking now her energy comes in again, I do not know if she brought you up, but there is a lot of her in you.

Sharon. Yes.

Joey. Thank you, she guided you along the pathway, she was always very protective of you; she is saying, "You always were a good girl and you always spoke your mind." I want to bring you back to when you were about thirteen or fourteen. I do not know what went on in your life at that time but I feel that there were many changes; I feel that you dreamt a lot and you rather knew what you wanted to be. You must have been like a square peg in a round hole. She is saying you had a lot of growing up to do and she understood that. You were old for your age. Do you understand that? You grew up fast because you had to grow up in hurry is what she is saying.

At this point for about forty minutes, Joey raised several personal matters and events in my life which were pertinent and evidential.

Later in the reading...

Joey.	I have someone here in Spirit tapping a cane, it is a woman, but I see the cane and this cane is to keep you in line. She is saying that this cane is also to let you know that she is watching over you and that she is your protector, your Guide.
Sharon.	Is this the same woman from the beginning, the one with the back?
Joey.	Yes, I do not know if she used a cane or whatever but she is coming in a different way now, because the cane is there and the cane is a symbol for you so that you can lean on the cane. What I want to say to you is that you are asking for help – and you are getting it. She is saying, "This time I am not coming as a relative, I am coming as a Guide." (I think that she wanted to make a distinction, but it is the same thing). Obviously she is very close to you and she protects you a lot.
	She liked flowered dresses you know, but as she comes now she is wearing a black dress with white flowers on it, not big loud things but conservative, like posies. She says, "I'm all dolled up." Her hats were important to her, and I feel a hat on my head. Because this is a special occasion, she got all dressed up as a sign of her respect for you. She is saying she helps to clear the way for you because you have

a lot of odds to conquer, you have to prove a lot of things to yourself. The message for you is that your grandmother is there and she is very religious, she repeats to you, what a friend we have in Jesus.

Normally, I would start a reading with a song but I heard her singing, In The Garden – I come to the garden alone – because she liked roses, sometimes you will smell roses. Because it is a very faint perfume, it is almost like a symbol for you. She will let you know her presence by that faint smell of roses, like rose water, because that was important to her.

Joey. I do not know if she had a bit of arthritis in her hand or if her hand was stiff, at one point...but she was musical." He asked did she like to play the piano. (Joey began to move his hands as if he was playing the piano).

Sharon. She played the piano.

Joey. OK, because I just wanted to do this (play the piano) but she liked her own accompaniment. She could sing to herself. She could wail like a banshee, it is not an expression she would use, but Lord, she poured her heart out, this woman.

Sharon laughs aloud at this.

Charity was important to this woman, the virtue of charity, so she obviously was very kind to everybody, even when they jumped on her. Do you understand if I put it that way?"

Sharon. She was very tender.

Joey. She said, "That was the way to go." You know she was ready to go when she went.

Sharon. I know. (I had a moment upon hearing this and I realized that I was answering just what needed to be said and not more. Joey seemed to be on a roll, so I really did not want to interfere with his reading.)

Joey. She was tired and it was quick because the load on her shoulders was very heavy, she worried a lot about her children and she was a real

	mother. She worried about everybody and she had to take care of everybody. "I am happy now, I am happy now," she says. Therefore, she comes to you with a lot of strength and a lot of glory. She is using this expression. She rather reminds me of Esther Rolle, the actor. You know the roles that she would play, the strong loving woman with nice energy, full of love and compassion. Grandmother's eyes were very soulful, WOW! those eyes. You could not fool her for a moment, she was very intuitive and she did not miss a trick.
Sharon.	(From the beginning to the end of the reading, I knew that Joey was talking to my grandmother and she was here and present. It was just impossible for me to meet someone in Bethlehem, Pennsylvania whom had never met my grandmother yet everything he said was right on.)
Joey.	She had a great faith in Jesus and I do not want to go on about it, but that faith carried her through everything. She is talking about a quilt of many colors. Do you know why?"
Sharon.	I have one in my bedroom. I sleep with it.
Joey.	She is talking about a blue room.
Sharon.	She liked blue a lot.
Joey.	Grandmother is singing away, "In The Sweet By And By" - She was very much like a child, because she was so pure, a pure soul. She provides the songs for you. She is saying, "Listen child, that cane is for you. It is to help you walk and help you weather your storms, so that you will never walk alone – remember that song." She liked that song, so remember.

I loved my reading, it made me feel like she was safe and I could live again.

Once I arrived at my grandmother's house in Virginia, I found open on my grandmother's piano, sheet music for "In

The Sweet By And By" which was one of the songs Joey sang during my reading.

I knew then for sure that Nana was at my reading and that Joey was the real deal, a true medium. I now realized this was not so scary after all. He also mentioned that her dress was torn in the back as the ambulance team had cut it while they were working on saving her. At the house I asked my mother about this dress and she found it and showed me the bag from the hospital with my grandmother's belongings from that day, and just as Joey said, her dress was torn in the back.

I had not seen or heard from Joey for years since he had relocated to Toronto for his job. One day in Montreal a client of mine mentioned she had heard a medium on the radio named Joey, and I knew exactly who it was. Since those many years ago Joey and I have become great friends and he has helped me through more of my family members' deaths. This has been an experience I've always had a hard time dealing with. For me, letting go of them because of the unconditional love I feel for them is something that is just not that easy.

By the way I have figured it out. The wish I had to be with my grandmother in Bethlehem (where Jesus was born) did not come to pass. It turned out to be a different Bethlehem. The way I got to have my dream of being with my grandmother in Bethlehem was the reading I had with Joey in Bethlehem, Pennsylvania, in which she came through for me.

Joey made that dream possible.

HELENA REATH

John Reath relates: I heard about Joey Crinita, a medium in Montreal, (a ten hour drive from my home) from astrologer, Lise Caron in July 2002. I tried to contact Joey many times by phone between July 2003 and April 2004. I left him messages but was unable to make contact. Finally everything came together, a client was to drive to Montreal from Moncton and Joey returned my latest call. I had about two hours to prepare for my journey to see Joey.

Joey. Your life for the last year and a half has been to expect the unexpected. You are a man who is never lost for words. I know that personally from speaking to you on the telephone.

The connection that I got here is someone who passed away suddenly. They are saying, "I didn't expect this. It was a hell of a surprise." I need to clear my throat because whoever is coming through never thought that they would be able to do this. There were new things that they had to learn, this person was not prepared to go, it was not an accident, it just happened very quickly. I feel sometimes at a distance because I am trying to wind my way back. With this soul, this Spirit, the feeling that I am getting is that I am not unhappy, I am at peace. I want to fidget with my hands here and I want to do this: (Joey moves his hands around). I do not know if they were very talented with their hands, so I can't wait to get my hands on other things now because I want to learn what it is to communicate over here. I am giving you a key and the key is very symbolic, and the key means, "John you need to get on with your life, you know that." Do you understand why I would say that to you?

John. Yes, she was extremely talented with her hands, she could do anything.

Joey. You need to do the things that you have to do.

I said to you before that you are a man never lost for words, but there are a lot of things that you never got to say, what was in here, (Joey points to his heart) because you kept a lot of things in. But she says,

"Know your heart, I know your heart." This is a very close relationship here.

I have to ask you a question, do you read a lot, please?

John. Yes.

Joey. I thought so, but you have always read and you read a lot more now and what she is saying is that, "I peek over your shoulder when you are reading and I lead you to certain books."

Would you understand that?

John. Yes, she gives me help.

Joey. Yes, and you feel that you are being led, and you are. She say, "I am setting things up for you."

This person liked everything in order, (he points to a table in the room where everything is neatly arranged). Everything in her life had to be in order, she liked order.

John. Helena was a true Virgo and liked everything in its place.

Joey. I've got tears in my eyes, there is a lot of love, a lot of emotion and what a sense of humour, a very nice lady and very proud, and if you notice that I am sitting up straight because she would get after you sometimes, she did not like people who slouched. Do you understand that?

John. Yes.

Joey. (As John observes Joey taking on Helena's conditions he said), "Sit up straight because I am sitting up straight. And I don't like things around my neck."

"By the way, she is not giving you what for. She always felt like she would suffocate if things got too tight about her neck. Do you understand?

John. Yes.

Joey. She didn't like tight spaces but she is saying, "Now I have the whole sky to roam in, the Universe and I am OK, she repeats, I am OK." You had to make quick decisions when she passed, you were freaked out and I do not know what the conditions were – but you were freaked out. Helena is saying, "Well, huh, that was one hell of a surprise, that's all I can say."

That is how I am getting it but she is laughing now because she says, "What a way to go." I can tell by her energy that she is very free and she has adjusted to Spirit. There must have been many candles lit for her, because I see many candles.

John. Yes, there were.

Joey. She says, "I like that, I like that and it is time to start putting things away. It is hard for you, but start putting little things away."

Have you been looking at pictures and letters and things like that and thinking of putting them in boxes?

John. Yes, sir.

Joey. John, you are not on your own and you never will be, and I need to tell you this for her. I have to repeat this for her." I am not going anywhere, this is my home." You understand that. She is still there, she is still there.

I do not know if you have a rocking chair because I saw a rocking chair and I feel that this rocking chair sometimes moves on its own. To me, the rocking chair is symbolic of the home. This is not an earthbound entity I am talking about, by the way. So she can hang around the house and it is fine, they do that, (Spirit), and they do little things to help you.

John. Yes, we do have the rocking chair which has been in Helena's family for many years, it is a family heirloom.

Joey. Is there a garden please?

John. Yes.

Joey. The daffodils ready to come up?

John. Yes,

Joey. OK. The daffodils will come up and she is going like this, (Joey makes a gesture with his hand to indicate the flowers growing), because she liked them she says, "I can't wait, I can't wait, and that is where my Spirit will spend a lot of time."

John. Helena loved to garden, it was her joy and she loved any kind of flower.

Joey. I like her energy because this woman was very in tune with nature and she believed in the little people like gnomes and things like that, like the little fairies. She says, "I believed in waste not, want not, when I was here."

John. She was very practical.

Joey. Did she do any kind of teaching, I have to ask you that, she taught by example?

John. She taught by example.

Joey. She says, "I always find my way home", and I feel that she is saying that because I feel that your door was always open. I feel that she took in strays. I feel that you would come home from work, (I do not know if you were on the road sometimes or sometimes you were not around) and you would find people at the house. She would say, "Oh! They had nowhere to go and I had to take them in." So, she was like a foster mother to many people. Would you understand that? Therefore, when she went, everybody was shocked.

John. Yes, Helena always had people in the house and had indeed fostered children. One occasion when I arrived home, Helena explained that we had a new person in our home. It was a miserable Winter's night and a young woman arrived at the house looking for a room. She was a student at the local University and had experienced a problem with some man who was the owner of the place where she was rooming. Celine had brought all of her belongings in her little car that night. On another occasion, the infamous 911 incident in New York, many aircraft were diverted to Moncton, New Brunswick. Helena went to the local Coliseum and rescued a man and a woman and their three month old baby. We had another young woman from Algeria who was associated with the University come to stay with us for a three week period. She stayed with us for thirteen months.

Joey. I am hearing a song like the Liverpool folk song, "Maggie, Maggie May" with all that energy and I am

	tapping my foot. She liked those old folk songs, she liked music.
John.	Actually, Helena loved the French Acadian folk songs. She was Une Vraie Acadienne, (a real Acadian). She liked to play the guitar and she liked to tap her feet and play the spoons, actually she was very good at it. One of her favourite bands was known as, "1775" (the band took that name as that was the year of the Expulsion of the Acadians by the English Forces). One occasion, at a show in Montreal, Helena got up on stage and took over for a performer because she felt she could do it better.
Joey.	OK, she says I am still doing it Honey, I am still doing it Honey. And she made me repeat it. She would repeat things to you two or three times just to make sure that you would remember. Therefore, that is why she has been repeating things to me, just as she used to do to you.
John.	That is correct she would often repeat things to me to make sure I got what she was saying.
Joey.	She is saying, "Don't let the buttons be falling off your coat." Do you understand that? She is talking about buttons here and stuff like that.
John.	I most certainly do. Helena was a seamstress by trade and she worked for the past thirty years in the Tailor Shop at the local Sears store.
Joey.	She took care of you; you were like her other child. I do not know how many children you have, but you were her biggest baby. However, she loved you, oh she loved you, but she liked you too. She said, "He was a bit of a devil sometimes." I want to say that because you have a good sense of humour. Therefore, you could be very naughty at times by the things you would say, but she got a big kick out of that and she could always hold her own with you. In fact, she says, "I made up my mind that he was the man I was going to marry and that was that." She had you hooked before you knew it. You understand that?
John.	Yes, I asked Helena to marry me on three occasions and she turned me down every time. Finally, on December 31, 1992, the last day of the leap year, and

	New Year's Eve, Helena asked me to marry her. Naturally I accepted and I said, "Thank you for asking."
Joey.	And she would occasionally remind you of that. She is still around and there still is lots of love, a lot of love.

(Joey comments that people retain their personalities when they pass).

I do not know if she had a devotion to the Blessed Virgin Mary. I must ask you that because what she is saying is, "I saw Mary, I saw Mary and that has helped me."

John. Yes, she did have a strong devotion to The Blessed Mother, so that would please her immensely.

Joey. Yes, she made a joke, "I am as happy as a clam."

I like this woman, she never lost her sense of wonderment about life, even as old as she got, she was not old when she passed. She was like a little girl and she was like Alice in Wonderland, which was part of her magic. She likes Alice in Wonderland, she liked that story and she likes those kinds of fairy tales. She read them and she could tell them, she was a good storyteller.

John. Oh yes, she was good at it and she loved to be the center of attention.

Joey. Yes, a good storyteller and she used her hands to express herself. But she says, "I died with a smile on my face." She walks beside you and she always will. Her main reason in a lot of her life John, was to make you happy. She took care of you. You were her little man and she is saying, "I'm going to look around", she would not be mad if you found someone else. It is not going to happen right now, it is not the time. But as you heal down the road, she says, "I want you to get out there more." Joey commented, "I do not think that it is your nature. She says, "Do not lock yourself in the house. You have to get out Honey."

I believe that you have gone to seek help in some ways. I believe in some ways you have sort of adjusted, there is no guilt, there is no blame, there is no anything.

John. I have a terrible feeling that I should have done more to save her life.

Joey. God decides that. Perhaps those decisions were not yours to make. You know that there is no guilt in her passing. It was her time to go and so the Spirit had already left the body. She knows you did whatever you could, so whatever it is, I am telling you that there is no guilt there.

John. I am not holding her back?

Joey. You are not holding her back in your grief; by the way, you cannot hold her back. She would not have come in as freely if you were holding her back. My Guide would have told me and I would have said, "John, let her go." She is fine and she has already found her way, do you understand that? She is a woman that could open doors. She is speaking metaphorically. She is telling me that if she wanted something, she would go and get it. She is saying, "I worked all this out; I came because I wanted to, so you are not holding me back. I came out of love."

(Joey stated that he could not guarantee a contact would be made, because if for some reason the Spirit could not or would not come, no medium can bring them in).

There is never a guarantee. Therefore, she came of her own volition because of her love for you. So she says, "Happy to see ya" (laughingly) and she is fooling around because that is how she used to cheer you up especially when you got home, because sometimes you would sulk. You would get very quiet and you would go into this space and it was very hard to retrieve you, but you were fine. She would worry about it sometimes if she saw you too quiet, because she would try to figure out what you were thinking about. You are a hard worker and you have worked hard all of your life. I do not believe that anyone has ever given you anything. You have worked hard in whatever you have done. You love people and you are very sincere, but it has not been an easy road for you. You have inner strength and at this time in your life you can look back and say, I did it my way, I made things work. I want to say she knew you inside out and sometimes when you

	got quiet, sometimes you would think, well maybe I do not deserve this, I did not deserve to be so happy. Would you understand why I said that to you?

John. Yes, over the years we shared love, achieved many real goals and had a lot of fun. Helena taught me respect, unconditional love, and how to laugh. We took many trips, we visited family, we travelled to Europe, vacationed in a couple of instances in warmer climates and we grew together.

Joey. Because she is saying, "Wrong, wrong, because I loved you, and this is very important for you to get, because we will be together again. I will be waiting for you when it is your time."

But she does not expect to see you for quite a few years. There is no linear time in Spirit and it is not measured as it is here. It is not that long and I repeat that you are not holding her back. I have to be clear on that so that you will know that. You have to go through the process of grief, but she still walks beside you, she is still in the house. I feel that you have accepted the fact that she is not here now on the physical, she is in another realm, she is still around and she always will be. She is saying that you can do something different with the house, even if you feel that you do not want to be there and you want something different for yourself, like an apartment or something different, she has no problem with that. She says, "I do not care, because wherever you go, I will go." She understands that she is in Spirit now and she is going to educate herself. She is looking for long lost relatives. She said she was always the one looking for long lost relatives, she is like a rescue person.

John. Yes, Helena was always looking for long lost relatives - very true, whether it was locally or while we were in Hawaii looking for and connecting with long lost cousin, Fiddler Joe.

Joey. Helena says that you are getting off your butt now and you are doing things and she is quite pleased about that. Make whatever changes you need to be happy and feel satisfied. When you talk to her, she gets it, by the way. She hears you and she says "I know, I am sad too." She comes with this energy sometimes when you are sitting in your chair and nodding off, you should feel a movement of air quickly passing above your head, she says, "That is me, whispering very softly to you."

You got a jewel when you got her because you had thought to yourself, how in the hell did she ever end up with me? Do you understand? In addition, she is saying, "Because I loved him." Helena was very independent and perceptive. Was she any kind of a healer, did she have anything to do with healing and did she want to be a nurse?

John. Yes, that is right, she really wanted to be a nurse and there were numerous instances when she took care of people. She had an uncanny knack for arriving at the scene of accidents, and more than once helped injured victims.

Joey. Because this woman could have been a Doctor, that is what I wanted to say, that is what I was getting, but I had to go around how I got it. She could look at people and she could tell what was wrong with them. She had those wonderful eyes and she had a natural gift, whether she used it or not all the time. She says, "Now I am more aware of it so I can take care of my own."

Did she go over on her ankle sometimes?

John. Yes, she had some problems. Helena was in a cast for several months after she twisted her ankle and fell in the mall parking lot. She did not appreciate being slowed down by an ankle cast.

Joey. She is laughing and says, "Yes, he can sell the house and make sure that you get more than it is worth." She adds, "He will know what to do."

Are you thinking of relocating from where you are?

John. Not far away, just two minutes, just around the corner.

Joey. OK, Good.

You can do whatever you want, she does not care. She always let you make your own decisions, and if she wanted something done, she was no fool. Do not worry, she would always let you know, she would fly it. She would give you the idea, put it out there and she would be quiet and let you think about it. She says,

"John, you were always the head of the household, and even when you thought you were, I always ran the show." She is laughing. She knows exactly what is going on, so she would guide you. She is quoting Robert Browning, "Grow old along with me! The best is yet to be." She is saying, "We are not going to have those golden years on this level but I will still always be there." She always wanted to care for children and she says, "I am doing that now in Spirit." Therefore, she is making herself useful. She sends you a lot of energy for your back. She used to rub your back, she says, "I still do that."

Joey comments she is a very lively connection. This love goes on and on and there are no barriers here.

Joey. You know that when you want to figure things out John, you take a blank piece of paper. You always have done that. So now, when you want to do that, just ask for her help and she will be there. You know that you have this hook-up and it is very strong.

John. Yes, it is something I do; it is where I sort out my mind.

Joey. Helena is telling me now that she is pushing up daisies - but she would rather have margaritas.

John. This was very special for me (marguerite being the French word for daisy)... because Helena kept a pail of margarita mix in the freezer, it was a special drink that she liked for special celebrations. Once again, her sense of humour shines through.

Joey. She is really proud of you. You put yourself through a lot to find out about your emotions. She says, "I am proud of you sonny boy", she keeps on telling me that you were like her son. She did not take any b--- from anybody, and she was very spiritual.

John. That is right; she did not take any b--- from anybody, and she did a good job of making me feel worthy.

Joey. And she was fun, she loved to cook and she loved to feed people. She learned that from her mother, she learned many things from her mother. She says, "I had a great family connection." She loved her family, they were different people; it was on a different energy. Do you understand this? She is what you would call an old soul, so your Helena has been around the block a few times. It was important for her to sow a seed, that is why this is so important for her. She said, "Do you think that I just sit up there doing nothing, like playing a harp?" Not her, too many other things to do.

Was there a painting of her?

John. Yes. I had a painting made of both of us together after she passed, does she like it?

Joey. She said, "It is not too bad you know", well, she is pleased with it so there you go.

She knows what is going on and she says that it is OK for you to enjoy the company of other females if you feel like it, it is OK. Socially, you can do whatever you want to do, wherever your life takes you.

I see red roses, she loved red roses?

John. Yes, red roses would have a special meaning for her. Actually, I had a vision of red roses shortly after Helena passed.

Joey. When you are sitting quietly sometime, take a pen and paper, think of some things and talk to her, and see what you get. There was a wonderful book called, The Betty Book, and it was about a husband and wife communicating by writing after Betty had passed away. Therefore, the only way one can make contact is by meditation and by being in the quiet. Here is my advice to you; because I do not want you to become like a nut job and get obsessed with this and thinking, well, she is always around. This is what I would ask you to do. You have to walk the spiritual path with practical feet. You have to be sensible about it, and I think that you are a very sensible man. I think that you would be able to do it because she is already guiding you. She is asking, "How the hell do you think you got here", and she repeats it, that is exactly how she would talk to you. She is there, so if you want to take her ring, put it down beside you along with a writing pad, there is your contact.

Helena is smiling at you, she had a great smile and she could break your heart with that smile.

John. She sure could and just before she took ill, she made numerous contacts by telephone with old friends. I feel that her Spirit knew that she was going. After she died, many people came up to me and told me that Helena had called them.

Joey. She knew those days when her Spirit was leaving the body, so she was ready to go.

John. Was she ready to go on December 22 or in the hospital?

Joey. When in the hospital, so in the hospital it was good, because her Spirit was already going more into the Spirit World.

John. Joey, she loved her father. I did not mean to interrupt you, but was he the one who gave you the information?

Joey. "Was her father thin in the face?"

John. Yes.

Joey. He was a farmer; he is coming in now. He is not huge, but a bit taller than you and I, just a bit, not much. He is wearing overalls and boots. He is saying, "I have lost a lot of weight now and I came to get her." He always liked you John, but he would give you the eye, and you would catch him looking at you. He would study you because he wanted to make sure that you were good enough for his girl. Would you understand that?

John. Absolutely, he was a farmer and he had a farm, although he worked on the railroad. Helena had a great affinity with her father, as did I. Helena's father referred to his daughter as 'pet crow' because when she was mad at her sisters, she would take their things and hide them and she had great eyesight - and crows can see very far, that is why he called her pet crow.

Joey. He came to get her, he is the one. Her family was waiting for her on the other side. So Spirit knew and now they are all together, she has found everybody. Just so that you know.

I am looking out the window because she always wondered what it was all about, what was in back of the sky. What would it be like, she was never afraid of death, and she loved life. She says, "Life was a gift to

	me, everything was a gift and God was always good to me, I am not afraid." She never worried about her health too much because she did not take things too seriously, and did exercise and she kept herself in good shape.
John.	When Helena had her heart attack, she was about one hundred twenty seven pounds and very active.
Joey.	She was extremely creative and she would change things in her house, she did not always want things to be the same. She would change items around and she said, "I made us a wonderful home" and she says, "When you have to rebuild your house, you put it together with parts of you and parts of me." And she will still be there; she says, "You will never get away from me." So she is saying that she will be there for you, she will help you.
John.	Yes, she was very creative and decorated everything very nicely.
Joey.	John, you have to take care of your health. She places her hand over your head because you have to make sure that your blood pressure is under control, that everything is OK. You have been through a lot in the last year and a half but it is coming down. Do you understand that?
John.	Yes.
Joey.	John, you have a very green thumb as well, you were very compatible, you two. Sometimes you were like one soul. She is saying, at one point you were like brother and sister and she says, "You were like my soul. We would finish each other's sentences and we would finish each other's thoughts and sometimes you did not have to talk, we would just communicate." And she laughs and says, "Don't forget it." Therefore, she does not want you to be sad, there have been enough tears. She says, "I am just looking at it from a different angle." She liked the water and the air of the sea, which she liked to breathe in. She was so close to nature and so in tune with the elements and very in tune with Spirit. That is why she is so strong. That is why I do not worry about her not being around. I do not worry about you not picking her up, because you

will, her presence is in the house. She says, "I'm there, I'm there", she comes and goes.

Keep on talking to her because you are not holding her back, you are not doing her any harm. You need to understand that there is nothing to be forgiven. She is physically OK. Meaning that in Spirit there are no physical imperfections or illness. She says, "That's my guy, you have always lived your life that way, your intentions were always good. Sometimes you have a funny way of getting things done because you could be stubborn and wanted things your own way". But she adds, "That's fine because he always got to where he was going." Joey adds, and she really stood behind you. She was a person who always adjusted to life. If she had a problem she would deal with it and she would wipe the dust from her feet and move on. She was not one to live in the past. She was not one to feel sorry for herself and she says, "I have no regrets."

She was a very realistic person and in the background I hear the song, "Quand Le Soleil Dit Bonjour Aux Montagnes". She liked that song. As I heard the song in the back of my head, she said to tell you that she is walking in front of you and she has the lamp, she is like a guiding light. I will be his Guardian Angel. So she is taking care of you. She walks with you. This is your whole message: Remember the perfect times and she is grateful for them. You were her pal, you were friends and she says, "I'll catch up to you, meanwhile, you need to get on with your life and you are doing remarkably well." She feels you are dealing with her passing and you do wrestle with your pain, and she knows this. She says, "I do not forget you and you do not forget me, but you are still here and you have a future here".

Joey. We are all travellers in eternity, you know that. She waits for you is what I want to say. She mentioned buttons before with your clothes; did she have a button box?

John. Yes, she was a seamstress by profession for many years.

Joey. You are fine; you are going to be all right. Helena says to tell you, remember that there is no time over there.

Now is the time for you to pick up the pieces, tell him how proud I am of him. She likes the idea that you are working on yourself and trying to understand yourself more and you understand the people around you. This has changed you a lot. I am proud of him and give him a big E for effort. Because she says, "I would never tell him what to do." Understand that? But she says, "I have been leading him." She has taken care of you since the day you were married and she says, "I'll always take care of him and as far as I'm concerned, we are still married. I am just in another place right now."

Comments from John Reath

My beautiful wife Helena officially died on January 5, 2001 at 1:40 am. Helena was fifty-nine years of age when she started her journey to the "next phase" on December 22 - fifteen days earlier.

Helena was lying on the couch and she had a smile on her face. I asked her what was going through her mind. She replied, "I was remembering when we first met and how well we connected." I was very struck by that and then went on to speak to her about how lucky we are to have each other to love and how fortunate we had been with our children and how things were coming together financially for us. Helena did not respond. I discovered that there was a serious problem. I called 911 and tried to revive her. The paramedics rushed Helena to the nearest hospital. She never regained consciousness.

On April 16, 2004 I met with Joey in person at his home in Montreal. It appeared that Joey was able to sense Helena as soon as we sat down for our consultation. It was immensely sad but very exciting at the same time. Joey was impressed with Helena's sense of humour. Helena really had a tremendous sense of humour and she loved music. Helena loved to tap her feet and play the spoons. She was, "Une Vraie Acadienne". Joey saw and sensed her real essence.

At one point Joey said: "Helena loved to garden." I confirmed that she did. Joey then went on to say, "She is telling me that now she is pushing up daisies - but she would rather margaritas" (marguerite being the French word for daisy). In addition, Helena kept a pail of frozen margarita mix in the freezer. It was a special drink that she liked for special celebrations. Once again, Helena's sense of humour was with me and that was very special for me. Joey told me that Helena was saying, "Don't let the buttons fall off my coat." Helena was a seamstress by trade. Obviously, it was one more direct connection.

Through Joey:

Helena referred to me needing my "quiet space" - another connection.

Helena was always looking for long lost relatives - very true, whether it was locally or while we were in Hawaii looking for and connecting with a long-lost cousin, "Fiddler Joe".

Helena always had people in the house and had indeed "fostered" children. I was very happy that I had one more last conversation with Helena through Joey.

Since December 22, 2001 the word, "connection" has been a key word in my vocabulary. I believe that Helena had already started to "crossover" when she said, "I was just remembering when we first met and how well we connected."

What a nice memory! I need to recall those words often and am so happy that Helena said them.

Joey helped assure me that Helena and I will always be connected.

Thank you, Joey

John Reath

Shawn Asling

Introduction by Jean Sexton

I met Joey Crinita thirty years ago. Over our span of friendship I've witnessed his gift of mediumship many times and have my share of personal experiences through Joey. Joey is many things, a teacher, healer, writer, and poet. Most importantly, he is authentic.

This is a telling of the manner Joey came to meet my long-time friends, Ilona and Greg Asling.

August 11, 2003 brought a great loss to Ilona and Greg. They, their youngest son Shawn and his girlfriend, Ashley were out on the water enjoying the day. Without warning, an accident occurred. Shawn drowned at Lawrencetown's Rocky Run, Nova Scotia. He was twenty-three years of age. His parents, family and loved ones were left to deal with the painful process of sudden grieving.

August 14, 2003 I telephoned Joey in Montreal to tell him of the accident, conveying only that Shawn had died. In my long-time friendship with Joey, I had never called upon him in this type of circumstance. However, I was deeply concerned for my friends and hopeful he would be able to provide assurance, comfort, something. Joey offered to tune in and see what impressions he might receive about Shawn's passing.

The following is a written summary of Joey's comments during the course of our telephone conversation:

- Do not be surprised if there are candles at this evening's visitation, more like a Vigil.
- Shawn wore his sweater around his neck/shoulders... preppy look. However, he was very traditional.
- He has blonde hair, beautiful. He is like an angel.
- Does he have a brother? They are very close, like twins. Shawn is in shock but he is all right. He is okay. He is not alone; someone is with him in Spirit. Joey felt it was a brother energy and asked if there was a miscarriage between the births of the brothers? (Shawn's older brother is Scott).

- Joey asked if it was a drowning. Did he bang his head? Shawn did not know what happened to him, it was quick. He was in shock and surprised, but he is okay and not afraid.
- Joey began to recite some lines from the hymn:

Abide With Me

Abide with me; fast falls the eventide;
The darkness deepens; Lord with me abide.
When other helpers fail and comforts flee,
Help of the helpless, O abide with me.

- Joey stated that Shawn was a Jewel in the Crown and much like an uncle who went young.
- He was artistic and liked the colour blue. Joey asked if Shawn was left-handed and said there is something about a gold ring…. perhaps a school ring?
- I knew it was unusual to make such a strong contact so soon after one's passing and Joey concurred with this, adding that Shawn wants us to know he is okay.
- Joey asked I not yet share this conversation with Shawn's parents because it was too soon. He did suggest however that I write down this conversation because it would prove helpful in the future.

August 25, 2003

Ilona returned to work, she needed to be busy away from home.

I went to her office that morning. She told me of poems recently discovered in Shawn and Ashley's bedroom. They were found under a Joe Louis cake, a favourite of Shawn's. Evidently, he was saving one, using it as a paperweight of sorts. Ilona was surprised not to have seen this in days prior and shared two of the poems with me. The words were quite frankly, astonishing. It seemed he had left a gift for loved ones. The following is one of Shawn's poems written in that Summer of 2003.

I was standing barefoot in the river, when the current ran off with my mind and the wind picked up my body, blew it up the mountainside.

Left alone I saw the river empty out into the sea and high up on the Mountain peak stood a statue of me.

The song of a sparrow was all that I could hear, it was brought over the flowing water by the wind to sing in my ear.

As I was listening to the tale being told by the babbling of the brook something arose from the storyline as if to have a closer look.

Its beauty was like that of none that I have seen before and inspired me to draw closer and find out a little more.

Shawn's girlfriend Ashley asked for his gold high school ring. Unfortunately, his parents could not give her the ring as Shawn had been wearing it at the time of the accident. It was lost to the water. Ilona then told me the background of the gold ring. On a visit to Hungary many years previously, her father gave her two rings with instructions to give one to each of his grandsons, (Scott and Shawn) upon their graduating from high school. Here was one of Joey's double-checks... he had mentioned in our initial conversation, "There is something about a gold ring." I was yet to share with Ilona and Greg my earlier conversation with Joey.

Upon returning home from visiting Ilona at her office, I telephoned Joey to relate the morning, in particular the gold ring and writings. He felt on some level Shawn knew and had left this as a gift... we spoke further of Shawn. In this conversation, Joey mentioned he felt September would have been a big month for Shawn as he was returning to University. Joey felt that Shawn had other plans as well.

Joey requested when I felt the time was right, to convey the following to Ilona and Greg: Shawn would get their attention with a sign. He felt it would be the sound of a flute or music. They will be somewhere and hear the sound of music. This will be from Shawn to get their attention. Again, Joey encouraged me to maintain notes. He felt strongly it would be appreciated and helpful to Ilona and Greg sometime in the future. I had concern when the time would be right... Joey said, "Not to worry, Shawn will set it up." He then asked if Shawn's parents were aware of my knowledge, interest and belief in Spiritualism and how they felt about the subject. Both Greg and Ilona were aware of my interest, to what degree I was unsure. They did however know of my long-time relationship with Joey. They knew he was a medium. If they understood what it meant, I do not recall.

Over the next several weeks, Ilona expressed a want to get together. She had things to share and sensed I did as well. This came up several times. We agreed it would occur when the timing was right and settled on letting it be.

October 17, 2003

Ilona telephoned and we planned a visit at my home.

I felt this evening would be the appropriate time to tell Ilona of my earlier conversations with Joey and decided to let the visit take its course. Soon after she arrived, Ilona asked me what I wanted to tell her. I enquired, why this question? Ilona expressed that she intuitively knew I had information for her. She did not know why, it was simply a strong feeling. She had been waiting for a time when she felt ready to receive whatever it might be. It seemed Shawn had indeed set it up! And now was the right time for me to convey Joey's comments and impressions regarding Shawn.

I had my notes ready and willingly shared them with her. As I read the notes Ilona confirmed a miscarriage between sons and that an uncle to Shawn had indeed passed at a young age as well. We spent several hours talking. Ilona felt our visit was meaningful and the timing was right. She was going through her process. An acceptance was forming. She asked if it might be agreeable to send Joey a particular poem Shawn composed and did I think he would be interested. I contacted Joey with Iona's request to which he acquiesced and oddly, requested a photograph of Shawn be included as well. As it unfolded, Shawn's poem did indeed interest Joey, as did the photograph.

November 1, 2003

This day found a friend and I paying an unplanned visit to Carol Ann McNeil's home on the ocean in Indian Harbour, Nova Scotia. In fact, it was via Carol Ann I initially made Joey's acquaintance thirty years ago in Montreal.

Unexpectedly, Greg and Ilona dropped in as well. It was very unusual that they did so. They spoke of an experience the night before, waking at approximately 2:00 am to the loud and distinct sound of running water. Both began to investigate for the obvious. It was not raining, the faucets were not running, the outdoor taps were turned off and the indoor water feature was unplugged, et cetera. Yet the sound continued, loud and clear and at the same time, comforting and calm. Ilona and Greg believe this was the message from Shawn to get their attention.

November 4, 2003

I informed Joey of these double-checks. He was interested to learn it was not music or the sound of a flute, however at the time of this 2010 writing, Joey feels that Shawn is still yet to make the music happen. Although water was responsible for Shawn's passing, he sent the sound of water. Ilona felt it was a further message to continue to enjoy the water they all so loved. She and Greg grew up around water and raised their sons around water. Understandably, they had difficulty embracing it now. It seemed to be a message..." it is okay."

Early 2004

Some months later, Ilona asked if it might be possible to meet with Joey in Montreal.

She and Greg wanted a reading and could I arrange it? I felt conflicted. I knew they were hopeful for information of Shawn. I informed Ilona that in any reading contact from Spirit is not a guarantee. It would be disappointing for them not to receive anything. (I thought and did not voice that this would be unlikely as I am long familiar with Joey's work). I further went on to say that Joey gives what is given to him and has no control over what he might receive. In response, Ilona replied that she and Greg would accept whatever the experience brought. I asked that she leave it with me. Privately, I had concerns because I fully understood the impact such a reading would have on Joey. As a sensitive medium he not only receives messages, he also feels the emotion. I knew should a reading take place, it would be a tough one, exhausting and draining for all present. On one hand, I did not want to impose on Joey. On the other hand, being familiar with his work as a medium, I felt strongly he would be helpful to my friends. I opted to make the request and left the decision to Joey. I let it be known there was no pressure to agree. It would be whatever it was meant to be.

It is important to mention here that although Joey encouraged me to note the related 2003 telephone conversations, he had not read the content prior to the writing of this book, seven years later. Joey works on a very quick vibration, giving impressions received as quickly as they come in. He does not recall the information after it is delivered and would have no recollection of the details of our 2003 conversations.

The Reading takes place at Joey's Montreal home.

On Saturday, March 20, 2004 Ilona and Greg Asling travelled from Halifax to Montreal to meet with me. The purpose of this meeting was hopefully to make contact with their son Shawn who had passed to Spirit on August 11, 2003. Ilona and Greg were strangers to me, as of course was Shawn. As stated in the introduction by my friend Jean Sexton, she had telephoned me on August 14, 2003 three days after Shawn's premature death. During my conversation with Jean, I shared the impressions I received. At the time, I was impressed to request a photograph of Shawn which is something that I normally would not do, as I do not read from photographs. I did so on this occasion and I would come to know the reason why later.

Prior to the meeting, I placed Shawn's photo on a table that is located next to the chair that I use during my readings.

I knew that this reading was going to be a very emotional experience for all involved. When Ilona and Greg arrived to my home, they told me they almost did not come because of the intense pain they were in and what if Shawn did not come through during the reading. We had not met before and this would be their first encounter with a medium. Ilona and Greg knew nothing about the process and what to expect. Jean had informed them how I work and that was all they knew. As a rule, I do not read for two people during a private sitting, so this was something new for me as well. I was keenly aware of the sensitive nature of this meeting and of the emotional fragility of both parents which was plainly evident to me as the reading progressed. I knew it was very hard for them to respond to my comments. Initially short yes or no responses were forthcoming, often through their tears. However, Shawn did a brilliant job of establishing his identify and the high level of his energy coupled with the strong emotions transcended the pain for a period of time as we were all struggling through this Spirit connection between a son and his parents. In the final analysis, Shawn showed up... this is the reading:

Joey. I usually start my reading with a symbol and I heard the song, "I'll Be Seeing You" in my head. However, I know what the situation is, it has been a long climb and I am waiting to see what happens as Shawn comes closer, and I can feel his energy. I know that he is quite tall. He is saying, "I am very strong and still wiry." Would you understand why I would use the word wiry?

Greg. Yes.

Joey. The first thing I want to tell you is, Shawn is saying, "I'm all right" I have to ask you something because in the picture here, his hair comes down like that, (pointing to Shawn's hair in the photo on the table), and Joey asked, "Did he wear it up sometimes so that it was a bit pushed up? In addition, it was more of corn gold than it is in this picture, it is blonder and he was blonder in person. I had to tell you that because the thing is the smile, it was a killer smile and he could always get his way with that. It is interesting because you are both dark in a sense, and he is blonde. He is saying," I am a bit of a gypsy too." Do you understand why I would say that?"

Greg. Yes.

Joey. Because he says that he had gypsy in his blood.

First, he knew how to swim and I know that he went by an accident. I feel what might have happened, he must have banged his head but he really did not know what happened to him. It was very quick and he says, "Before I knew it, I was over here."

Did he at one point wear moccasins, brown moccasins, and loafer sort of things?

Greg. Yes.

Joey. He has them on now. He says, "I am really relaxed." He must have had long legs, I am putting my legs out here (Joey stretches out his legs); he is saying, "You know I did not trip over anything." In his life he always felt he was God's child, (Joey says, I have to give it to you that way), because in his life doors and paths were always open for him and he says, "I knew within my heart." He did not know that he was going but he felt that he had a destiny to meet. Would you understand that?

Greg. Yes.

Joey. He would talk about that and sometimes he would meander in his mind, (that is the word I want to use) because I feel that even when he was younger he had a very good way with words. You understand?

Greg. Very good.

Joey. He could express himself well and I know that he learned to speak at a very early age, so this boy was very articulate. I do not know if he had an interest in shells or marine life. I see shells. I feel that since he was a child he would collect many things. He was a collector of everything.

Greg and Ilona. Yes, he would collect everything.

Joey. Shawn says, "I would drive my mother nuts."

He was like a garbage man, he had a wooden box he threw everything in and you would have to go and clean everything out. Do you understand? At one point he put something in there that smelled, he was about eight years old and he is saying, "My Mom had to go and clean it out, she was always doing that", and his hands were always dirty, but he says, "I'm all clean now." As he grew up he always wanted to build; he is saying that he could build castles in the sand, but he says, "I also could have built buildings, that is what I wanted to do." I do not know if he studied architecture or not.

Greg. Yes.

Joey. I feel that he could have done it, (Ilona interjects, yes), he could have done anything that he set his mind to, and his hands were so expressive.

(Joey gets up from his chair and approaches Greg and gives him a little nudge on his shoulder and says, "How are you doing old man?" Shawn is playfully saying. "Don't be mad, don't be mad."

Joey asks Greg, "Do you understand?" and returns to his chair.

At this point, Ilona responded for Greg that Shawn would do this all the time.

Joey. Did he have an old kimono that he would wear, a blue thing?

Ilona. Yes, yes.

Joey. Yes, the old one and he says, "It looked like a rag sometimes." He loves that and he is saying, "Don't throw it out." So, he wants to tell you that when you go into his room, which you still do, and you talk to him, he is still there; he says, "I am in the house."

Joey continued, "Now I have to ask you this, because I feel that he went looking on the other side. Did he have a grandfather that had something to do with the sea or the navy or something of that sort."

Greg. No.

Joey. Sounding surprised, "Why would I get that, obviously he has found himself a mentor on Spirit side."

Ilona. He loved the sea.

Joey. He found himself a mentor because he said, "I got myself a boat" and he repeated it.

As gregarious as Shawn was, he was extremely outgoing but he liked to be alone. A part of him could be very quiet. He got that quietness from you Greg. You and he had that communication, where you could just look at him. He is very much your son, I can see him looking at you now and he says, "I was better looking Dad, you know that." He is saying, "I could communicate with my father without words." Joey asks do you understand that.

Greg. Yes.

Joey. And he never told you a fib because you always, always caught him, occasionally he would try to get away with things. I see him slipping out the back door. Do you understand?

Greg. Yes.

Joey. In addition he would be very quiet; this kid could be as quiet as a mouse.

Greg. Yes.

Joey. You would not even know that he was in the house and he would be working away. He was very artistic and so he could do little creative things. I must say that he was a very bright young man and he still is, because we grow in Spirit. The innocence about him was so apparent. When people looked at him they would first think, this kid does not know anything about life. One would look at him and he was so happy-go-lucky. One might think of Shawn as a new soul.

Ilona. Yes.

Joey. He was like an angel that someone let loose on the earth plane and he is saying, "I knew everything. I knew all about sex when I was thirteen." Because he used to read, he made up his mind to get into books and he liked to find things out. You could not hide things from him, he was like a detective.

Greg. Yes.

Joey. Shawn is saying, "I would have made a good cop and I would have made a good carpenter." He had all of these talents and he said, "God was very good to me and let me tell you Mom, they needed me over here." Just so you know, he is now working with children on the Spirit side. We just do not go up there and play the harp all day. Shawn says it would break his heart when he would see little children with special needs, "I am doing that now, I'm taking care of little kids." He is like the Pied Piper, that is exactly what he would have been, and that is what he is doing on Spirit side.

Ilona. He loved it.

Joey. He liked music, he is strumming on a guitar and he is doing, On Top of Old Smokey. He said he would drive you crazy when he first started to learn.

Ilona. Oh, yes.

Joey. He says, "I wasn't the greatest player but I got better as I got older."

Greg. He sure did.

Joey. He knows that he drove you nuts and you would think, my God what is he doing? Shawn was so happy. You provided a loving home for him and you two gave him the ideals which he incorporated within himself. This boy walked the talk. It is interesting that I call him a boy, he really was a man, but he was like a boy. He is like the eternal child, he is still like that and that is how he is.

What is all this about colours? Did he have all his shirts and stuff colour coordinated, or could he not see, he could not do it right. Do you understand?

Ilona. He was so horrible with colours he could not match.

Greg. He would put anything with anything.

Joey. Exactly, that is what he is telling me. I would say colour coordination was not his cup of tea. He did not care about that, everything was a mishmash, he would just wear what he would wear. He did not care about that kind of stuff. He just enjoyed life and he liked to read.

Joey. I do not know what this is all about, he was a good swimmer.

Ilona. Oh yes, a very good swimmer and he could have been even better. As a baby he was so comfortable in the water.

Joey. Yes, because he is talking about breathing in the water. He loved the water. He still loves the water; he says he is nature's child, he belongs to the Universe. There are some souls that come and in their young years make their mark and then it is time for them to move on.

Shawn says, "I was a gift to you and God only lent me to you for a while, but I had to go home." He had to go home and he knew it, there was a part of him that knew it and this kid did not waste a second.

Ilona. No, never.

Joey. That is why he says, "I lived every part of my life." He did not like sleeping that much, he would say there is too much to do. He would say, let's go, let's go."

Ilona, Yes, yes.

Joey. He would just move, he had to have things done, anything that he set his mind to, he could do. He could work in a garden if he wanted to and he liked that. He says, "I always liked to make things grow." He liked daffodils and he liked the Spring. Spring was important for him; it was a time of renewal. It was the time when life started. I do not recall when he passed but I feel it would have been a later time in the year.

Greg. August.

Joey. Because he liked the Fall as well, he says, "I am sorry I could not be around on this planet to watch the leaves change", but he is still around and he watches everything. This boy is a very loving and active Spirit. You never see him without a smile on his face. I am watching him now and he has that grin, because he is happy. He says, "I am at peace."

Joey. What is this with a blue blazer?

Greg and Ilona. He never had one.

Joey. But he has one now. This is symbolic. Shawn says, "I am going to school now." He is now educating himself. He says, "I am going to finish University." He could have written. He could have been a very good writer as well because of his love for the English language. He had a faculty, an ear and could have learned other languages if he had chosen to do so. He would listen to people. He must have been a very good mimic. I would say that this kid would never miss a trick, because he was so bright.

Greg. No, he did not and he learned from life.

Joey. He got along well with older people. He liked older people and he always respected his elders. When he was a young boy, he was still an old man, because at times he would shuffle along (and that is the word that I am using). He would just mosey along and he was all eyes, just looking around. Even in the Spirit World now, he says; "I know I can fly." He looks around, this Spirit is so bright and his mind is so bright that he is constantly still learning and taking care of all of his friends. (Joey made a gesture with his arms as if to gather other people into his arms.)

Greg. He always did that.

Joey. He is still doing it, so he could bring everybody together, one world for peace. If he would have stayed on the earth plane, he could have made a great politician but he would not have done that. He said, "He had too much integrity." It is just that he wanted to bring people together. He is saying that he had all of his wits about him, so he is still in his prime. He says, "I got work to do up here."

I now see a picture of an old lighthouse and it is symbolic. Shawn is saying, "I could go to a lighthouse and look out." He likes old things, he liked to watch, he was always watching for something. I feel that it was this sense, he knew he was not here for too long, although he would not verbalize something like that. There was a part... like, you would think; "I wonder what he is thinking sometimes." Do you understand?

Greg. Yes.

Joey. Because at times he would go off. He would be present with you all the time, and there also was a very serious side to him. He would contemplate many things about life, what he was doing here. He was just so fascinated with everything. He just loved it.

I hear the sound of birds. He must have liked birds.

Ilona. Yes, that is right.

Joey. Bluebirds, bluebirds, I am seeing here and jays, do not forget the jays, and he liked the Jays.

Ilona. He loved the jays.

Joey. He also liked the Blue Jays baseball team. The kid had an eye on everything. He was very aware of what was going on in the world, very aware of what was around him.

Joey further stated. And as I am doing this, I am working with energy, because he is trying to send you healing. He is sending energy to you.

Joey addresses Ilona directly, "Sometimes when you would be sitting, especially after he had passed in the first few months and I know that it is very hard for you, I feel as if I wanted to slip a pillow behind your back and behind your head and Shawn would stand behind you often, and you would feel it, because you would talk to him, but he could not get to you. Do you understand that?"

Ilona. He touched me.

Joey. He says," Yes, yes. I was reaching out."

	Joey continued and Shawn says, "Ma, you ain't seen nothing yet", and he repeats, "You ain't seen nothing yet." He would say this, he would tease you, but he is doing it out of love to let you both know that he is around. He was able to make this contact today. Now, he has green shorts on, long green shorts that he just showed me. He says, "I got a good tan" (because he tanned really well), he says, "I do not know how, because I did not get it from you two." He further says, "I am all set for Summer," because that is how he is relaxing. He just drifts in, and it is just that he comes with so much love. He is in the house. He is definitely around you. Do not think that this boy is far away because he is not. He says you know I prayed in my own way, and he always did that. He was not one for being very religious.
Greg.	No.
Joey.	But he prayed in his own way. He understood what was up there, he says, "I am still looking for angels with wings." He has adjusted to being in Spirit. It was very easy for him because it was almost as if he went home in a sense, (although his home was also here) and he knew it. Through the years you will know that he will be around, particularly at Christmas. He liked Christmas, The Holidays, and those festive occasions. He says, "I am always there, I'm always there." I am seeing a chest of drawers here with socks. I do not know if you have been going through those lately.
Ilona.	We had to take them out.
Joey.	Shawn says that you can give some of them away, especially the grey ones, the thick ones. You know, because it does not matter, because it is all right to give some of my things away. You keep what you need. He says, "I do not need a shrine; because I am here, I am always here." Nevertheless, you do whatever. He would never tell you what to do but he just knows how hard this is and he misses you too, because there was a lot of love, your family was full of love. He loved you both so much and you two brought him up so well. This boy was a free Spirit. You taught him the meaning of love, and I do feel that it was a karmic relationship with you two. He is always part of

	this family. He was meant to be born into this family, I have to ask you, when he was being born, did you have an easy birth or did he take his time?
Ilona.	No.
Joey.	He could not wait to get out and he never stopped.
Ilona.	No, the doctor had to tell me to put my book down, the baby is coming. I said I am almost finished. Greg went to get a tea and they had to call him back, he almost missed him. He wanted to come.
Joey.	I have to ask, was there a poem that he was writing and he never finished?
Greg.	Yes.
Ilona.	A bunch of them.
Joey.	OK, because I just see this and he is saying, "I finished some of them now." In addition, he is saying, "If you want to Dad, you could do this." Joey went on, "Take some of them, do not rewrite his work but just maybe sit and he will inspire you and let you finish them for him. In addition, he will work with you. He is saying, "You could do that and I will not get pissed off." His work was very private to him. You understand that?"
Greg and Ilona.	Yes.
Joey.	Therefore, there is a lot more depth to your son than you realized. When you found some of the stuff he wrote after he had passed... WOW! He is an old soul because he has been here so many times before. Did he like archery?
Greg.	He did not participate in it, but he knew about it, oh yes.
Joey.	I had to ask you that, but it does not matter because I saw the bow and arrow and when I said that he was an old soul, he proudly said to me, "Well, I was a knight in a past lifetime, so I know this kind of stuff." He liked England by the way, he liked The British Isles, the Old Country.
Greg.	Yes.
Joey.	He was a true Canadian spirit in many ways, but he liked the old places. He would have wandered through

Europe. That was his intention. He said, "I have done it now and I am going to do it all the time." Joey adds, "Because in Spirit they can go wherever they want, right". He brought a lot of information with him and I believe that he could have read Latin. He understood it. He said, "I am going to learn that now," and he is saying, "I am going to pick up many of the things that I wanted to do."

Joey addressed Greg directly and said, "I am looking at your watch. Shawn says, "My father knows that I never had enough time to do anything, I never had enough time." (Shawn is checking his watch). Joey continues, "I feel that when you bought him his first watch it was like a big deal and I do not know if he broke it, what happened?

Greg. He broke it.

Ilona. He lost or broke everything.

Joey. Shawn says, "But it was only things." He was not attached to anything, and he did not give a hoot if it was broken.

Ilona. If something broke, he kept it broke.

Joey. He never threw anything away. He was like a pack rat. He had stuff from when he was seven or eight years old just there lying around, because that was his sense of history. He says, "I left a lot of these things for you on purpose" because he knew that he was not going to be around. Therefore, he left things. He states, "That is why I never threw anything out, I knew my journey here was short. Sometimes I looked over my shoulder and I would just wonder what was going on." He knew his life would be completed in Spirit this time around. "But," he says, "I will be back."

I do not know if you have other children. I do feel within the next couple of years that a child will be born into the family who will be very much like him, with many of his mannerisms and many of his energies. It is not going to be him. He says, "It is not going to be me." Because he is not reincarnating. Shawn says, "But I am going to influence this." You wait and see, he is going to influence it. Do not tell the others. I want this for your double-check. I want this as proof for you.

You are going to watch this child grow and you are going to say, there is Shawn, there is Shawn." Particularly, he says, "When the kid gets old enough to start messing around with paintings and mixing colour up, I am going to set something up, so you will know it is me." He intends to play a joke with painting and colour. In addition, he wants you to know that his influence will be felt there.

(Since this 2004 reading, Tae Shawn Asling was born on August 25, 2004 to Shawn's older brother Scott and his wife So yeon).

Joey. I see many margaritas here.

Ilona. He liked to drink, he liked to party.

Joey. He says, "OK, but I like the other margaritas (daisies) too." I do not know if he is having a party, but he says I will celebrate with margaritas.

Ilona. He loved to party, he would party anywhere.

Joey. Yes, Shawn says, "I was a cool dude." He did not use that lingo, but he could fit in anywhere. This man had friends; from all walks of life, everybody liked him. He was everybody's pal and just boom! He says, "I'm the Pied Piper." That is how he describes himself and he knew it. He knew that this was his gift to humanity. He says, "I thank you for giving me the love that you gave me, the way that you raised me and the freedom."

Now you must have had a big house, because he liked to run.

Ilona. Yes, outside in the open air.

Joey. He liked to run and he says I always had all the freedom that I wanted at home. At one point, did he get something for his ankle, a little bracelet or something? (Joey was touching his left ankle.)

Ilona. No, at one point he had some injury on his ankle quite some years ago and it was his left ankle.

Joey. OK, because my ankle... I just saw something over it and Shawn says , "I don't have that anymore." As you know in Spirit there is no physical incapability. So, he is saying everything is gone now. There is no physical stuff. There are no physical limits. He adds, "In a way,

I like that", because he is free. You could symbolically put this boy on a pony, I do not mean he rode a pony but he is like the wind. He says, "I am like the wind." Do you know that poem, "Do Not Stand at My Grave and Weep," because he is very much a part of nature. Joey makes a gesture of moving his arms and hands about and says, "What I am doing now is moving the energy about for Shawn, he understood that one could move energy. By the way, he was a healer. I would not be surprised that at some point he did want to become a Doctor. He could heal people and I will tell you how I mean it. His friends would come to him with all of their problems and he would reach out (Joey demonstrated) and he would like to put his hands out and touch them."

Greg and Ilona. Yes, yes.

Joey. He was very tactile and as he reached out to them, there was a lot of energy that came from his hands. If you held his hand it was hot. That was the power that he had. He said, "I could heal people, I am still doing it, I am still taking care of my friends."

Greg. I do not doubt that at all, he is taking care of his friends.

Ilona. We do not know much, but we know he helped. So many people loved him.

Joey. Did he help someone with his back, what did he do?

Greg. I had a back problem and he was aware of that.

Joey. Well, I think that he is helping you. I wanted to put my hand on your back. (Joey stood and placed his hand on a specific area on Greg's back.)

Greg. That is exactly where it is.

Joey. Shawn is saying, "Don't worry Pop, I'll fix you up."

Greg. That is what he would call me, Pop, old person.

Joey. He would tease you about that and the white hair. He is repeating again, "Don't worry Pop, I'll fix you up." So just know that he is around and that he watches over you, both of you.

I am very excited and I must tell you this right now, because Shawn is around. Why I agreed to this reading is because I like his energy so much. In speaking with our mutual friend Jean, I described Shawn as such a Light Spirit.

Greg. Yes, yes.

Joey. Last Wednesday (March 17) at about three o'clock in the morning, I was awakened from a deep sleep. Now this is not unusual for me, as I see Spirit very clearly... I am frequently awakened from sleep by a Spirit entity, but it is still startling. I usually sense a presence, and there they are, standing by my bed. On that morning, standing at the edge of my bed is this tall guy with long blonde hair, smiling and peering down at me. His energy was very light and I noticed his teeth. He gave me a great smile and his hair was arranged high on his head, (Joey made a gesture of tall hair) as though it was puffed up. He was wearing a green sweater. I thought to myself, who are you and my usual reaction is to say, "God bless you", which I did. He then disappeared as quickly as he had appeared. I was still sleepy, nothing clicked for me and as usual I went back to sleep without giving this too much thought. The next morning while I was having a shower, I had an epiphany. It was Shawn who had come to visit me. I immediately went to check the photograph that I had in my possession and without a doubt it was Shawn. That was my double-check. I recognized him instantly. This was the reason why I was impressed to make the unusual request to Jean to ask Ilona to send his photo along with the poem she wanted me to have. It was now perfectly clear to me. I was not going to share this with you because I thought you would think I was crazy. However, Spirit does indeed work that way and Shawn has been waiting for you all week. He is around and he has now made that connection with me. This was solely for me, and Jean does not know because I have not spoken with her of this. I was debating whether to tell you or not. In fact, what I did was enlarge his photo for myself so I could have a closer look at him. I wanted to make sure it was Shawn and indeed, it was.

Again, it was 3:00 am when I was awakened, and he was tall. Greg, you are tall but he is about as tall as

	you are and the hair was much longer than in the picture, and it was sticking out and long, long.
Ilona.	Yes, six feet tall and blonde, blonde, blonde.
Joey.	Yes, he just looked like an angel; his hair was sticking out and the teeth and his smile. Do not forget I was lying down so he looked very tall to me and his presence was full of Light. He is definitely around, there are no ifs, ands or buts about it. He will be around and he continues to be in the house. It does not mean that he is earthbound or anything like that.
Ilona.	No, he is not earthbound. He is happy.
Greg.	Is he taking care up there?
Joey.	He is fine. He is a pure Spirit and he is taking care of you (to Ilona) and your husband.
Greg.	Is he lonely?
Joey.	No, because when the Spirit is free it is such a feeling of Light because you are a part of God. You are part of the Universe, there is no loneliness there. They do move on and yet they watch over you and he will always be there. However, he is not in some cold dark place.
Greg.	He was loved.
Joey.	He has it and he knows that. He will bring the love to you through the years. Now he is singing, "Oh My Darling Clementine". He is being funny and he must have teased someone about their big feet because he is doing this now (Joey makes a gesture of big feet). Through the years he will let you know that he is all right. You will both know that he is here. It is very subtle, it may be just that you are sitting in your chair in your living-room.
Ilona.	We already feel him.
Joey.	Maybe sometimes you will be nodding off and he will be with you and know it is not your imagination. That is where he comes through to you and he knows that, moreover, he comes in and then out. He says, "He has things to do."
Ilona.	Of course he does.

	We had an experience around 2:00 am with the sound of running water. (As referred to in detail in Jean's opening comments.)
Joey.	Shawn is teaching. This child of yours is a child of Light and so he knows what he has to do. He is out looking for relatives and he is out looking for other people. He said, "I am going to try and find them."
	Was there a child that never touched the earth plane please?
Greg.	Yes.
Joey.	I thought so, it is a boy, it is a brother in Spirit and he has found him.
Greg.	That is good.
Joey.	He is older than Shawn is by two years?
Greg.	Yes.
Joey.	Shawn says, "We named him in Spirit, we call him Peter because he really is my brother", and he says, "Ma, Ma, you know that Peter means rock, that is the symbol which Jesus used when he said to Peter, "You are called Peter, and upon this rock I will build my Church," and he Peter said he was not around just to collect rocks. "My brother Peter knew how I used to collect rocks," said Shawn. Peter is now saying that he was Shawn's guiding star and that he met him when he went into Spirit. When they met, Peter knew Shawn because he looked exactly like him, except your other son Peter is a pure Spirit, he is an angel who has never touched the earth plane. (This is what happens with stillborns and miscarriages.) He is pure Spirit and he will stay in Spirit. His hair is blonde, long and down to here. (Joey points to his back to emphasize the length.) However, he says he looks just like him. They are friends and he, Peter, is showing Shawn the ropes. Shawn says, "So I want you to know that" he continues, "Now that I have told you that, we will influence the new generations to come, the new kids, the new family. Tragedy or something like this will never happen again, but I had to go home."

	Shawn is showing me an old wooden door like a shed door and it is made of brown wood. Is there a door like that?
Iona.	Yes, it is in his room.
Joey.	Oh! He is laughing at me.
Ilona.	It is a shed door.
Joey.	OK, he is knocking on it now and he says, "I hear you knocking but you cannot come in. I like my privacy", but he is showing me the door and he says watch for the knocking occasionally, that is what you will get on the doors. Just a little tap. Spirit can do that; just wait. This boy is very strong. Shawn says you know when I make up my mind to do it, then I am going to do it. Moreover, this was his pose. (Joey stands with his hands resting on his hips to demonstrate how Shawn would do this when he was a kid, and you knew what was coming next.)
	When he took that stance you both knew you had lost the ball game.
Ilona and Greg.	Yes, yes.
Joey.	Shawn is saying he is going to do something for you so that you will know, and he is very determined about this. He also adds, "Do not worry about me, I am fine." He repeats, "I am fine."
Joey.	Speaking to Ilona directly, I have to bring you a yellow rose.
Ilona.	A yellow rose?
Joey.	Yes, in fact I tried to buy one for you yesterday but I could not find one. I wanted to give you a yellow rose from Shawn.
Ilona.	I gave a yellow rose to him.
Joey.	So here is your double-check. Symbolically he is giving it back to you, the yellow rose. It is important. These are the little things, how he lets you know that he is very aware of what is going on. He jokes it is too bad that you had to come all the way here to find that out, he says that it is now time for you to move on. In that sense your grief will always be with you.

	Is there a pillow with embroidery on it please, some kind of a pillow with something embroidered on it?
Greg.	There are Hungarian pillows with embroidery on them.
Joey.	He was going to throw one across the room. A pillow is going to fly one day. He is saying, "I am trying to think of things to do to attract their attention."
	Let me tell you about Spirit, do not look for these things, it will happen when you least expect it.
Ilona.	No, we know now.
Joey.	They will do it; these two boys of yours are two of a kind. Let me put it this way because Shawn is saying it this way, "You've got your angel who has never touched the earth plane, Peter was a miscarriage and you have him. You have an angel and a half angel, you have two of us up here looking after you. I know that you need looking after at times. I will try and give you whatever evidence I can so that you will know that I am around."
	He is crooning a bit and I hear... for it's a long way from May to December. He is singing, "The September Song". I do not know what was to happen in September, what he had planned. He says you know it is a song about young people growing old and falling in love with somebody new and I fell in love too and I feel bad about that, my fiancé, my girlfriend, but she will move on with her life and find someone new and I bless her too.
	I feel that she is doing that now and Shawn added, "That is fine."
	Shawn is saying my family is very important to me. And then continued on to say, "I do not even have a toothache." Joey interjected why he would say that, because he never had problems with his teeth and that just means that he is OK, he is fine. He is flying with the angels, that is what he is saying, and he repeats it. This boy, I keep on calling him a boy and he is a man, but he has the essence, the innocence of a young child, he was very pure.
Greg.	He was a child, a pure rascal.

Joey. Well, angels with dirty faces is one of my favourite expressions and that is exactly what he is except that now he has a brother up there that he likes to get into trouble with. He is enjoying that. He is also serious. He says that he will pass on information, I don't know what this is.

Greg, I feel that for you this stuff is all new, he is going to give you some ideas and he says, old stuff. I see an old book here. I do not know what he is doing or planning. I feel that he is going to look and get some old information about classical stuff or something, that you would not have even have thought about. All of a sudden you are going to see yourself drawn to books and looking stuff up. He is going to be there and he says, "I am going to show you how to find stuff, Pop." He is going to give you something with information or a book that you will know comes directly from him because he says, "I am taking care of you." I see him standing in front of you and he is standing you on your feet and he says, "Pop, I am helping you to get back on your feet" and especially in the area of your work, would you understand that? He says to you, "Thought you couldn't do it", and he says, "I know, please do not let me be the cause of that. It is the time now. Let us start making things happen again. You have got to start being creative again." Would you understand that?

Greg. Yes.

Joey. Shawn is saying, "You know what, I could do it." In addition, he is looking at you like a rogue, like a kid. Therefore, he is helping you in your business. I do not know what you do, but Shawn says ,"I am helping you put things together and I am helping you to learn how to say no. Would you understand that? Let me put it this way, if somebody offers you a deal, it is not the time to do it and do not sign any new deals or contracts that have to do with partnership or anything like that. I do not know what this is all about but do not do anything until after the end of October. Towards the end of the year you could, but not right now. You sort of have to take back what is yours. Do you understand? And he is saying, "I'm helping you, I can be there guiding you."

	I am seeing somewhere and I am walking through a doorway, I feel that it is an old place. An old house where I have to bend down to get into the door. Would you understand that?
Greg and Ilona.	Yes, we do. When you go downstairs in our house you have to duck a little bit.
Joey.	Oh, that is it because Shawn is talking about that. He is saying, "I am there when you go there." So when you go to the basement or wherever in the house, just know that he is around and do not make any mistake about it. He is around.
Joey.	Ilona, do you put things in jars, kind of like pickling?
Ilona.	No, not pickling but I know people who do. I do take some things out of boxes and put them in jars.
Joey.	OK, because he is showing me this and he says, "She is still doing that", and he would laugh sometimes and say to you, "What are you doing that for?" Ilona, you are very creative in what you have to do and I do not know if you have anything to do with marketing or trying to put things out there, but that is the feeling that I get and Shawn is saying, "Ma, you have got to market yourself better." Would you understand that? He says, "Don't worry about that, because I am going to start taking control of it, I have nothing to do a lot of the time."
Ilona.	Yes, I am trying to market better.
Joey.	Shawn says, "Ma, you are a jewel, a bright and shining star," and he says, "I am going to help you." He is helping you both to get back on your feet because this was such a blow. He says, "I am propping you up." He walks beside you a lot so this whole thing has brought you closer together in your relationship and he says, "I am here."
	You have both of your boys standing behind you right now, they are here. You got two of them, you got more than you bargained for now. Know that perhaps you cannot always see him right now, and you probably will not. He will appear. He can do it. I know because I have seen him. You will know that he is in the house. Shawn is saying that you have a big mirror in your bedroom.

Greg. Yes.

Joey. Shawn says to look in the mirror one day, do not stare at it. One day you will be walking by it and you will see something. I think that it already has happened but it will happen again. He is trying to draw your attention. He said this is a completely new thing for you and when people have to deal with these things, it is very, very hard. But he says, "I am there and be not afraid."

I do not feel that he was a religious person in that sense, but he is saying, "The Lord is My Shepherd".

Greg and Ilona. We say it.

Joey. He is saying that to both of you so that is why he is joining in, to let you know. He is saying, "It is true, it is true, and believe it. It's true, you have a Shepherd."

Are there purple flowers somewhere out in the garden?

Ilona. Yes, a lot of them. Purple flowers.

Joey. Because Shawn loves those purple flowers. He says, "That is where I am around. They put me with nature." That is where he hangs around. Know that he knows about the purple flowers and he is happy. He said, "Why don't you put a bench there so Scott can sit down," he does not like him to get tired. Why he is saying that is because he used to harass his brother Scott sometimes. That is the word he used. He is saying give him a bench so he could sit down because he is older and he gets tired, and both of the boys will be there.

(This is an excerpt from an email to Joey from Ilona received September 21, 2010)

One more thing: he was talking about Scott a lot, that he is working too hard in the garden and he needs some rest. Scott never was interested in gardening before. After Shawn's death he spent every moment and late nights with a headlight on in the garden. I know that somehow he connected there with Shawn, growing, nurturing nature together with his brother. They always took care of each other. I have a home movie, Scott made it years ago, they were camping together in British Columbia in the Winter and

Shawn was cold in the tent at night. Scott stayed up all night with the fire, and very often ever so gently covered his brother. When I see him in the garden, that is the picture I see.

Joey. So, Shawn is in tow with Peter now. You have an extra child. You both know that. There they are, they are pure Spirits and he is with him, so now you have two of them to protect your house. Shawn tells me he did not like fire, he would light fires but he did not like fire and he says jokingly, "I think that I might have been burned in one lifetime". Because sometimes, he was clumsy.

Greg. We would light a fire every Saturday night. He did not want it. He just came home to live with us with his girlfriend Ashley. Later he wanted to go to University, he wanted to go and get a good job in Vancouver.

Joey. He came home for a reason. He came home to be with you.

He is talking about his ring, he knows you cannot find it now because it is gone. He says, "I'll find it one day. You can take turns wearing it if you want." (Joey makes a gesture symbolically placing a ring on his finger, and says the ring was symbolic).

Greg. It was a symbolic ring, he knows we wanted to find it.

Joey. Did he like many cereals? He liked to mix them?

Ilona. Yes, every morning or evening or afternoon, he would have bowls of cereal.

Greg. Yes, he would mix and match different colours of cereals.

Joey. OK, I see him doing it and he is still doing it.

He brought a lot of Light into your home. That I can say. He was a love child and I do not mean that in a bad way. He was full of love this boy.

Ilona. He gave too much love.

Joey. Shawn says, "God loved me so much that he wanted me for His own, He took me back." Joey adds Shawn is doing work in Spirit so he is not sitting by and playing a harp, he says, "No harps for me." He might be up there chopping wood because he could do physical things, he liked that too.

Ilona. And he loved animals.

Joey. It was time for him to go. That is his message. He made his life here count and he would keep little notes. I do not know if his handwriting was small at times, but he could crunch things in. (Joey imitates someone writing very small precise words).

Ilona. Yes, yes.

Joey. He will grow in Spirit, but when he manifests he will always come back like a young man at a young age. I have just seen a picture of The Sistine Chapel. I do not know if he was interested in art of that type or if he wanted to go to Europe to see that stuff, but he says, "I've seen it now, I've seen it now." For him the world holds a sense of wonder.

Greg. He loved to travel.

Ilona. He loved to go on adventures.

Joey. Yes, and this is the greatest adventure of all and he will learn. He did what he had to do and that is why his life was so full. This boy did not waste time. His life had a sense of urgency. He knew that he had to move on, he knew his time here was limited. He said," The arms were there to welcome me and I saw a Light." Then he met his brother, the child that was a miscarriage who is called Peter. They named him in Spirit and he was there to greet Shawn. Therefore, that made it very peaceful and that is why he was able to adjust. This is what happened. Joey added, total strangers could have greeted Shawn and in five minutes he would have been there shaking hands with everybody saying, "Hi, how are you doing."

Ilona. That is exactly right.

Joey. He is saying, "I am making new friends now you know, and I could meet all my heroes." So know that you had a very special gift. In addition that he came here to enrich peoples' lives. Think of him now as in a different dimension, you will see him again. You know all through your life that he will always be there.

Shawn says, "Tell my mom when it is time for her to go that I will be there. I will reach out my hand and take her over the bridge." It is a Light bridge by the way and he will take you over the bridge. Therefore, that is his way of saying that you will be safe always. Know that he is always with you and he is with you when you travel.

Greg and Ilona Asling's message to Joey, July 7, 2004.

Hello Joey:

Both Ili and myself had looked forward to meeting with you for some time with the hopes of learning more about Shawn's present "life", we had hoped for many things to come of meeting with you including comfort in knowing that Shawn is well and also that we might find some way to ease the pain and sorrow of missing him. Our meeting was truly amazing and it accomplished more than what we could have hoped for! We were very impressed at the time of the meeting and even more so later after listening to the tape and remembering the many things that you spoke of. I feel certain now that Shawn is with us constantly and that somehow my warmest wishes and hopes for this life and the next will come true.

While you were in contact with Shawn he asked you to tell me I could finish off his writing. We told you then that after his accident we found several poems, or lyrics, written by Shawn, some of which were unfinished. When you read the two pieces that are attached I think that you will find them quite amazing, particularly knowing what happened to Shawn within weeks of his writing them. We thought immediately, and we still do, that Shawn wrote these notes and left them for us. He may not have known how or when he would be leaving us but he sensed that he would be leaving before the rest of our family. His writing is an amazing gift that first had us mesmerized, how could he have written these things? From that moment we felt so very grateful that he had left us a message and that his departure wasn't the complete waste of life that we felt but perhaps he really had gone on to a place where he was needed more. That you reported him taking care of younger children perhaps is the answer…. did they need him more than we did? When we found these notes we were in Shawn's room, surrounded by his belongings and reading his handwritten lines, nothing else could have made us feel closer to him at that time. Although they seem cold and impersonal when read as an "attachment" I think you, more than most, will find Shawn's poems enlightening. We're interested in your comments.

Ili and I are pleased to have met you Joey, we felt that we had the benefit of striking up a special relationship with you due to our mutual friendship with Jean. Of course the fact that Shawn got along so well with Jean also made this a most natural of get-togethers. We would like to keep in touch and look forward to seeing you again.

Sincerely,

Greg and Ili

Following is an email message dated September 21, 2010 from Ilona to Joey referencing the draft of the March 2004 reading.

Dear Joey,
Thank you so much for your e-mail, and of course your writing.
Greg and I both trust Shawn and you with your writing. Please just feel free to say what you remember.
I would like to add something which was one of the most important parts for me. When we arrived and walked into your apartment, immediately everything felt warm and good inside me. And then you said that Shawn is waiting for us, he is already there. Later you said he woke you up earlier that week in the early morning and you recognized him from his smile and blonde hair. He was standing by your bed. It felt so good. The reason this is so important to me is because I don't want to do anything which may give him any kind of difficulty, ever. I would love to and I always want to spend time with him, but only at his wish. I don't ever want him to feel sad to see me broken. I want to honour everything about him, even his passing, with the purest and deepest love for him. So it was comforting for me to know that he was just as much looking forward to our meeting as we were.
If he comes to meet you again, just please tell him that I miss him very much and I love him.
I hope to meet you again, soon.
Ilona

Comment from Joey:

Ilona is referring to Shawn's 3:00 am Spirit visitation to me on the Wednesday prior to the Saturday morning reading with his parents. This provided me with the double-check that Shawn was more than anxious to communicate with his beloved parents. However, I did not communicate the visitation to them until well into the actual reading.

EPILOGUE 2010

Shawn Asling
Unfinished Lyrics Summer 2003

No I can't remember the day I was born.
But I'm glad I caught the life I was thrown.
Now with both hands clenched I hold on.
I know that it could get taken away and like that I'd be gone.
No Lord no no no I don't need to be warned.

I keep my head up and I try to do no wrong.
I listen to what my heart says and it is going strong.
I push my way forward and always keep keeping on.
Don't know much about my road but I hope it's long.
I've felt the rays of sunlight and I've been there when it stormed.

-Shawn Asling

LINDA ZACCARDELLI BORSI

The following is an account of consultations given by Joey to Gemma Zaccardelli Vincenzi and her father Vincenzo Zaccardelli on separate occasions. It took the passing of my sister Linda, eighteen months younger than I to convince me that there is an afterlife.

It was a devastating day for my family and me on January 28, 2005 at 3:45 am. Our bright light superstar succumbed to the ravages of a brutal disease, Scleroderma. There would no longer be visits with Linda in her many hospitalizations where we cried, laughed and prayed, many times together.

Selfishly, I wanted this to continue because Linda was still here. After Linda's passing there was no will or enthusiasm for routine daily life for quite a while and life seemed pointless. A big void was unbearable. I listen to a lot of radio. One Saturday afternoon I was listening to the Laurie and Olga Show on CJAD, a local station in Montreal and they had Joey Crinita as a guest on the show. I listened with interest as he did phone readings for people calling in and discussed his gift. I took his number down and put it aside. I have always heard of the many charlatans in this field.

When I finally made my first appointment, little did I know how my life would change forever giving me renewed hope and purpose in myself and the world around me. I also know that Mr. Joseph Crinita is the real deal. I would like to share communications from my sister Linda from the Spirit World.

Sunday, June 25th, 2006 at 11:00 am was my first reading with Joey. He was preparing to go on holidays and made an exception on seeing me on a Sunday, which I truly appreciated. Linda, my dear sister did show up and the information relayed to me was no doubt from my dear sister, Linda. I couldn't believe when I heard Joey say from Linda, "It's about time you showed up and I like what you did with your hair." I had delayed making the appointment and I had recently put streaks in my hair which I had never done before and she always wanted me to do it, as she was the one who was into making herself up. Joey then related to me the following words from Linda: "Darling, thank you for being my friend and I still whisper in your ear." In my frequent hospital visits with Linda, she thanked me for everything but most of all thanked me for being her friend and constantly whispered in my ear. He then talked about her love of piano music. Linda was passionate about the piano, took piano lessons in her adult life and had her older son take piano lessons.

Joey described her energy as a combination of Evita Peron and Auntie Mame, which was a fact. Linda was a very outgoing strong loving personality. She made the analogy to Joey that that she and I were like Dean Martin and Jerry Lewis, I being the straight man and her the comedy act, which is very true, and has been for years. Joey then asked me about a photograph of Linda and me when we were five and seven years old. I had recently had a picture of the two of us in front of our house where we grew up all dressed up in our Spring coats and hats copied from the original and it is placed on my mirror in my bedroom, which she once occupied.

Joey inquired, "Do you have a devotion to St. Theresa, The Little Flower?" I responded, not really. He asked me to keep it in mind, and check it out, as he had received an impression of The Little Flower. I asked my mother if she had given Linda a St. Theresa medal. She advised she had given her religious medals but not of St. Theresa.

Sometime later, low and behold I found a chain letter about St. Theresa handwritten by Linda in 1997 in a book on my wall unit in the living-room. The instruction was to send it to four people. I never did this in 1997. I sent out the letter to four people carefully selected on June 26, 2006, the day after my reading with Joey, nine years later. One of the people chosen was our cousin who I did not have any contact with in awhile. This cousin and Linda celebrated their First Communion together and I had recently viewed home movies of this event. When this person received my letter, she proclaimed, "I am getting a letter from Linda!" She relayed this to me when we saw each other at Lakeshore General Hospital visiting a sick uncle a few months later. She advised me that when she received the letter, her older son Michael instantly said, "Just do it!" She also made me realize that my handwriting is very similar to Linda's. Receiving this information about St. Theresa has been a life changing experience and this to me is undeniably a direct communication from my sister.

This reading also revealed Linda's immense love for her two sons and her continued commitment to them and to my parents.

My second reading with Joey: I met with Joey for a reading on Saturday, January 17, 2009. Joey noted this date on the tape and said that he usually does not do this but felt it was important. Two very important revelations were made on this date, which amazed me.

Joey told me through his Guide that Linda was learning to pray and was committed to The Blessed Virgin Mary in the Spirit World. This was very evidential to me because the Saturday before she passed away, I was sitting across from Linda and she looked at me abruptly and said," Lets pray". I said OK please go ahead. She said, "No, you lead with the Hail Mary and the Our Father as you know the traditional prayers and you know that I do not." We had the most amazing afternoon connecting and I now have proof positive that this continues in the Spirit World. That Saturday at the Jewish General Hospital was like a training session as I led the prayer and Linda followed my lead. This piece of information had to come directly from Linda as there is no way that Joey could have known this.

Joey then said that Linda had said to "Look out for a blue jay in a Summer garden - it will be me!"

In July 2009 I purchased a Our Lady of Lourdes statue for the front yard of my father's property. I went to the nursery affiliated with Notre-Dame-des-Neiges Cemetery, here in Montreal which is the location of Linda's resting place and in the office there were many objects for sale. One of the objects was a Blue Jay that caught my eye and which I purchased and placed on the ledge on my bedroom window. This is where Linda slept when she lived where I live now.

Reading with Vincenzo Zaccardelli: Linda's father on Tuesday, September 30, 2008.

At the beginning of the session Joey said that Linda was asking, "Papa can you see me? Papa can you hear me? Not a hallucination, not a hallucination, not a hallucination!"

My father has had visions of Linda - they are not dreams and he is the only one who experienced this. Linda advised him through Joey that she had been working on this for three years as a gift especially for this occasion. This is a great comfort for my father. She is still working on speaking to him so he can hear her voice. Linda wanted my father to know that she is in his home.

Through Joey, Linda acknowledged all of the praying that Gemma does.

Linda advised that The Blessed Mother acknowledges and hears Gemma's prayers. Gemma prays the rosary everyday and Linda is now praying in heaven as well. Joey mentioned that Linda loved the Ave Maria as sung by Barbra Streisand, and that she liked Streisand. Ave Maria is Linda's favourite hymn and the movie, "The Way We Were" with Barbra Streisand and Robert Redford was one of her favourite movies. Through Joey, Linda said to my father, "I'm still doing my nails." This was important because Linda did her own nails one week before she passed. Joey mentioned the little dog Piccolo, a shitsu lhasa apso. This is Gemma's dog and Linda advised Joey that the dog sees her. At night there have been times when the dog gets up and seemingly looks like he is playing with someone. My father also has had visions of Linda with this dog in her arms.

During sessions with Joey for my father and me, Linda has advised that when it is our time she will be there to meet us. She also stated that she is the Guardian Angel for the whole family. In the reading with my father, she declared that she set the whole thing up in finding out about Joey, and I am convinced she did. Joey check out your address - 3450- Coincidence? I think not. Linda passed into the Spirit World at 3:45 am.

My experiences with medium, Joseph Crinita have given me renewed hope that there is so much more to come, and life on this earth is not all that there is.

Note from Joey:

I requested Gemma to share Linda's story because of her amazing Spirit and because she is such a good communicator from the Spirit World. There is always a beautiful energy when Linda comes through. I emailed Gemma my request on April 14, 2010 and on April 25, 2010 I received the following from Gemma:

This email from you came right after my mother-in-law passed away on April 11. When I read this I was getting ready for the first day viewing. I do believe that Linda communicated with me again. In our telephone conversation yesterday, you advised me that Linda is already comforting her, which is wonderful.

JACK GRAY

Jim Hawkins shares the following:

I was introduced to a "New Age" Church by a friend when I was working at Douglas Aircraft in Santa Monica in the early fifties. This is when I learned about reincarnation and it gave me a completely new perspective on life. Now I understood (or so I thought at the time) why people came to this world with their problems and physical conditions. In the early seventies I attended lectures by Dr. Joseph Murphy at a local auditorium here in Los Angeles and when Dr. Murphy retired in the middle seventies, I started studying Science of Mind and reading Thomas Troward's books.

In October of 1977 I met Jack Gray and immediately felt a strong pull towards him. We both seemed to be interested in the same subjects, such as Victorian architecture, furniture, paintings and after some time of "dating" Jack moved in with me in June of 1979. Jack was a kind, generous person, highly intelligent and with a good sense of humor. Shortly after this I found out that Jack was a confirmed atheist and so we decided not to discuss any religious ideas together. I continued with my studies of Science of Mind and in 2003 I found some books by Elaine Pagels on Gnostic sayings that were around at the time of Jesus. I had wanted to find some literature on Jesus that was close to the real sayings of Jesus and not what appeared in the New Testament. Elaine Pagels had just written a book on St. Thomas and I found this on Amazon and also a book titled, "The Disappearance of the Universe" by Gary Renard, which I purchased.

"Disappearance" opened up a whole new world for me and led me to "A Course in Miracles" which changed my life completely. "Disappearance" explains what "A Course in Miracles" is saying and leads you into a changing of your mind about this world and what happens in it.

I would love to have shared this with Jack but it was not to happen as he had such a closed mind about all of religion. Jack and I shared our lives together for 28 years until he entered into a nursing home in March 2007 and passed away on December 27, 2009.

On a quiet morning in early March 2010 while I was in the bathroom I experienced a telepathic "conversation" with Jack that revealed he was well, happy, at peace and said that everything was beautiful where he was. He also said that he did go towards the Light that I told him to do many times. He said that he did believe in the afterlife now and that he was OK. I know that this was a valid experience for me since it has previously happened to me so I was not shocked or concerned upon hearing his voice speaking to me in my head. After being together for so many years Jack and I often communicated without words as many couples are wont to do in long time relationships.

I met Joey Crinita on the evening of July 8, 2008 while he was visiting Los Angeles.

Introductions were made through my friend Ron Sexton and the three of us went to dinner at Hamburger Hamlet. Joey and I hit it off immediately by discussing old movies and in particular the movies of Susan Hayward who as fate would have it turned out to be our favorite actress.

During that initial encounter Joey did not mention that he had an interest in Spiritualism nor the fact that he was indeed a medium, although I was aware of this through Ron and his sister Jean. I have now met Joey socially a few times during the past few years, however I have never seen him on a professional basis for a private reading.

On the evening of April 22, 2009 after dining at Maria's restaurant on Pico in West Los Angeles with Ron Sexton and his sister Jean, Joey visited my home in West Los Angeles.

As we sat in the living room Joey commented on the high amount of positive Spirit energy and the peacefulness within my home, he commented on how the house seems to embrace one. This house has been my family's home since 1955. I would state at this time that Joey had never met Jack and did not know anything about him. During a run-of-the-mill casual conversation which followed, Joey spontaneously told me some interesting facts that he was receiving from his Guide.

These facts included:

I had made the right choice in putting Jack into a nursing home and that he is getting good care and that Jack would be with us for a while longer.

I would be around for some time and when it was time for me to go, it would be quick.

I would be taken care of in the meantime and did not have to worry about finances.

My health is OK and he also stated that in this life-time that all my Karmic debts have been paid and that my Karmic slate was clear.

My Grandmother on my Mother's side was in the house and looking after me and that I was protected by my angels in my daily life.

I again met Joey on March 2, 2010 after Jack had passed away in December 2009.

On this occasion Joey relayed a message from Jack through his Guide to me in which he advised me to stand up for myself and not to give anything away that I did not want to. He reminded me that I did not owe anyone anything. Jack went on to thank me for letting him win arguments through our years together, which by the way was a true fact.

Joey also mentioned the name of Molly, who dropped in to say hello, she was a good friend to Jack and I and had passed over in 2005. He also mentioned an older woman named Mabel as a Spirit Guide who was rather large in the body with a big backside and who had attached herself to me and the house and protected me.

On March 14, 2010 on the occasion of a dinner to celebrate Ron's birthday at the home of Joey's sister Irene, Joey and I were having a quiet chat and without any prompting on my part Joey spontaneously shared the following which came through from Joey's Guide Wana. Joey advised me that Jack's Spirit was present in the room with us. He then went on to describe in detail the telepathic conversation that I had with Jack earlier that month, which I had not related to anyone. Joey used the same words I had telepathically heard from Jack thus confirming my experience which was unknown to him at the time.

The conversation in which Jack related that he was OK, he was at peace that he now believed in the afterlife and that he would wait for me. Here was my double-check as Joey repeated the words back to me verbatim.

Again Jack reminded me not to be intimidated by anyone and to stand up for myself.

Joey reminded me that I am protected by my angels who silently watch over me and that people who are difficult towards me will be taken out of my everyday life so that I do not have to deal with them. He stated that Jack was wearing a yellow sweater that he liked and which I recently found in his chest of drawers. Joey mentioned the television show, "Rumpole of the Bailey" and said that Jack mentioned that he was beginning to sound like Rumpole himself. This was another confirmation as Jack and I liked to watch that show together for years. Jack said he will wait for me and we will visit the Colosseum in Rome and Florence together in Spirit. This was something which Jack and I previously discussed when Jack was alive and we never got to do it. Jack said that "he was wrong" about God and Spirituality and he knows differently now. He thanked me for telling him to go towards the Light, which is what Joey told me to tell him. Jack appreciated that I had let him decorate our house and that I did not interfere, as Jack loved old Chinese antique furniture and our home was quite liberally decorated with such, along with numerous works of art. Jack said he was going to teach again, a fact unknown to Joey, that Jack was indeed a teacher. Jack said that he was very happy.

Note from Joey:

I purposely requested Jim Hawkins to share his and Jack's story not only to honour their life-long relationship, but because of the fact that Jack whom I had never met personally was a confirmed atheist until he died at the age of 90. Yet, through Jim's prayers and his encouragement for Jack to seek the Light, Jack found his way into the Light in Spirit and was able to manifest to Jim telepathically assuring him that he was waiting for him in the Light, confirming that love is eternal and endures even after the change called death.

CHAPTER X
SPIRIT NUDGES

INTRODUCTION

On occasion, we get a nudge from Spirit and from the Universe. When that happens, it behooves us to pay attention to what I refer to as the Little Joys of Spirit.

Simply, these are things that command our notice and give pause. Some events are evidential and affirm that Spirit is indeed aware of the events shaping our lives. When deeply personal experiences occur in our lives, they leave a mark and are often food for the soul.

There may be more to serendipity than what meets the eye... are we not led to where we are destined to be?

AMELIA EARHART

In July 1970, a week after my friend Gloria and I returned from Camp Chesterfield, (the Spiritualist Camp in Indiana), I was home on a Wednesday evening. I had decided not to go to the week-night service at the First Spiritual Church that started at 8:00 pm. I received a telephone call at about 7:00 pm from Joe Lewis, an acquaintance from the Church. We chatted for about twenty minutes. During the call I mentioned I was not going to Church that evening. However, out of the blue I felt an urge to go to Church, which was approximately a fifteen minute walk from my home. I made it with a few minutes to spare before the service was about to commence.

When I entered the Church, the speaker for the evening, Colleen Gregory, was standing at the back of the Church. When she saw me, she put her arms around me and said, "Joey, I am so happy to see you." I was a bit taken aback but did not pay much attention as I politely returned her greeting. For the record, I am not the type of individual who you would throw your arms around unless you know me really well. I am by nature reserved. When I was a younger man, particularly at that stage of my life, people would have thought twice before entering my personal space. Colleen later told me she wondered what in the world I thought of her cheerful greeting and if she had offended me. For no particular reason she was overjoyed to see me that evening. At the time, I did not know Colleen well, though we did have a passing acquaintance as members of the Church.

The service was about to start. I took a seat next to Sandy Palmer who happened to be Colleen's niece. Colleen delivered her inspirational talk. She closed with the reading of a poem entitled, 'Courage' which she informed us was written by Amelia Earhart. I, of course, knew nothing of the poem at this point. You could have knocked me over with a feather. Upon hearing this I immediately nudged Sandy to tell her, "I just saw her in Chesterfield, she is a Guide to me." I was astonished! This was something I had not expected and almost had not gone to the service that evening.

As I recall, after the service I did not speak with Colleen and went directly home. Later that evening I received a telephone call from Colleen asking me if what Sandy had related to her was so. I confirmed that it was. When I spoke with Colleen I was curious and anxious to know why she had chosen that particular poem to read. This was my double-check. When we next met, Colleen gave me a blue bound book entitled: 'Wings An Anthology of Flight' by H.G. Bryden. The book was published in 1942. The poem appears on page 248, written on a Sunday afternoon by a then thirty year old Amelia Earhart.

COURAGE

Courage is the price that Life exacts for granting peace.
The soul that knows it not, knows no release
From little things;
Knows not the livid loneliness of fear,
Nor mountain heights where bitter joy can hear
The sound of wings.
How can Life grant us boon of living, compensate
For dull grey ugliness and pregnant hate
Unless we dare
The soul's dominion? Each time we make a choice, we pay
With courage to behold the restless day,
And count it fair.

-Amelia Earhart

Colleen and I became firm friends after this experience. As it so happened, Colleen also led a development class within the Church. Amongst her students was a Polish couple, Steve and Anna Zabrinsky. They were recent immigrants from Poland to Canada. Evidently, a few months later during the class, Anna received a clairvoyant message for Colleen. This is what she related to Colleen: "I saw a woman standing beside an old airplane, the woman was wearing a leather jacket and wore a scarf around her neck. She said that you did not know her, but you would know who this message is for. It is for a Joe and she wanted to say hello to him." Anna being a recent immigrant from Poland had no idea who the woman was. Colleen knew instantly who the woman was and for whom the message was intended. I accepted the message with pleasure. Soon after, I was given a gift of a photograph of Amelia from an employee at The Montreal Gazette, a local newspaper. I continued to find books on Amelia Earhart and through the years I keep an eye out for a Spirit Light whenever I board an aircraft. I obviously have no fear of flying.

In June 2009 Colleen wrote her version of these events:

The year was 1970 and I was preparing to give the Wednesday evening talk at the First Spiritual Church of Montreal. As was my wont, I spent some time the evening prior to the talk preparing a few notes. I had an outline in my mind of what I would say but needed an appropriate ending. Then I remembered that some thirty years past, a close school friend of mine had shared a poem entitled, Courage by Amelia Earhart. I began searching for it amongst my papers and clippings; however, because I had not seen the poem for a very long time, I could not find it easily. The more difficult it became to locate, the more obsessed I was with finding it to read the following evening. At last, the poem emerged from the depths of my souvenirs, in a book called, Wings An Anthology of Flight. The following evening at the end of my talk I said I would like to close with a poem by Amelia Earhart entitled, Courage. When I came away from the platform, my niece Sandy Palmer was waiting to talk to me. She related what Joey had revealed to her at the service. I called Joey later that evening at home. I did not know him that well at the time, but I was curious and felt privileged to have been part of this story.

Note from Joey:

Since her disappearance July 2, 1937, there has been much speculation as to what happened. The mystery of Amelia Earhart continues to intrigue. As recently as December 14, 2010, seventy-three years after her disappearance, an article appeared in The UK Guardian as well as other various media outlets. The experience I related concerning Miss Earhart at the séance held by James Tingley unfolded exactly as I described.

JUSTIN AND THE PLAYPEN

On August 5, 1980 my father Joe died suddenly of a massive heart attack. At the time of his death, my parents were living on 6th Avenue in Verdun. My mother Emma could not stay in the house after he died. The following month, she and three of my sisters, namely Sally, Susie and Gloria, and my late brother Frankie, all moved to a large seven room flat on Evelyn Street in Verdun. At the time, my nephew Justin, born on February 19, 1980 was seven months old. Prior to his death, my father would often care for Justin while his mother, Gloria was at work. Gloria and my father had a very strong connection. Since the time of my father's death, my sister Gloria shared a large double bed with my mother during this period of grief as Emma did not wish to sleep alone. This was in a spacious bedroom just off the kitchen in the rear of the house. One evening Justin fell asleep in his playpen located in the center of this same bedroom. Gloria decided to let Justin sleep where he was as she tucked him in under his blankets. He lay peacefully asleep in the playpen and she went to sleep as well in the double bed beside my mother. At approximately 3:00 am Gloria was awakened and turned to find her sleeping infant son, Justin lying in the bed between her and Emma. Gloria instantly jumped out of bed, checked the playpen and discovered that the blankets had not been disturbed. They were neatly tucked in, exactly as she had left them while Justin slept. She awakened the family to determine if someone had moved the baby. The household had been asleep and knew nothing of the baby being moved. Needless to say it was quite an eventful night. With the exception of Justin and his grandmother, no one slept the remainder of the night. It is not possible for a seven month old infant to move himself from playpen to bed without assistance. We suspect it was Grandpa Joe – recently passed one month earlier into Spirit, taking care of his grandson. To this day, Justin as an adult claims that this was an impossible thing to happen. Ah... but it did.

ASSISI - 1985

The last time I had been to Assisi was on a four day visit in October of 1978 when I buried the ashes of my nephew Nicholas on the 29th of October on Mount Subasio, in the serenity of the beautiful oak forest. Nicholas was born on September 21, 1977 and lived only thirty days. He passed into Spirit on October 22, 1977. Upon his death I promised his mother, my sister Susan, that I would bury Nicholas' ashes in Assisi where we believed he would be close to and watched over by St. Francis.

On Saturday, May 25, 1985 I had returned to Assisi along with my travelling companions, Noella Martinez, Robert Negro and Elizabeth Bruni. We arrived in Assisi by train from Rome. We could not conceive of visiting Italy without coming to Assisi. On the afternoon of our arrival, I set out with Elizabeth to visit Nicholas' final resting place. I had an idea where I had interred his ashes, but I was not totally sure. We set out in the afternoon and walked quite high, up into the mountain and into the verdant oak forest searching for Nicholas' grave. I had not marked the grave. I knew it was under a giant tree and that I would be led to the spot. We finally stopped and I felt Nicholas' presence. I clairvoyantly saw Nicholas, as a teenager. Although he would have been eight years of age at this time, he chose to appear older to me indicating he had grown in Spirit. He was tall for his age, had beautiful olive skin, dark hair and deep brown dancing eyes.

I remembered Nicholas as an infant in St. Mary's Hospital in Montreal. He was in a convulsive state most of the time, but whenever I visited, he would lie still with open eyes and stare directly at me. As I stood silently here on Mount Subasio, I heard his voice in my head as he told me he had friends in the Spirit World. He was happy and asked to be remembered to his mother and he thanked me for taking care of him. (Prior to my October 1978 trip to Assisi, I was working at a Church service with Elizabeth McIntosh. We both gave clairvoyant messages at this service. Whilst I was on my feet delivering Spirit messages, Elizabeth was seated behind me on the platform. She received a message from Nicholas for me which she related after the service. He thanked me for bringing him to Assisi and wanted me to know he was growing in the Spirit World. He had now fulfilled his purpose as a spiritual being by his Spirit touching onto the earth plane.

Through the tragedy of his death, he brought our family closer together. An interesting part of Elizabeth's message was that Nicholas had shown himself, not as an infant but as a young man. This was how I saw him on that day.)

Elizabeth Bruni renders her experience of what she witnessed that afternoon. "This is what happened in the deep of the forest on Mount Subasio. Joey suddenly stopped walking. He stood quite still and lifted up his arms above his head in an attitude of prayer. It was a dark day and as he prayed, the sun's rays shone through the tops of the trees down onto Joey alone. I was standing off to one side of him. A Light totally surrounded him. It did not shine on me. I have never experienced anything similar to this before. I was in awe. It was as if he was transported into another realm. When I say there was Light, there was Light. I have never seen anything thing like it. This was more than solely the rays of the sun... he was shining. I just stood there and stared in silence as he prayed. Joey appeared to be transformed right before my eyes. There was a great sense of peace and tranquility in the atmosphere surrounding us. We both received an infusion of energy at the same time. It was as if a bolt of lightning had gone through my body. Joey said Nicholas was here in Spirit with us and with that, Joey walked directly to the spot under a big tree where he had buried Nicholas' ashes. Joey related that Nicholas said: "Thank you for coming back to find me and thanks for taking care of my mother."

We stopped and prayed and meditated for some time before we took our leave.

When we first arrived at this spot on Mount Subasio, we were both very warm and thirsty. It was quite a hike up from the bottom of the mountain. However, after this experience we both felt energized, as if the heat was not a problem. We were aware the walk down the mountain would be over an hour. Luckily for us, we were about three minutes into our trek down when a beige Fiat Uno stopped. The occupants were a husband and wife who spoke Italian only. I speak Italian and was able to converse freely with them. They offered us a lift to the Gates of Assisi. During our conversation I determined that they had recently returned from a trip to Canada, they had a wonderful time and were very happy to be able to drive us into Assisi."

SATURDAY EVENING - MAY 25

Later that evening, Elizabeth and I went for a walk through the narrow and ancient streets of Assisi. Our travelling companions, Noella and Robert decided to retire early. The night was as black as pitch and there was not a star to be seen in the sky above. The town is very poorly lit and one can very easily become lost.

As we quietly strolled through the narrow streets, I recounted stories of St. Francis and his little band of Friars. At one point, I remarked to Elizabeth I sensed we were quite near the home of Bernardo di Quintavalle, although I was not exactly sure where it was. I recounted that Bernardo was Francis' best friend and when on a rainy Spring evening (April 15, 1208) Bernardo invited Francis to sleep overnight at his house due to upcoming inclement weather. At the time Francis had been sleeping outdoors for long periods. Bernardo ordered a bed prepared for Francis in his own room. Francis, in order to conceal his sanctity pretended to be asleep. Francis, thinking that Bernardo was fast asleep, began to pray repeatedly saying the words, "My God! My God!", whilst at the same time he wept bitterly and remained on his knees in prayer throughout the whole of the night. Bernardo upon witnessing his friends' great piety was so very moved that he asked Francis if he could follow him.

Elizabeth and I had now been walking for quite some time and were becoming fatigued. I suggested we stop for a rest. We found ourselves standing before a building shrouded in darkness. We could make out some side steps which led to a landing about three feet high. We easily lifted ourselves unto the landing. We sat and continued to talk as we rested on the stone landing. We remained there approximately twenty-five minutes until we noticed the hour was getting late. It was now one thirty in the morning, time to return back to the Albergo Umbria where we were staying.

As we lifted ourselves down from the landing, we saw a plaque above the entrance door. We had not seen it in the darkness when we first arrived. The plaque was inscribed in Latin:

HIC S. FRANISCVM AD COENAM ET CVBITVM B. BERNADVS QVINTAVALLIS EXCEPIT ET IN EXTASIM VIDIT.

Translated: HERE THE BLESSED BERNARDO QUINTAVALLE RECEIVED SAINT FRANCIS TO DINE AND SLEEP AND SAW HIM IN ECSTASY.

Unbeknownst to us, we had been sitting on the landing in front of Bernardo's home all the while. We were quite moved by this realization.

SUNDAY - MAY 26

We four had spent the afternoon walking about the Basilica of St. Francis. By the time we arrived back in the town, all the restaurants had closed. We had not remembered that after lunch the restaurants close between 4:00 pm – 6:00 pm. It had been a long day for us and we were very hungry. As fate would have it, we passed a restaurant which was in darkness, but nevertheless we approached the restaurant, opened the door and entered. We were met by a woman, who turned out to be the owner of this family-run establishment. She informed us the restaurant was closed. We were about to turn and leave when she graciously invited us in, and made us welcome.

We were served a fantastic meal of grilled vegetables including mushrooms and peppers with pasta and a delicious salad drizzled with balsamic vinegar. The whole family waited on us displaying a natural exuberance as only the Italians do with their love of food. They watched us eat heartily. We could see in their eyes they enjoyed watching us eat. To our minds, this was another little miracle of Assisi.

BILL MCINTOSH

In 1992, in the city of Perth, Scotland, Elizabeth McIntosh experienced a life threatening cerebral aneurysm. During the time she was recovering in the hospital, her husband Bill began to have prostate problems. The following is a recounting by Bill of what took place:

"I went to visit Elizabeth in the hospital. I was in agony from the pain I was experiencing because of the prostate problem. It had just come upon me and no one knew about it. I entered into the ward where Elizabeth was. I saw her sister Nancy and her brother-in-law Matt were with her standing by her bed.

Elizabeth is lying in bed and as soon as she saw me she said, "Did you see that Doctor who is looking for you?" I responded, "What Doctor." I watched as Nancy and Matt made signs in the air by turning their fingers around in a circular motion to indicate that Elizabeth is off of her rocker.

Elizabeth then said to me, "You must have seen him, he is dark, he is black and he wants to see you, and he is going to keep you in hospital for two days." Of course, by this time my brother-in-law Matt is almost under the bed with laughter.

"There had been no Doctor in the ward looking for me."

However, by now I was in total agony and the pain was almost unbearable. I made my excuses and go downstairs to the emergency room. I advised the emergency staff about my symptoms and the pain. They showed me into an examination room, closed the door and instructed me to wait. When the door opened, who came in to see me? A black Doctor! He examined me and said, "You are going to have to come in for a couple of days."

ROBERT 'BUZ' MEYERS AND THE PAINTNG

In the Fall of 1984, Buz Meyers was guest speaker for an astrological group in Montreal. On his free evening, he came to visit me at my apartment in Westmount. Buz was quite taken with some of the artwork in my home. He was particularly drawn to an 18 x 24 portrait of a young knight in armour hanging in my living room. As he was leaving the apartment at evening's end, I spontaneously removed the painting from the wall and gave it to him. For many years the painting hung in his office in Euclid, Ohio where he read his astrological charts. Buz relocated to Virginia Beach, Virginia some years later and brought the painting with him. Buz passed over on March 12, 2000. The annual For Purpose On Time Community Conference, which he and Vickie Greene founded was scheduled for that October in Virginia Beach.

I was invited to come and speak in Buz's place. The conference took place at the Surfside Inn in Virginia Beach. Understandably, Buz's untimely death left a huge void in the lives of his many devotees and friends. We were all deeply saddened by this loss. In order to help defray outstanding debts left by Buz's passing, an auction of many of his personal possessions was held. I had come to this conference at the behest of my friend, Jonnie Ruth Kuhn and I really did not know many of the people within the group. I had not seen the President, Karen Malfregeot for many years. On the evening of my arrival, I met up with a long-time friend, Frances Lombardo and we went to dinner. When we returned to the hotel, we stopped in the auction room to browse. There was quite an assorted array of items. What caught my eye was a painting propped up against a wall. Of course, I immediately recognized it as the painting which I had given Buz years earlier. It had slipped my mind. I mentioned this fact to Frances as we walked over to examine the painting of the young knight.

On the back of the frame was a sticker indicating the painting was framed at Gemst Art Gallery in Montreal. This painting had always been one of my personal favourites, and I intended to place a bid on it at the upcoming auction. Frances informed Vicki and Pete Greene, who were close personal friends of Buz and conducting the auction about the history of the portrait and how it came to be there. When I encountered them the next day, they informed me that Frances had made them aware of the connection and they returned the painting to me. They would not hear of any exchange of monies, they felt this was what Buz would have wanted. I was very touched by their kindness and likewise, very pleased to have the painting returned to me. I carried the painting back home on the plane to Toronto. It now hangs in my bedroom here in Montreal. It has come full circle and is a fitting reminder of Buz.

RON JACKSON AND THE FLICKERING LIGHTS

In February of 1985 I was invited as a guest speaker and to publicly demonstrate clairvoyance at the Salute To Astrology Conference for the National Council for Geocosmic Research, (NCGR) chapter in Houston, Texas. The chairpersons of the chapter, Susan Certain and Peggy Larson had assigned a volunteer to assist me during the conference. Ron Jackson and I immediately hit it off. Susan and Peggy arranged an interview with Warren Roberts, a well-known Houston television personality. I went on her morning show to publicize the conference and my book, The Medium Touch. I thoroughly enjoyed the interview. I found Miss Roberts to be a charming woman and in typical Houston style, made to feel most welcome.

A tape of the interview would become available only after I returned to Montreal. Ron offered to pick-up the tape when it was ready. This took some time. In the ensuing months I asked Ron to give the tape to my friend Gillian Payne who would keep it for me. Gillian and I were close friends. I frequently visited with her in Houston. As events unfolded, Ron and Gillian were to eventually meet over the tape. Gillian and Ron married. In some small way I feel I was the link. I would visit with them in their home. I thoroughly enjoyed Ron's company. He was a brilliant human being, a competent astrologer and a walking encyclopedia of knowledge. Ron was a well-read interesting personality with a boyish charm and a grin to go with it. After his death, I would at times feel his presence while speaking with Gillian on the telephone. Even now, many years later he often clairvoyantly pops up during telephone conversations between Gillian and I, frequently in his lemon yellow pullover and always with a grin. I was extremely fond of Ron and was delighted when he and Gillian married.

Gillian relates the following:

I met Ron Jackson on February 1, 1986 in Houston, Texas – on the doorstep of his renovated house on Driscoll Street. We took an immediate dislike to one another. He was arrogant and lectured me as how to copy a video tape without erasing it and I defensively feigned a level of technical expertise I did not possess. As I left with Joey Crinita's tape in hand, I thought to myself, "If I never see you again it will be too soon."

So fourteen days later we met again at an astrology lecture given by Rob Hand. He used Ron's chart to illustrate his lecture and I dimly realized that there were some connections between us astrologically. Within two months Ron and I were gloriously happy, inseparable and had moved in together.

In addition to being a fine astrologer and intuitive, Ron was very empathic. He seemed to have a very strong connection with me as he would always know when I was eating something particularly good, (he could taste it in his mouth) or when I was feeling a strong emotion or pain – positive or negative – as he would feel it too. He was seropositive for HIV and managed his health very well. We had a wonderful life together.

Seven years later he died on a rainy Thursday morning, January 7. It was a big shock in some ways, although in the last couple of months his health had deteriorated and he had lost all his energy.

I had lost my best friend, my lover, my husband, my astrological colleague and my partner in life's adventures.

Over the years I had anticipated how I might feel when Ron died but had no concept of the tumult of conflicting emotions I would experience. I was upset and heartbroken but at the same time felt the most extraordinary sense of euphoria and a 'soaring' sensation. It was as if I had one foot in one dimension and the other foot in another. And that was exactly what had happened. Somehow, maybe it was because of our closeness, I was able to share in the way he felt now that he was 'free' and in Spirit. I could feel the incredible power of his joy now that all the stress and conflict associated with living life on Planet Earth had been released. It felt like a cork that had been held down in water under pressure had suddenly been released and had gone rushing to the surface. His vibration had shed all his physical discomfort, worry, judgment and resistance as he rocketed into that higher vibration. Ron's irrepressible joy and laughter were so strong that I could empathically participate in his experience.

It didn't last forever; maybe a week or so, but from time to time during the long slow process of grieving I would catch an echo of those intense triumphant feelings of release to remind me of his joyful return to Spirit.

We had talked about his death in practical terms and we both knew he would die first. I told him that I expected many signs of life from him and he needed to get busy once he was in Spirit making sure that I knew all was well. True to form he did not let me down.

The first thing that happened was all the phones stopped working. We had Sony two-line handsets on all four floors of our house. They all died at the same time. I found a Sony retailer and took them in for diagnosis. The repairman looked at the internal workings of the phones, one by one, and then asked me for the power supplies that plugged into the wall. He carefully examined them and said "Well lady, I don't know what you've been up to but what you have here is an impossibility." He pointed to the fried internal circuitry of the phones and the perfect condition of each power supply. "It can't happen like this." Apparently the power supply should have been as damaged as the phones, if it had been a power surge - and that seemed to be the cause of the phone damage. I had an inkling of who might have had a hand in this.

The lights in the house developed minds of their own. Ron had invested in a very expensive remote light control system that allowed you to turn lights off and on in any room in the house from any floor - of which there were four. However, now every light in the house would spontaneously flare on full blast at the same time in the middle of the night and then would annoyingly fail to respond to the system remote to turn off. At 3:00 am I would trudge up and down the staircases turning lights off physically. It finally became so unmanageable that I abandoned the idea of remotely controlling anything electrical and regressed to a 1950's mindset - turning it off and on by hand.

Jackson did have a wonderful sense of humour and this was definitely his idea of fun. I still have the flickering light demonstrations from time to time and know that Ron is close at hand - and still laughing.

NORM PERRY - JOEY - JONI JAMES

On January 18, 1978, I was invited to be interviewed on Canada AM. This came about at the suggestion of a friend, Ron Stannett, who at the time was a cameraman on the show. Ron was friendly with Helen Hutchinson who co-anchored the show along with Norm Perry and Harvey Kirck. In a conversation with Ron, Helen Hutchinson expressed an interest in interviewing me on the show. I was looking forward to the interview with Helen. I liked her after having briefly spoken with her by telephone. On a cold January morning, I flew from Montreal to Toronto for the live interview. I was employed at Eastern Airlines at the time and the manager, Mr. Al Schreiber graciously gave me the morning off. In fact, a television was placed in the employee lounge so staff could watch the show.

I arrived at the CTV studio about 20 minutes before the show and was ushered onto the set. I saw Norm Perry being miked for the live interview. This was a change from what I had expected. I was under the impression Helen was interviewing me. I later learned five minutes prior, Norm Perry decided he would conduct the interview.

Norm Perry introduced me on camera and then directly proceeded to ask a question, "Mr. Crinita, do you mean to tell me that my grandfather who passed away twenty years ago is here with us right now?" I thought the question absurd and I responded by asking him, "Are you nuts, where do you think he is, hiding under the rug?" (there was a rug on the set). I was quite put off by this question and thought that Norm was trying to make me look ridiculous. We then went on to discuss psychic phenomena. Norm raised the subject of charlatans and fraudulent mediums. I agreed there were charlatans in the psychic field but I added if we did not have real hair then we would not have wigs. I had nothing to hide and was certainly not afraid to answer Norm's questions. Norm Perry was very well informed and although the interview was short, I felt that it went very well. I was told after leaving the set, Norm who was still live on air said, "You know, I like that young man." When I walked off the set, my cameraman friend Ron, said to me, "You little so and so, you'd think you've been doing this your whole life." That was because I did not back down from Norm's questions. After the show, we all had breakfast together and I caught an Air Canada flight to

Montreal and was back at work by 1:00 pm. I have yet to see a tape of the show.

In 1996, eighteen years later, I was living in Toronto and working at the Head Office of Travel CUTS. On many a Saturday, I would take a leisurely stroll down Yonge Street and often end up at Sam The Record Man music store. I had become friendly with one of the managers, namely Kelley Jackson whom I had met at the store in 1994. Kelley really knew her business and was always most helpful. We often chatted about music and I kept Kelley current on any CD that my friend Joni James was in the process of releasing. I had the inside scoop as it were, because of my frequent contact with Joni.

One Saturday afternoon in 1996, Kelley mentioned that Norm Perry periodically came into the store. Evidently, he was a Joni James fan and was particularly interested to know whether the Joni James sings Hank Williams album would be released on CD. Kelley had spoken of me to Norm Perry telling him of my close connection to Joni. He expressed an interest to meet me. We did meet on a Saturday afternoon in the weeks that followed. During our meeting Norm informed me he was a long-time Joni James fan. When Joni performed at the Capitol Theatre in Toronto in the 1950's, she was his first celebrity interview. As an avid collector of Joni James music, he was very pleased to hear that Joni was still performing and re-releasing her albums, particularly that the Hank Williams album was about to be released on CD.

He expressed a desire to contact Joni. I said I would speak with her to obtain permission to provide him with her contact information. I agreed to meet with him after I had spoken with Joni. During this discussion, I did not remind Norm that he had once interviewed me. I contacted Joni and she did remember Norm Perry very well. She recalled the interview. It was Norm's first interview and he was a very nervous young man at the time. Joni had put him at ease and they had a very good interview. Her recollection of him was as an extremely nice young man. Joni gave permission to provide Norm with her home address and telephone number.

At a subsequent encounter at Sam's, I gave Norm the information. He presented me with a photograph of Joni and himself taken at the time of the interview. I took the opportunity to remind him of our previous meeting on Canada

AM many years prior, and gave him my opinion of the grandfather question. He did not recall me or the interview. However, he did state, he would never have intentionally attempted to make me or anyone look foolish in any manner. I assured him that this was not the case, because I had nothing to conceal. Joni later advised me Norm telephoned her and they had a lovely chat. As for myself, I like the irony of this tale and I wonder how the interview would have gone if Norm Perry had known of my connection to Joni James way back then.

DONALD ROYER

The strangest thing has been happening to me since my mom Fernande Royer passed away on December 22, 2001. Buttons have been falling off all parts of my clothing at an alarming rate, from the sleeves of a suit jacket twice, a buttoned sweater and the tie button of a shirt, all in a little over a one month period. I was thinking to myself, I have lost an odd button in my life, but never at this rate.

When my mother passed, I took her old sewing kit which my brother Bert was about to dispose of in the trash. Today, February 21, 2002, my wife Debbie was about to sew my many missing buttons back onto the garments. She needed a certain colour thread that she did not have and thought of my Mom's sewing kit. She found two ounces of pure gold hidden in the sewing kit amongst the thread. Coincidence! Isn't that interesting? The popping buttons steered straight to the gold. I will be sharing the proceeds with my brothers Bruce and Bert. For myself, that is my button popping double-check.

ELIZABETH McINTOSH – A RED WINTER ROSE

Gordon Higginson, the noted British medium was appearing in Edinburgh, Scotland. Although we were permanently living in Canada, my husband Bill and I always went home to Scotland for the Christmas Season to be with our families.

My sister Nancy lived in Edinburgh and had a garden. Even though it was December, the roses were still in full bloom. We went to see Gordon Higginson's demonstration. Prior to leaving from my sister's home, I snipped a red winter rose from the garden and wrapped it in cellophane to protect it from the cold. We arrived quite early to the Church where Mr. Higginson was to appear. Prior to the service, I took the red rose and placed it within a fold of the curtains that surrounded the platform. (This red rose was a gift for my late mother-in-law, Mrs. Dorothy McIntosh. She had also been a medium and loved roses which I always gave to her. This was a symbol between us.)

That evening I did not receive a personal message from Gordon Higginson. However, during his demonstration of clairvoyance he did remark, "To the lady who put the rose in the curtain, your mother-in-law says thank you." That was proof for me. Sometime later while Bill and I were teaching a workshop at the Life Spectrums Conference in Elizabethtown, Pennsylvania, I went to have a spiritual portrait drawn of myself by the intuitive visual artist Arthur Douet. During the sitting, Mr. Douet said to me, "I don't know why I am doing this, but the lady said to put the rose on your portrait." And I got the rose from Bill's mother. This was further proof for me.

HEATH LEDGER- JANUARY 26, 2008

On January 22, 2008 Heath Ledger died at his apartment in New York City. Like countless people in the world, I was shocked and saddened by the untimely and tragic demise of this talented actor at the age of twenty-eight. When I heard the news, I immediately prayed for his soul, which is something I do whenever I hear of someone's passing. I pray for them and ask that they be led into the Light.

On the evening of Saturday, January 26, I had been speaking on the telephone with my sister Irene in Los Angeles. We talked until just past midnight. Amongst the things we discussed was the passing of Heath Ledger. I went to bed at 12:30 am. Prior to sleep, I routinely pray for people whom I know are in need of healing. Additionally on this evening, I particularly prayed for Heath and specifically asked that Wana and all of my Spirit Guides help lead Heath towards the Light. I had been remembering him in my prayers every night since he had passed into Spirit. About 1:30 am I was awakened by a presence. (This is not unusual for me because this is how I see Spirit, very clearly. Spirits usually appear by the side of my bed, they sometimes appear above me just hovering over the bed. I am mostly always asleep or just drifting off into sleep. When I sense someone in the room, I wake up to see Spirit. I have never asked anyone who has made the transition to appear to me, these visitations are always spontaneous.)

I opened my eyes and standing by the side of my bed was the Spirit of Heath Ledger, whom I instantly recognized. He was wearing a black windbreaker, a green shirt and black pants or jeans. Most noticeable was a black ski beanie on his head. There were strands of long dark hair visible from under the beanie, he had a little moustache and a goatee. I called out "Heath"! and he responded with a very slight half smile. The look on his face was one of surprise or puzzlement as if he did not know where he was. I sensed that he was probably surprised to be in Spirit.

There was no mistake that this was Heath Ledger, especially when I spoke his name out loud and he reacted. It was over in a second as these Spirit visitations are for me. The telepathic impression I received from him was that this was something he had not expected, his death was accidental and a big surprise to him.

After this experience, I immediately got out of bed to write the details. As I have stated, I've seen many Spirit people, however this was the first time that I had ever made a note of such an occurrence. I believe that my Spirit Guides received my prayers on Heaths' behalf and this was their way of letting me know that he was being led into the Light.

DOLORES MARTINEZ - DECEMBER 13, 2009

On Sunday December 13, 2009, I was to attend A Walk in the Light Workshop at Joey's home. That morning, I left my home early in an attempt to do some Christmas shopping prior to collecting my mother, Noella to be at Joey's home before 1:00 pm. I had to rush to the Bombay Shop to take advantage of a one day special and of course, I was in a rush and pressed for time.

As I hurried through the shopping mall, the most wonderful Christmas tree caught my eye. The tree was decorated without lights, garland or bows. It was decorated solely with teddy bears of all colors and sizes from top to bottom. I was amazed at how beautiful it was. It was a feast for the eyes. I stopped for a while to take it all in.

That afternoon during A Walk in the Light, Joey gave me a message from my Dad Jose, who is in Spirit. He said he would turn music on for me in my home and to warn my husband Rejean in advance. It took only two days to manifest. On the morning of Tuesday, December 15 as I was coming out of the shower, I heard my husband Rejean screaming my name, "Dolores hurry, hurry come here." I ran out of the shower grabbing a towel and still dripping wet when I heard the music. It came from a Christmas music box which we never crank because to us, it is only a decoration. We have never played it. I looked at Rejean and I said to him with a serious and 'angry face', "Please don't joke around, this is not funny." He looked back at me and swore on his deceased brother's head that he had not touched the box at all. I then smiled and looked up towards the heavens and said, "Thank you Dad."

In addition, on the same Sunday afternoon after Joey gave me the message about the music, he spoke looking directly into my eyes, stretched out his arms and said, "Before your father leaves, he wants to give you a teddy bear for Christmas." WOW! That made my day, and so did Joey because there was no way that he would have known about my seeing the teddy bear Christmas tree that morning. I had not told a soul, not even my mother. Joey and I did not speak before the meeting. But my father Jose knew!

SUSAN HAYWARD

In 1963, as a teenager, the first Susan Hayward movie I saw was, With a Song in My Heart. This was my introduction to my all-time favourite actress and began my life-long admiration of the star. Not unlike millions of other fans, I followed Miss Hayward's career and never missed any of her films. I appreciated Miss Hayward both on and off the screen. I could relate to Edythe Marrenner, (her true name) and her Brooklyn roots because it was akin to Griffintown where I was born and raised. I lauded her enormous talent and personal strength of character which she managed to convey in her on-screen performances. She inspired me and thus she became someone whom I looked up to. I was deeply saddened to learn of her serious illness in 1972. My sister Susan found an address published in a magazine where one could write to Miss Hayward in care of United Artists. I selected a get-well card with the twenty-third psalm inscribed. I remember it was light green in colour. I mailed it hoping it would reach Miss Hayward. In the card I thanked her for the many years of joy which she had brought to me through her work and I wanted her to know that I was remembering her in my prayers. That was really important to me, after all, she was my heroine and I held her in the highest regard. Susan Hayward died on March 14, 1975.

In the Spring of 1977, I made my first trip to Los Angeles. Through my friend Gaby Desmarais, I was introduced to Valerie Douglas who was then a publicist employed at Guttman and Pam, the Public Relations firm. During the course of a conversation, I asked Valerie if she had met Susan Hayward in person. She replied that she had not, but she had often seen her in person and she was indeed truly beautiful. Valerie then asked me if I had ever sent a card to Susan during the course of her illness. I was somewhat surprised by the question and replied in the affirmative. I had indeed sent Miss Hayward a get-well card in 1972. Valerie went on to inform me that in 1972 she was employed by United Artists who were handling Miss Hayward's mail at the time of her illness. One morning, two pieces of mail came across her desk, both addressed to Susan Hayward. It was Valerie's responsibility to screen and read the mail. She recalled one letter was postmarked Atlanta, Georgia and was written by a Doctor on staff at a hospital in Atlanta. In his letter, the Doctor explained that although he had not met Miss

Hayward personally, he felt the need to write to her. It was a nine page letter relating to her illness and offering Miss Hayward encouragement.

Along with that particular letter was a card postmarked Montreal, Canada. Valerie recalled that it was signed by a Joey. The card remained on her mind because of the Canadian postmark and also because it had arrived in the post with the Doctor's letter. Valerie stated that she forwarded both letters on to Miss Hayward that same day. This bit of news pleased me immensely and I found it more than interesting that of all the people I should meet on my first trip to Los Angeles, it was Valerie Douglas who had raised the subject of the card without any prompting from me. I trust that Susan did indeed receive my card.

In the Summer of 1979, a friend and I motored down from Montreal to Carrollton, Georgia. I wanted to pay my respects at Miss Hayward's final resting place. Her simple grave is located in front of Our Lady of Perpetual Help Church. She rests alongside her husband Eaton Chalkley. Her former home was located directly across from the Church. I prayed at the gravesite and then entered the little country Church which was open. (It is interesting to note that on two previous separate occasions, two individual friends of mine had visited Susan's grave. On both occasions the Church was locked and there was not a soul to be found, and no response at the rectory door). There is a side altar where I stopped to pray for Susan. At the time, the altar was very tastefully decorated with an exquisitely patterned light green material which covered the back part of the altar. A beautiful golden crucifix also adorned the altar. (The last occasion I saw the altar it was somewhat changed, however the green material was still in place). My companion and I visited the Church for quite some time as we sat in silent contemplation. It was a very hot Georgia day and I was thirsty. There was no one about when we arrived. I decided to knock on the screen door of the house next to the Church, which I assumed to be the priest's residence and ask for a drink of water. My knock was answered by a cheerful greeting of "hello brother" from within the house.

With that, Monsignor Michael Regan, a jovial Irish-American priest with laughing blue eyes and a smile and personality that could sell Killarney, invited us into his home. We were ushered into the living room. I headed directly for a green wingback chair and made myself at home. I told Monsignor why I had come to Carrollton. He informed me the last time Susan Hayward came to Carrollton was to make the final arrangements for her burial, approximately six months prior to her passing. She was at that time accompanied by a nurse and by her brother Wally. She had sat in the very chair that I was now sitting in.

Monsignor referred to me as a devotee of Susan Hayward and we spoke of her at length. He shared his personal experience of a very down-to-earth woman who demanded no special accolades and who could be seen driving her pick-up truck along the dusty roads of Georgia. Mrs. Chalkley, as she was known to the locals had apparently won the hearts and the respect of her neighbours and they protected her privacy. I remarked to Monsignor Regan how much I liked the Church and he took us on a tour and pointed out the side altar which I had prayed at was decorated by Susan herself. She had apparently flown in a decorator from California to assist her. She had purchased the beautiful golden crucifix for the altar whilst filming The Honey Pot in 1966 at Cinecitta in Rome.

We spent quite a few hours visiting that day with this wonderful kindly priest. It did not matter to him that I was gay, a Spiritualist and a lapsed Catholic. We were invited to return and stay the following weekend. We gladly accepted Monsignor's invitation. Monsignor told us the Chalkleys had built this home and then donated it to the Church. I felt honoured to be staying in the house. This held great significance for me.

Through the years I corresponded with and occasionally telephoned Monsignor Regan. I visited him again on September 26, 1982 and on November 3, 1991. Whenever I happened to be in Atlanta, I made it a point to visit Carrollton, to visit Susan's resting place and see Monsignor Regan. At all of our meetings, Monsignor would always encourage me to return to the bosom of Holy Mother Church. Monsignor Michael Regan passed on August 19, 1999. He was a priest for fifty-two years and truly a man of God who fervently lived his faith. Due to my high regard for Susan Hayward, I was able to meet this remarkable human being. The following is an excerpt from a Christmas Church bulletin which Monsignor Regan mailed to me.

December 20, 1983

As I was wondering recently about the contents of this brief communication at Christmas, I realized that this would be my eleventh Christmas from Carrollton.

Moreover, it occurred to me that I never explicitly referred to the fact that our Church cemetery here is visited regularly by people from all over our country. They come to visit the grave of Susan Hayward who with her husband Eaton Chalkley, donated the land on which our parish buildings stand. Together, they were the major benefactors of our parish back in 1962 when the Church and subsequently the rectory were built. Eaton Chalkley died in 1966, Susan in 1975. Among the visitors who have come to visit Susan's resting place, I have met many who have come to pay her a debt of deep gratitude for helping them to discover their better selves through the inspiring characterizations she played on the screen. The lives of some of these visitors have been completely turned around. The parts she played showed them the way toward self-discovery or self-recovery. My own experience in encountering such vivid indications of the influence of the media should not have come as a surprise to me, but they have been truly startling. The media can build up or break down. Fortunately, Susan Hayward, Lord rest her, really let her Light shine on the screen, and she served as a tremendous instrument of goodness in the lives of God only knows - how many people. There is a Latin dictum: exempla trahunt- example drags.

Michael Regan

I once asked Joni James, (my other inspiration since youth) if she had ever met Susan Hayward in person. She related the following:

Joni and her husband Tony Acquaviva lived at 1027 N. Roxbury Drive in Beverly Hills. Joni and Toni were friends with Susan's son, Timothy Barker. Tony had transacted some business with Tim. Tim's fiancée, Ilse and Joni were friends. Joni hosted an engagement lunch for Ilse. Joni, being the excellent cook that she is, prepared a sumptuous home cooked Italian meal for the occasion.

A half hour before the scheduled time as Joni was finishing the meal preparation, the door bell rang. Joni answered the door and standing before her was Susan Hayward, who introduced herself with a friendly, "I'm here." Joni invited Susan in. Susan made herself at home and as she observed all of Joni's gold records on a wall she commented, "Quite an achievement." In response Joni said, "Thank you" to Susan and, "Look at what you have achieved, an Academy Award." Susan smiled graciously.

After lunch, Susan remarked to Isle as she pointed to the gold records which adorned the wall, "You see what Mrs. Acquaviva has achieved and how busy she is. I hope you appreciate what she has done for you." Joni was quite impressed with Susan. She was beautiful and a no nonsense, down-to-earth woman. Joni recently said to me, "If I'd known how much you liked her, I would have introduced you." That I thought - would have been something!

On a July 2008 visit to Los Angeles, I was introduced to Jim Hawkins through our mutual friend, Ron Sexton. Jim and I hit it off instantly. He is a very gifted artist and a soft spoken gentle soul. He has an interest in metaphysics and we share a common interest in the cinema. Additionally, through conversations we discovered that our favourite actress is Susan Hayward. Of course, with me that qualifies for immediate friendship. In 2009 while visiting Jim's home one evening, we were discussing one of Miss Hayward's films. Jim excused himself, saying he had something to show me which I might find of interest. Jim left the room and returned with something in hand.

He handed me an original working script of With a Song in My Heart. I was quite impressed. He informed me that he had acquired it a number of years ago in Pasadena. There are notations on the script and it obviously belonged to someone who worked on the film. That evening when I returned to my sister's home I excitedly shared the news of the script. The following week I met with Jim again. He said he had a surprise and presented me with the script as a gift.

I was moved to tears and very touched by his generosity. He could not have given me anything that would have pleased me more. I now have the script numbered 409 in my possession. The original title for the film was, You and The Night and The Music, is penciled out and With a Song in My Heart is written in. The cover reads: Final Script May 11, 1951. For me, this is more than a gift from Jim.

Again, of all of the people in Los Angeles. ... and so it goes.

CHAPTER XI
THE SPIRITUAL STEPS

THE SPIRITUAL STEPS

1. Wondering
2. Lights On
3. The Search
4. Realization
5. Re-evaluation
6. Crash
7. Reaching Out
8. The Dark Night of the Soul
9. Enlightenment
10. Going Forward
11. Remembrance
12. Living in the Light
13. Repeat Performance

INTRODUCTION

There is no set formula or process of awareness that collectively dictates the soul's evolution. Each individual needs to work through the process and experience step by step and stage by stage on a personal and solitary level. This does not mean that we will experience the process alone. There are and will be fellow travellers in eternity who will have had similar experiences. From them we can learn.

Ultimately, the spiritual journey is a singular one and individuals need to work out their own personal relationship to The Eternal One. The steps can serve as a focal point and a gauge for us in our quest. There is no time limit on spiritual awareness as it is a constant process. Spiritual steps are the natural progression along the pathway of a soul's evolvement. One step at a time.

1. WONDERING
Who am I? Where am I going? Why am I here? And of course, what is it all about? These thoughts filter in and out of the consciousness. For some people these questions come on a daily basis and for others at different intervals of life when one is given to serious thought about individual existence and reason for being. The thought usually passes, and we put it aside to ponder when time permits or when we are in a more reflective space.

2. LIGHTS ON
This usually happens after we have had an experience out of our normal frame of reference that has to do with the workings of the soul. Frequently, it is the death of a loved one. Other possible circumstances are the loss of power or position, a personal tragedy, a life threatening illness or a near death experience. Any one of these can be the trigger which causes one to question the meaning of life. We begin to ask in earnest, "Is this all there is?" We start to question our belief system and heed the tugging going on inside. The "things of the Spirit" to which we have yet to relate, now begin to make sense. The word "spiritual" is no longer foreign or strange. The Light begins to penetrate our consciousness and we realize in our humanity, we are indeed fragile.

3. THE SEARCH
We decide to find out what is going on. Our curiosity is piqued. We want to know. We pray for guidance. We ask questions of others, read books, attend seminars, workshops, meditation classes, tune into media, surf the net and seriously pursue the spiritual pathway. The neophyte begins to perceive things in a different light. We discover the spiritual masters and intellectually absorb their wisdom. We find new interpretations for "old truths" and slowly begin to perceive the inner meanings of their teachings. We begin to question our beliefs and open many doors on our pathway to the soul. We seek out spiritual teachers and gurus. We discover we are not alone on this journey to awareness. There are other people travelling this same route. We are travellers in eternity. We recognize and find one another.

4. REALIZATION

The process of self-realization has begun. We think, "I am really a part of this; there is more to me than meets the eye." We begin to accept our spiritual nature. We have come too far to turn back, however we are fearful of the future. We wander into our heads and set up barriers. "What do I have to give up?" "Am I worthy?" "Will I make it?" "Can I sustain it?" "Is it worth it?" "What is the price I will pay?" And of course, some people ask: "What will people think?" We realize the Light within cannot be extinguished. We have become peaceful within ourselves and conscious of that subtle peace within our being. We decide to go for it and get on with our search. We learn to pay attention to our personal spiritual experiences. We become more aware of happiness, exhilaration, peace, pain and anticipation on a deeper level. We are on our way. Other people begin to recognize the transformation. They may not always identify exactly what the change is. However subtle, a change has indeed occurred and some people around us may begin to feel threatened.

5. RE-EVALUATION

A profound change has taken place on the inner level of our being. We begin to reassess our life, to take inventory of our behaviour and relationships. We make new friends, we change others and we start to connect with and build our spiritual family. We recognize kindred souls. We start to get our act together and handle unfinished business in our personal relationships. We become more honest with ourselves and with the people around us. We approach our life with a more positive outlook. We may even notice our sense of humour has improved and we learn not to take ourselves so seriously. Our old attitudes are falling by the wayside; we are becoming more in harmony with our higher nature. Life is not so hard and things take on a rosy hue. We are joyful and more accepting of ourselves and of others. There is a peace within, at the very core of our being.

6. CRASH

I used to be different but now I'm the same. Life catches up with us. All the spiritual insights and growth we've experienced seems to have disappeared. Did we make the whole thing up? We still have problems to deal with in relationships, jobs and the world in general. What happened? The changes we implemented in ourselves appear to be falling apart. We fall back into old habits and mindsets we thought we had overcome and changed. All the good resolutions seem to have come to naught. We are no longer motivated to meditate or pray. This is the time for our inner faith and the lessons we have learned to sustain us. So we stay with it and we hold on. We are reminded of the words of the mystic, St. John of the Cross: "Without light and apparently without strength, even seemly without hope, we commit ourselves to an entire surrender to God. We drop our arrogance, we submit to the incomprehensible reality of our situation and we are content with it because senseless though it may seem, it makes more sense than anything else."

7. REACHING OUT

We worked too hard to get where we are and to enhance our spiritual awareness. We have climbed the mountain. We do not deny our experiences. We know we have transformed ourselves. We cannot and we will not go back. We pray for understanding, for strength and for the gift of faith to sustain us in our quest. The door has been opened so we walk in, fortified by prayer and meditation which are the keys to the life within and we learn to appreciate the beauty of silence and to cultivate solitude. We utilize our inner sanctuary and we create a sanctuary in our home, or a favourite outdoor spot, a sacred place where we can be alone in the quiet to meditate and pray as we strive to listen to the inner promptings of our being. We are committed to our soul's growth.

8. THE DARK NIGHT OF THE SOUL

The dark night of the soul is a familiar phenomenon in spiritual life and for many, a necessary stumbling place on the path to enlightenment. If we have it all together, then why is it so lonely, cold and difficult at times? Have we been led down the garden path? Are we just rationalizing? Has The Eternal One forsaken me? Have I been deluding myself? Our life is a mess and we feel totally alone. Our relationships are falling apart and friends desert us. Our loved ones are leaving the planet and we see only chaos and despair. The world seems upside down and we are overwhelmed by the circumstances in our life. We have been diligent in our spiritual quest so why are these things happening? Our ego gets bruised and our unconscious drags up our phobias, imperfections and our shadow, the darker side of our nature. We experience the roller-coaster effect of great clarity and of total darkness within. Digging through darkness is how we find the door to the Light. We begin to understand that we reach God either through inspiration or desperation. We have experienced both to the fullest. We ask once more, "Why is this happening to me? Did someone turn the light off when I wasn't looking?"

9. ENLIGHTENMENT

We made it. Everything falls into place and we are one with the Universe. We are more in touch with our humanity, our spiritual dignity and our personal relationship to The Eternal One. We strive to love unconditionally, simply for the sake of loving. We see God in every flower, every sunset and in all of creation. We are aware and accept the interconnectedness of all living forms. We surrender to the Divine Will. We allow it to be worked through us. We accept and we grow in consciousness and in Light. We get out of our heads and into our hearts. We learn to be. We are the living manifestation of God's most wondrous creation and we are at one with the Universe and at peace with ourselves. We let it be what it wants to be. We are co-creators in the Universe and we are responsible. We see the living Light within ourselves and within our fellow travellers in eternity. We go to sleep at night, wake in the morning. We are still the same, yet we are different.

10. GOING FORWARD

We begin to walk the talk and live our beliefs by conscious action. We integrate with the Spirit and we realize that we have always been that way. We just did not see it. We move forward with an assured sense of self and a knowing which comes from understanding that we operate from our higher nature. We live in the awareness that what we say and what we do matters in the Universe. We can and do make a difference.

11. REMEMBRANCE

We understand the reality of our spiritual nature and we accept and know we did not get here on our own. Although the spiritual journey is a solitary one, along the way we have been inspired, led, encouraged, taught, moved and loved by other beings that have functioned as our spiritual mentors and guides. As we strive to walk on the path of Light we remind ourselves to be grateful, to love unconditionally, to give a blessing, to be conscious of our words and actions, to release an old grudge, to forgive ourselves and others too, to share our experience, to support others in their need, to be respectful of all creatures and the planet, and to remember that wherever you are... BE there.

12. LIVING IN THE LIGHT

We have heeded the yearning from deep within our soul and have answered its call. We've travelled the spiritual pathway, done the inner work, put in our time and energy and aligned ourselves with people of like vibration. We believe we have it all together. We believe we have it all figured out. We utilize our inner spiritual resources to give us the strength and understanding which allows one to better cope when the world about us becomes chaotic and unsettling. With time, we have become more sensitive, more finely tuned to the vibrations of other people and of the world we live in, and yet occasionally we find ourselves not so sure, or not as aware as we perceived ourselves to be. There are instances when we are not able to penetrate the veil which seems to engulf us, or to fathom energies which surround us although we are aware that they may not have anything to do with us on a personal level. Nonetheless, they have an affect on us and one must remind oneself the sensitive soul will unwittingly tune into the energies of the world about them. We need to acknowledge these energies for what they are and not become bound up in negative vibrations. In time, through prayer and meditation, clarity comes. This is the way of the spiritual warrior and the seeker on the pathway. It is part of living in the Light, for always, those who live in the Light need to experience and be aware of the shadows which always lurk. How else can one bring Light where there is none, if we do not understand and know for ourselves? The reward for one's spiritual endeavours and living consciously in the Light is that we have the opportunity to become angels in the making, whilst we live our daily life here on the planet.

13. REPEAT PERFORMANCE

Guess what? The process starts all over again. We have come to the point with Socrates where we can say with certainty: "The only thing that I know is that I know nothing." Our search for spiritual awareness is continuous, and not always easy. We learn in the process of living on the planet. We learn from our experiences and from each other. Every time we think that we have completed one stage, with each new step we take, each new road we travel, we are reminded that there is still yet a further one to go. The journey is infinite and eternal. There are no shortcuts. And no one ever said it was easy. Many are called, but few get up.

CHAPTER XII
THOUGHTS TO PONDER

INTRODUCTION

The following are several discourses I've delivered at various conferences. Included are personal thoughts I have put to paper that until now, have not been made public. I am also including random inspirational thoughts I've penned over the years. Although these writings may differ in style from this book's narrative, they are part of my work and I now offer them as thoughts to ponder.

THE POWER OF THE SOUL

The maxim, as above so below, is well-known to the spiritual seeker. As we wind our way along the journey of life, we come to see the Divine manifest in many instances during the process.

As mortals possessing a spiritual nature, we learn to rely on the homing device of intuition or an inner knowingness which are soul qualities.

We are born into this world with our allotted tasks to perform based on the karmic lessons that we either need to learn or teach. On the soul level, we are truly enlightened as to the purpose of our incarnation. This awareness stands us in good stead when confronted with hardships in our lives, be they the result of a life-threatening illness, the death of a loved one, emotional upheaval or unexpected and drastic changes in our circumstances. For many, a severe shock frequently serves as a catalyst for the soul's evolvement. In our humanity, we rally each in our fashion and within our individual time-frame. Like the Phoenix, we rise from the ashes victorious over tribulation to put our lives into perspective. Once we have triggered our spiritual alarm system and begin to pay attention to the inner voice of the soul's goading, we are able then to accept and handle our life situation on a more conscious level. There is little doubt that individuals who have acquired a spiritual anchor appear to use their inner resource as a means of coping with the difficulties of life. The soul, constant and wise, provides us with the inner knowledge that everything will be all right, even in the midst of the darkest night. Once the soul is illuminated and the Light has pierced our inner being, however subtly, it becomes our beacon and our guide.

It is only when we give thought to our particular life's mysteries from a spiritual or karmic point of reference do we fully appreciate the inner meanings of our circumstances and accept the inexorable lessons of life which we have chosen in order for us to develop as spiritual beings in this material world. Each soul is unique and forms its own individual pattern as it winds its way along the path which it has selected to travel.

It is only after one consciously calms the Spirit through various processes including prayer, meditation and contemplation, that clarity prevails and one becomes centered or focused on the spiritual perspectives which foster individual growth experiences. We are constantly in the process of learning and sharing our karmic lessons while fulfilling the mortal role which we have accepted to play as our part in the Universal scheme of things. Peace of soul is acquired through the process of becoming more whole on all levels of our being. The eternal soul, indestructible and constantly evolving is a source of unlimited power. When one experiences and understands on the soul level, one knows. We are not deterred or unsure when we heed the soul's command. We have an inherent sense when something is right for us. In the process of listening to the soul's voice we become more in tune with the Divine Will, which is the desired outcome of our existence.

There are instances when the curtain is drawn aside slightly, and with a certainty indicative of the Spirit, one is able to comprehend the reality and validity of our spiritual thoughts. These are often granted to us unexpectedly. Realization frequently appears like a bolt from out of the blue. Strength of purpose and unswerving faith are characteristics of the soul and coupled with a sincere commitment to our higher nature, enables the soul to realize its particular destiny.

Life is not without hardships. However, few humans live a charmed existence free from the unexpected and unwanted experiences prove to be difficult life-lessons. This is a condition of living on the planet. For the spiritually aware, life may appear to be paradoxical. On the inner-soul level, one accepts and understands that on the outer-material level, one cannot always see clearly. This often occurs when we get caught up in emotional reactions or go into our heads. The power of the soul sustains us in times of crisis and need. Our spiritual generator is part of the Universal Mind as we are part of The Eternal One.

How we cultivate our spiritual garden is entirely up to each individual. We are provided with the tools the moment our Spirit enters the body and from our initial cry to the world. We move on and into the physical manifestation of life to perform our accepted role. We must be ever mindful of who and where we are on our inner level. In times of angst we must not forget to stop and take a deep breath, and go within to empower ourselves to revitalize our soul.

The power of The Eternal One is infinite and we, who are divinely programmed creatures in possession of an immortal soul, are part of the all powerful essence. Souls are singular and the human attributes of the individual are but a dim reflection of the essence of the beauty within. The soul is eternal, always was and always will be. It is the Alpha and the Omega, and the manifestation of God's omnipotence.

The soul is the seat of our power. The soul is who we truly are.

BEING AWARE

Like all things worthwhile, there is no easy way. We are led to the path of awareness by various experiences and after making a series of choices our Spirit sets out on the path best suited to us. We incarnate with complete awareness on the spiritual level, an awareness which lies within the deepest regions of our being and is the seat of power. We know that it is there, that it exists and that it is a part of us, yet it is often hidden from us. Not unlike the beautiful and elusive butterfly, awareness suddenly appears before us - we see its beauty and as quickly as it comes in all of its splendour - it disappears out of our reach as we attempt to grasp it. Power goes hand-in-hand with awareness and being aware makes us responsible. Awareness means power and power is the knowledge that we can do anything we choose. For example, we can master and harness the shadow part of our natures. We can accomplish this by first accepting that we do indeed have a shadow part of our nature which occasionally reveals itself. When we recognize this part of ourselves manifesting then at that time, we must strive with the willingness to be all that we can be and experience ourselves as powerful spiritual beings, making positive choices in our lives.

Our spiritual power is as natural as the rain - it builds from within and when utilized properly for right choices and causes, it is a force which cannot be contained. It is generated by the soul and is fierce in its determination once set in motion, with a fervour akin to a wild fire that will not be contained, which brings to mind the metaphor, when your heart is on fire. The zeal which accompanies power can sear, can comfort and soothe. Powerful human beings who possess a high spiritual level of awareness operate from the latter. They use their power to heal, to bring comfort, to create and build strong spiritual foundations both for themselves and their fellow creatures, with whom they share the planet.

Our individual power is part of the essence of who we are. When we are in touch with our power we feel secure, complete and whole on all levels of being. We are a force to contend with. We can move mountains and scale the heights if need be.

When we choose to dissipate our power we then become unclear, unfocused and not in control of our lives. In order for us to become in touch with our power we must go within. Symbolically one needs to close one's eyes and visualize boring a hole into the darkness of our being with a powerful laser beam intended to reach our inner core, which is the seat of our power, the source of inner strength and awareness. If one chooses to give one's power away through negative habits, then after a period of time they will prove to be harmful both to the Spirit and the body. Negativity does not add, it only erodes and dissipates.

The identical experience occurs when we make wrong choices in our life's experience which are not conducive to our spiritual growth. The soul is not governed by time as we know it. One could choose to remain in a less than positive circumstance for many years until one is ready to tap into one's inner resource which has up until then been clouded by murky vision. In our humanity we often choose to be where we are because of the lessons our soul needs to learn. These lessons of life take on the form of patterns we repeat over and over until we get it right and make a conscious choice of breaking these patterns which steal our aliveness. The paradox is that on some level we do choose negative growth experiences which can be converted into opportunities for positive awareness.

Once one attains mastery of the self which is the key to the proper utilization of spiritual power, one can then rise as the Phoenix from the ashes to control the spiritual, mental, physical and emotional levels of our being. Once we come to know ourselves, we can then proceed to move out into the world secure in the awareness we can overcome all trials and tribulations no matter how devastating. For within ourselves, lies the source of our spiritual strength which is our link to the Creator. What we give away today, we can recoup tomorrow. In the twinkling of an eye, we make a choice to do what is needed for our survival to restore balance and to maintain dignity of spirit and our personal base of power. We know our limits and when our soul's own voice commands us to act, we then follow. The soul tells us when enough is enough. The lesson has been learned, the price has been paid. It is time to move forward.

Our personal and spiritual power is the sum total of our experiences. From this we learn and grow. How we choose to utilize that awareness is entirely up to us. We are only as powerful as we allow ourselves to be. There is no limit to the power of God and we tap into that power through prayer and meditation and remind ourselves to look inward and not up because it's an inside job!

Part of our human condition is to learn from our mistakes which are often a result of us giving our power away to others for various reasons. Be this in the area of relationships with parents, family, significant others or to one's job or a group cause. One must be vigilant and mindful of the fact that if we willingly give our power away, it should not come at our personal expense. For there are always persons and situations that will take and absorb our power giving little in return. For always in this world, some are givers and some are takers.

THE GIFTS OF SPIRIT

What are the gifts of the Spirit and where are they manifest today? They are all around us, within each one of us and can be summed up in one word, Love.

The eye of the Spirit is the seat of the soul. People have experienced: Glimpses of clairvoyance, flashes of intuition, a sense of precognition, feelings of apprehension, heightened awareness and prophetic dreams. In instances when we experience Higher Sense Perception, heed our inner voice and experience phenomena outside of our normal frame of reference, we are tapping into the realm of the Spirit, and to things which most frequently pertain to these matters. It is true that every paranormal or psychic experience is not necessarily of a spiritual nature. However, the majority of our out of the ordinary occurrences do belong to the spiritual realm.

These are the cosmic attention getters, the Universe's way of switching on the Light as affirmed by those who have undergone a near-death experience and have seen the tunnel of Light. These result in a questioning mind, which at times is tinged with the familiar, "This cannot be happening to me" or "This has got to be my imagination", and more often than not, the proverbial, "I must be losing my mind." Psychic phenomena has finally come out of the closet, and people are now openly sharing their personal paranormal experiences.

The gifts of the Spirit are available to all on variant levels and are found through the seeking. Prior to setting out on our quest, we may want to stop and inquire of ourselves:

What is the purpose of attaining and utilizing the gifts of the Spirit or things which have to do with our spiritual growth and well being?

What is the good of obtaining spiritual awareness and not putting it to use?

Why have insight if we will not see?

Why have sensitivity if we do not practice compassion?

Why seek truth if we are not honest with ourselves and others?

Why speak of unconditional love if we do not love ourselves and others?

Why ask for guidance if we will not listen and use it?

It is true we are spiritual beings encased in a physical body and we live in the physical material world. We are travellers in eternity who are seeking to become. We are in the process of becoming God-like mirrors of perfection. In our humanity we must be willing to accept ourselves and others as we truly are - fragile and vulnerable. Though we are fortified with spiritual strength and knowledge, we must contend with the daily experiences of living on the planet.

As we grow in consciousness we begin to integrate the gifts of the Spirit into our being and our life. This integration is reflected in who and what we are and in the picture which we present to the world. The greatest gift of the Spirit is the gift of healing in whatever form it manifests. People who are capable of love are capable of transmitting the power of healing by allowing themselves to be used as a vessel in the service of others.

There are various aspects of healing and it occurs on many levels. As in the act of physical healing, the laying on of hands or absent healing, wherein we send healing thoughts and energy to another. With the healing of compassion our hearts acknowledge that we understand and indeed we do understand. Compassion brings with it the realization: But for the grace of God we ourselves could be in very different and dire circumstances.

One of the primary aspects of spiritual healing is centered on forgiveness and the willingness to forgive those who have caused us hurt. We in turn must be able to forgive ourselves. With true forgiveness we experience detachment and unconditional love for all humankind, for our family, friends, enemies and most importantly, ourselves. The gifts of the Spirit have their foundation in Divine Love, which we as the children of The Eternal One are the recipients of. As we journey on this planet we learn and we grow in understanding as we struggle with our humanity and our foibles.

Spiritual service and evolvement need to have their foundation in pure motive and a loving heart. It is only then that we receive the spiritual grace that is accompanied by a serenity of Spirit by which our faith is fortified.

Do not take your spiritual gifts for granted. Utilize your knowledge, your experience and common sense to become a bright Light in a dark world. Let your example be as a beacon of Light to your fellow travellers and seekers in the cosmic scheme of things. The gifts of the Spirit are numerous and sundry. They are found in inspiration, creativity, clairvoyance, healing and wisdom and in the ability to appreciate life. To dream and be sensitive to the needs of others, these gifts manifest in the world today and are part of the spiritual reservoir of humanity. Each individual on the planet has received the legacy of Divine Love. We are all loved by The Eternal One. This is our common thread, the common gift is our ability to give and receive Love. Our humanity makes us all equal in the eyes of the Great Spirit. Use your particular gift as a basis to build on; and commence with your own life. Ask yourself: Are there situations in my life in need of repair that love can resolve? If the answer to that question is yes, then take your gift into your hands and use it. Use your ability to love as a foundation for all your life's experiences. Do not squander and waste that gift, and do not neglect your spiritual needs and your spiritual life. Use what you are given for the evolvement of your soul and for the spiritual enhancement of all with whom you come into contact.

THE WALKING WOUNDED

The eyes are the mirror of the soul and the reflection we cast before us in a sense reveals who and what we are, although the picture which we present to the world is not always accurate. It may not be in sync with the essence of our spiritual nature. Like the chameleon, we learn to hide in the shadows of our being to protect ourselves from harm's way and from pain. For some people the poignant memories of childhood, the pain of separation caused by the death of a loved one, the loss of love, health or material security cast a shadow on our Spirit and for a time can weaken our resolve and dim our Light.

As human beings we strive to maintain control over the happenings of our daily life experiences. We do battle with ourselves and at times with others, in futile attempts to change events which are shaped by our destiny in the roles which we have chosen to play in this lifetime prior to this incarnation.

When we are in conflict with our Higher Self we do not always choose the wisest course, because of the barriers which we have consciously or unconsciously placed upon ourselves. We can intellectually grasp the lessons of life at hand but one must feel on the heart level, in order for the soul to register and profit. Few mortals travel through life without battle scars brought about by adversity. Each individual has their unique tale to tell, their own particular form of hardship to bear. It is part of the human ethos and few are left untouched. The reality of the wounded healer is clearly evident to all who have known misfortune.

In shamanic tradition it is only after a wound or initiation period that the selected individual becomes transformed. The scars of the shaman or wounded warrior are their badge of courage and rite of passage into the ranks of healers and into mysticism. Tribulation leaves its mark on all and from the ashes of personal anguish, we can rise to meet a new day and live to fight and win our next battle. We are the walking wounded, not the victims of circumstance but the victor in the soul's domain. As we regard the eyes of our fellow travellers in eternity, we see within the flame of survival. Those who pursue the way of the Spirit have made a choice in life. A choice to be the best person they know how. A choice to live the courage of their convictions. A choice to examine old wounds, to heal from within whilst moving on in the process of becoming. We will recognize each other by our actions and by the Light which cannot and will not be hidden. We are the walking wounded. We are the children of the planet. We rise to meet the light of each new dawn as we move forward with our heads held high in the sureness that we are not alone on our sojourn. We cannot fail if we remember that we learn from each other and the life experience of another may serve to fortify us in our endeavours.

We are divinely programmed for survival - and with dignity of Spirit we reflect the lessons of our lives. We, the wounded, are not hindered.

THE JOURNEY TO THE CENTRE OF OUR BEING

Let the inner become the outer and the outer become the inner. Appearances are not always what they seem to be and that which appears to be what is so, is not necessarily what is.

Our realities are governed by our culture and belief system and for many people on the spiritual pathway, a sudden shift in consciousness is no great feat. It is only with a profound desire for change and awareness that one is able to leave one's set of beliefs and embrace new ones, while often times holding on to the foundation which is instilled in us at a very early age. That foundation often turns into the stepping stones for future spiritual growth.

From the known to the unknown is the path of the spiritual pilgrim. Past experience and current understanding are the stepping stones of faith and inner realization. The life that we lead is the only tangible measurement of our soul's true worth, for that is what we demonstrate on an ongoing and daily basis. Our actions and spiritual activities reflect the fountain of spiritual insight and strength which flourishes within each one of us. That spiritual strength, our inner resource, lies at the very core of our being and it is to that core that we retreat in times of stress or tribulation. Indeed we journey to the centre in search of hope to banish despair, to search for serenity, to cancel turmoil and upheaval. It is imperative for us to have an inner sanctuary where we can go in times of chaos. Therein we find our own refuge from the storm and the calming waters of spiritual grace offers a healing balm which both nurtures and fortifies. The journey to the centre of our being is not always a serene one and frequently it is not without outer interference.

The circumstances and events of our life can wreak havoc on our daily existence. Unexpected upheavals on the emotional level cause us to stop, look, react and attempt to retain control of our lives by entering into the space within, regardless of what outer turmoil we may be experiencing. Paradoxically, we may be seeking inner serenity in the midst of a raging storm. It is then we must hold on to our faith in ourselves and become our own anchor. When we are caught unaware by unforeseen or unexpected events, we need a moment to catch our breath and time to pull back, to examine and understand what is occurring. By taking deep breaths we can feel the soothing prana, the breath of life supporting us and helping us to become focused in a real and present sense, in the here and now.

We must handle the realities of living on the planet and learn from the experiences which arise from that. This can be achieved by a combination of spiritual centering and practical comprehension. We need to understand and to allow that which is located in the centre of our being to come to the fore into our minds and hearts in the form of intuition. As above so below and as manifest on the inner so it is manifest on the outer. We move in cycles. We grow in reason. We learn with time. The spiritual centre is not so separate from the physical, the two are one and the same, the spiritual sense resides within the physical house of the body. With constant attention being paid to both levels of Self, we can hammer out the chinks in our armour and forge our own personal metamorphosis in our life. Yes, we need to journey to the centre of our being and we also need to be here and now at the same time. One cannot be separate from the other. We are the citizens of the planet, evolving, resolving, growing and learning each at our own pace and in our own way. It does not matter how fast we move as long as we do move.

Our spirituality is our person-hood and it is also our humanity. Within that humanity is cloaked all the tools needed to do the job to move ahead, to realize our dreams and be secure in our personal choices of life experiences and direction. We, as the children of The Eternal One are both human and divine. We are both the leader and the follower, the giver and the taker, the spiritual neophyte and the oldest of souls. We can be wise and foolish at the same time, we can be sure and unsure simultaneously. We are unique by nature and yet we are all the same in our vulnerability and humanity. We can reach out or we can withdraw. We, as human beings, are so simple and yet so complex. And so, it is within the understanding of our differences and the acceptance of our sameness that we come to reside with one another in peace, compassion and harmony. We are our own best resource, that resource lives within. Use your resource, your spiritual awareness and extract from the very depths of your soul that which you require for physical, spiritual, mental and emotional strength. Find your source, your innate centre and share it with others without fear of diminishing your power. Always remember there is plenty more where that came from - it is The Eternal One's power house which belongs to each and every one of us. You are your best reservoir of spiritual strength and grace. There is no such thing as failure in the mind of God.

During our solitary and private moments, if we take the time to pay attention and heed our inner voice, we are entering into the centre of our spiritual nature, our individual Holy of Holies without the trappings which we have acquired simply from the process of living on the planet. Be singular in your purpose and steadfast in your spiritual endeavours. The journey to the centre is not hampered by time or space. It is not constrained by situation. It is the reality of here and now, of looking and truly seeing, of listening and truly hearing. The journey is inevitable and unavoidable if we truly desire to be who we are. It is an inside job! Once we arrive at this understanding, it is then we are truly able to look outward and view the world from a different perspective in the knowledge that inner strength is power and all power comes from a Source much higher than ourselves. That power is at the centre of the Universe and of our being and is simply called God.

QUO VADIS - WITHER GOES THOU?

The world is moving faster and life in the fast track is the norm. We are affected individually and collectively by the happenings of our time. The illusive veil of the planet Neptune is ever apparent because we cannot fathom many of these occurrences: The Tragedy of September 11, 2001, the economic downturn, the blatant greed of individuals and corporations, the lack of concern for the environment, war and upheaval based on religious and social differences. Having said this, we must not be lulled into a false sense of security. For in reality there is no security, and there never was. We cannot guarantee what will happen tomorrow to any one of us. As we are aware, in the twinkling of an eye the course of one's life and indeed the lives of millions of people, can be changed and altered as we have witnessed by the 2004 Tsunami in Thailand and 2005 Hurricane Katrina in New Orleans. As finite beings living in a material world, we are governed by the natural and spiritual laws. The laws of cause and effect are ever in motion and there is an invisible cord which links us all together by the virtue of our humanity.

The world stage has become much smaller. Cultural, political, religious and language differences are now the norm as human-kind attempts to raise it's collective consciousness and act in concert as demonstrated by the United Nations interventions in various international areas of concern for Human Rights. It is no small wonder that the sensitive individual who is committed to his personal spiritual evolution will have his energy field bombarded with all manner of feelings and impressions which are placed on the ether as a direct result of the existing conditions on this, our planet.

In the process of living, our emotions are assaulted and fear overwhelms us as reflected by the following; the fear of intimacy because of sexually transmitted diseases and the continuous presence of AIDS in this world, the fear of sitting in the sun because of skin cancer, the fear of growing older due to the youth-oriented culture. True, you must be vigilant in certain aspects of life. However, with all of our fears there is a chance that you may become insular and self-centered. We must be willing to look at the big picture, keep a spiritual perspective and in moments of uncertainty, be ever mindful that man is Spirit having a human experience. Therefore, it is our spiritual nature that governs our behaviour and how we relate to the world around us. Fear is divisive and causes people to separate and not unite. The Eternal One has implanted within each individual a homing device that is singular and unique, it is 'the small still voice within'. We can choose either to heed that voice or ignore its promptings. We will be guided if we learn to be still and listen. It is within our nature to question where we are going and to be in control of our personal destiny. As we grow into awareness of the Self, we become more adept in the navigation on the seas of life. The spiritually inclined individual has at his fingertips, many tools for self-development and therefore many opportunities to put into practice what you learn from the service to others.

We are continuously being asked to examine our principles and belief systems as we tune into the daily happenings on the planet. Our senses are bombarded daily with issues of bias, abuse, genocide, murder, robbery, character assassination, morality, political intrigue, free choice and the irresponsible handling of the natural environment based on opportunistic accumulation of wealth. As citizens of the earth, we are involved in these issues whether we want to be or not. It is therefore imperative for one to have clear focus and a sense of wholeness of being. This is achieved through soul-searching, meditation and prayer combined with a firm commitment to be the best person we know how to be.

We need to be true to our higher purpose, to walk the talk, to be constant and to possess the wisdom to know the difference between right and wrong based on our own spiritual perspective. We can then move forward with an open heart and mind. The one thing we can all be sure of is that ultimately we are heading in the same direction and will make our exit through the process of physical death. What we do up until that time is entirely up to us. You must simply be prepared to ask the question at the end of our journey: "Lord of my being, have I done well?"

CHAPTER XIII
MEDITATIONS

I created the following two meditations for use in my Workshops. I offer them in the hope that they may assist you on your spiritual quest.

I suggest that you meditate in a quiet and private place to avoid distractions.

If you record these meditations, please do not listen to them while you are driving a vehicle of any type or operating machinery.

Prior to entering into the meditative state, I suggest that you recite:

The Robe of Light Mantra

I clothe myself in a robe of Light composed of the love, the power and the wisdom of God.

Enveloping me and inter-penetrating me, not only that I may be protected, but so that all who see it, or come into contact with it may be drawn to God and healed.

-Author Unknown

INTRODUCTION TO THE HEALING DOVE MEDITATION

The purpose of this simple meditation is to send healing energy to those in need by bringing them to mind whilst visualizing a healing dove that will function as your conduit for the healing energy. Always be mindful that God is the healer and humankind the channel.

THE HEALING DOVE MEDITATION

Close your eyes.

Be aware of your breathing.

Take a deep breath.

Inhale through your nose.

Exhale through mouth.

Clear your mind of all the cares of the day.

Breathe in the vital life force.

Be aware of the rhythm of your breathing.

Relax.

Bring your awareness to the center of your forehead.

The area which is known as your third eye.

In your mind's eye visualize a snow white dove.

This dove is the symbol of the golden healing energy of light and of love.

Rest your hands on your lap with your palms turned upwards.

Visualize a white dove perched in the palm of your opened hands.

It is standing poised for flight, to fly to wherever you may send it.

Visualize the person you wish to send healing to.

Bring them to mind, visualize them well, healthy and full of the vital life force.

See them in their home or wherever they might be at this moment.

See them quietly resting in a chair or in a bed.

Send the healing dove to that individual.

Visualize the dove leaving your hands and flying from this spot and directly to the other person.

The dove is carrying your love and light and a golden healing energy to this person.

Visualize the dove arriving at its destination and hovering over the person's head.

From the center of the healing dove emanates a beautiful golden light which envelops the person.

See the golden healing energy coursing throughout every cell of their being.

Visualize a stream of golden energy completely surrounding the person and covering them with a radiant light.

Stay with your visualization and know that this dove is your healing messenger.

Remain in the silence.

The dove, its message now completed is ready to return to you.

Visualize the white dove leaving the individual and returning to you.

Visualize the healing dove alighting on your open hands.

Acknowledge this dove that has functioned as your messenger of golden healing energy.

Know that the healing energy has gone forward from you in love to another individual and the thought acted upon.

Relax, feel and see yourself encompassed by a golden healing energy.

Feel the energy flowing throughout your entire being.

Be with yourself and let your Spirit be replenished.

Be aware of the energy in the center of your forehead, your third eye.

Know that the healing dove is always at your disposal.

You can recall it to mind anytime you wish.

Be aware of your breathing.

Take slow and steady breaths.

Inhale through your nose.

Exhale through your mouth.

Open your eyes.

INTRODUCTION TO THE HIGHER-SELF

The higher-self is the highest part of our nature, and within that part of our being resides all the wisdom we need and all the love we can ever radiate or receive. The higher-self is the receptacle of all of the power that we require to achieve our goals and objectives. All of these things are contained within our higher consciousness. Because we are Divinely programmed, it is within each one of us.

When we live consciously and in the Light, we might ask ourselves the question: "Is this for my highest good?" and our inner voice will always let us know. However, in our humanity we do not always heed our inner instincts. Occasionally if we don't hear the answer that we desire, then we do not listen and we choose to ignore our inner guidance. Occasionally, we may sabotage ourselves. It does not matter why we do it. At times it is merely out of sheer laziness or to be contrary. The important thing to remember is that being aware makes us responsible. It is then that we need to accept responsibility for our lives and actions.

When we live consciously, the higher part of our nature, (the highest-self) comes to the fore. It then becomes evident that we live in our power, awareness, truth and Light.

We are all unique.

Your truth may not be mine.

Your light may not be mine.

Your ways may not be my ways.

Your reality may not be mine and what works for you may not work for me.

There is one mandatory condition for the relationship with the higher-self and that is: harmlessness... **no hurt may be caused**.

If we have caused any harm or hurt another, (and we all have), then we need to make amends in any way that we can by asking for forgiveness. This can be accomplished on a physical level or by mentally sending out a thought.

How do we become in tune with the Higher Self:

- Acknowledge that your higher-self exists by bringing it into your consciousness.

- Make a habit of asking the question: Is this for my highest good and for the highest good of all concerned?

- Name it - Choose a name for the higher part of your nature and use it. Make it a name that has meaning for you.

- Live in the here and now, be conscious, be awake, be aware of your life and of your actions. Be deliberate and passionate in what you do, live in your power.

- Be cognizant of the dual part of our human nature, the higher part and the shadow part. We possess both. If something does not feel right, listen and pay attention to your inner voice.

- For the purpose of this meditation, visualize your higher-self as a hologram, a three dimensional duplicate of your physical body and send your higher-self before you. This concept is helpful in real-life situations for varied circumstances. Simply visualize your hologram arriving before you to pave the way. Let your energy arrive before you do physically.

MEDITATION ON CONTACTING THE HIGHER-SELF

Close your eyes.

Become aware of your breathing.

Inhale through your nose.

Exhale through your mouth.

Be aware of the rhythm of your breathing.

Visualize yourself seated in your chair as you are at this moment.

Know that you are safe and protected in this space and that you are going to reach out and tune into the highest part of your spiritual nature.

Think of your higher-self as your cosmic twin.

Relax.

Inhale through your nose.

Breathe deeply and forcefully exhale.

As you do so, visualize before you a three dimensional hologram of yourself.

This is a replica of your physical body on the spiritual level. There are no physical imperfections with your higher-self.

This image is whole; it is light, powerful and serene.

Observe the light which radiates from within. It is constant, strong, bright and powerful.

Visualize yourself standing up and being face to face, eye level with your higher-self.

Step into the hologram, this is a part of you.

Feel your body merging into with your higher-self, move your arms and legs if you wish as if you were trying on a diving suit, feel comfortable.

Be in touch with the higher essence of your being, your power, your light and your energy.

Stay in the meditation.

Be aware of the rhythm of your breathing.

Bring to mind an incident in your life when you consciously chose to operate from your higher-self, the highest side of your nature when you could have chosen to act otherwise.

Recall the incident and how you felt when you choose the higher road.

Be with yourself and stay in the meditation.

Now let it go.

Relax.

Bring to mind an incident which is not yet resolved, when you knowingly were harmful to someone else and you did not operate from your higher-self.

If there is a need for forgiveness, use this opportunity to ask for forgiveness now, while you are merged with your higher-self. Do not dwell on any negative or hurtful situations. Be willing to release all to the Universe.

Then let it go.

Be willing to move on from this time forward.

Be aware of the rhythm of your breathing.

Take slow deep breaths.

Now step out from the hologram.

See yourself as separate.

You are now facing your hologram.

If you feel so inclined, take this opportunity to give your higher-self a name.

Make it a meaningful name for you.

Use this name to connect with your higher-self, whenever you choose to do so.

Let it serve as a reminder that your higher nature will constantly guide you.

Learn to trust your inner instincts.

You can depend on your higher-self.

Make use of it in your daily life, in your interactions with others and always choose the higher road.

Be aware of your breathing.

Relax.

Prepare to come back into the present.

Breathe gently, open your eyes.

CHAPTER XIV
PRAYERS, POEMS, BLESSINGS, SAYINGS... AND THE LIKE

From untruth, lead us to truth.

From darkness, lead us into Light.

From death, lead us to immortality.

Om peace, peace, peace.

-Ancient Vedic Prayer

This is the sum of all true righteousness:
deal with others as thou wouldst thyself be dealt by.
Do nothing to thy neighbor which thou
wouldst not have him do to thee hereafter.

-The Mahabharata

God Be In My Head

God be in my head, and in my understanding;

God be in my eyes, and in my looking;

God be in my mouth, and in my speaking;

God be in my heart, and in my thinking;

God be at my end, and at my departing.

-Sarum Primer

Sioux Prayer

O, our Father, the Sky, hear us and make us strong.

O, our Mother the Earth, hear us and give us support.

O, Spirit of the East, send us your Wisdom.

O, Spirit of the South, may we tread your path of life.

O, Spirit of the West, may we always be ready for the long journey.

O, Spirit of the North, purify us with your cleansing winds.

Cherokee Prayer

O Great Spirit, help me always to speak the truth quietly,
to listen with an open mind when others speak,
and to remember the peace that may be found in silence.

Irish Prayer

May you have a world of wishes at your command.
And God and His angels close at hand.
May the long time sun shine upon you, all love surround you.
And the pure Light within you guide your way on.

Lead, Kindly Light

Lead, kindly Light, amidst th'encircling gloom,
Lead Thou me on!
The night is dark, and I am far from home,
Lead Thou me on!
Keep Thou my feet; I do not ask to seet
the distant scene; one-step enough for me.
I was not ever thus,
nor pray'd that Thou shouldst lead me on;
I loved to choose and see my path;
but now lead Thou me on!
I loved the garish day, and, spite of fears,
pride ruled my will. Remember not past years!
So long Thy power hath blest me,
sure it still will lead me on.
O'er moor and fen, o'er crag and torrent,
till the night is gone,
And with the morn those angel faces smile, which I
have loved long since, and lost awhile!

-John Henry Newman

What lies behind us
and what lies before us
Are tiny matters compared
To what lies within us.

                         -Ralph Waldo Emerson

If I can stop one heart from breaking,
I shall not live in vain;
If I can ease one life the aching,
Or cool one pain,
Or help one fainting robin
Unto his nest again,
I shall not live in vain.

                         -Emily Dickinson

Our birth is but a sleep and a forgetting:
The soul that rises with us, our life's Star,
Hath had elsewhere its setting,
And cometh from afar:
Not in entire forgetfulness,
And not in utter nakedness,
But trailing clouds of glory do we come
From God, who is our home:
Heaven lies about us in our infancy!

                         -William Wordsworth

Psalm 121

A Song of Degrees

I will lift up mine eyes unto the hills,
> from whence cometh my help.

My help cometh from the Lord,
> which made heaven and earth.

He will not suffer thy foot to be moved,
> he that keepeth thee will not slumber.

Behold, he that keepeth Israel
> shall neither slumber nor sleep.

The Lord is thy keeper:
> the Lord is thy shade upon thy right hand.

The sun shall not smite thee by day,
> nor the moon by night.

The Lord shall preserve thee from all evil:
> he shall preserve thy soul.

The Lord shall preserve thy going out and thy coming in
> from this time forth, and even for evermore.

-The Book of David

The Robe of Light Prayer

I clothe myself in a robe of light composed of the love, the power and the wisdom of God.

Enveloping me and inter-penetrating me, not only that I may be protected, but so that all who see it, or come into contact with May be drawn to God and healed.

-Author Unknown

Crossing the Bar

Sunset and evening star,
    And one clear call for me!
And may there be no moaning of the bar,
    When I put out to sea.
But such a tide as moving seems asleep,
    Too full for sound and foam,
When that which drew from out of the boundless deep
    Turns again home.
Twilight and evening bell,
    And after that the dark!
And may there be no sadness of farewell,
    When I embark;
For though from out our bourne of Time and Place
    The flood may bear me far,
I hope to see my Pilot face to face
    When I have crossed the bar.

                -Alfred Lord Tennyson

Give us grace and strength to forbear and to preserve.
Give us courage and gaiety and the quiet mind,
spare to us our friends, soften us to our enemies.

                -Robert Louis Stevenson

To be what we are, and to become what we are capable of becoming, is the only end of life.

                -Robert Louis Stevenson

MORTE D' ARTHUR

And slowly answer'd Arthur from the barge:
"The old order changeth, yielding place to new,
And God fulfils Himself in many ways,
Lest one good custom should corrupt the world.
Comfort thyself: what comfort is in me?
I have lived my life, and that which I have done
May He within Himself make pure! but thou,
If thou shouldst never see my face again,
Pray for my soul. More things are wrought by prayer
Than this world dreams of. Wherefore, let thy voice
rise like a fountain for me night and day.
For what are men better than sheep or goats
That nourish a blind life within the brain,
If, knowing God, they lift not hands of prayer
Both for themselves and those who call them friend?
For so the whole round earth is every way
bound by gold chains about the feet of God.

-Alfred Lord Tennyson

They will come back, come back again,
as long as the red Earth rolls.
He never wasted a leaf or a tree.
Do you think He would squander souls?

-Rudyard Kipling

Mychal's Prayer

Lord, take me where You want me to go;
Let me meet who You want me to meet;
Tell me what You want me to say,
And keep me out of Your way.

-Mychal F. Judge O.F.M.

Prayer of St. Augustine

Thou, who art the Light of the minds that know Thee;
the life of the souls that love Thee
and the strength of the wills that serve Thee;
Help us to know Thee that we may truly love Thee;
so that to love Thee that we fully serve Thee,
whom to serve is perfect freedom.

-St. Agustine of Hippo

O Lord, support us all the day long, until the shadows lengthen and the evening comes, and the busy world is hushed, and the fever of life is over, and our work is done. Then in thy mercy grant us a safe lodging, and a holy rest, and peace at the last.

-John Henry Newman

I sought to hear the voice of God and climbed the topmost steeple, but God declared: Go down again, I dwell among the people.

-John Henry Newman

My Lord God, I have no idea where I am going.

I do not see the road ahead of me.

I cannot know for certain where it will end.

Nor do I really know myself, and the fact that I think that I am following your will does not mean that I am actually doing so.

But I believe that the desire to please you does in fact please you.

And I hope I have that desire in all that I am doing.

I hope that I will never do anything apart from that desire.

And I know that if I do this you will lead me by the right road though I may know nothing about it.

Therefore will I trust you always though I may seem to be lost and in the shadow of death.

I will not fear, for you are ever with me, and you will never leave me to face my perils alone.

-Thomas Merton

I have spent my days stringing and unstringing my instrument, while the song I came to sing remains unsung.

-Tagore

The heart has its reasons which reason knows nothing of.

-Blaise Pascal

Men never do evil so completely and so cheerfully as when they do it from a religious conviction.

-Blaise Pascal

It is by suffering that human beings become angels.
— Victor Hugo

To love another person is to see the face of God.
— Victor Hugo

To refrain from imitation is the best revenge.
— Marcus Aurelius Antonnus

Where there is sorrow there is holy ground.
— Oscar Wilde

We are all in the gutter, but some of us are looking at the stars.
— Oscar Wilde

There but for the grace of God go I.
— John Bradford

A well spent day brings happy sleep, a well spent life brings happy death.
— Leonardo da Vinci

Those who have a deep and real inner life are best able to deal with the irritating details of outer life.
— Evelyn Underhill

Heaven's light forever shines, earth's shadows fly.
						-Percy Bysshe Shelley

Lord, I believe; help Thou mine unbelief.
						-Mark 9:24

I will not leave you comfortless: I will come to you.
						-John 14:18

Peace I leave with you, my peace I give unto you: not as the world giveth, give I unto you. Let not your heart be troubled, neither let it be afraid.
						-John 14:27

All my ways are pleasant ways, all my paths are peace, in quietness, and confidence shall be my strength.

God is at the center of this experience and God is love.

In the center of all Light I stand, nothing can touch me there.
						-Isabel M. Hickey

Far away there in the sunshine are my highest aspirations. I may not reach them but I can look up and see their beauty, believe in them, and try to follow where they lead.
						-Louisa May Alcott

The Lord bless you and keep you;

The Lord make His face to shine upon you,

And be gracious unto you;

The Lord turn His countenance upon you,

And grant you peace.
						-Numbers 6: 24-26

Words of Wisdom

So live your life that the fear of death can never enter your heart. Trouble no one about their religion; respect others in their view, and demand that they respect yours.

Live your life, Perfect your life, Beautify all things in your life. Seek to make your life long and its purpose in the service of your people.

Prepare a noble death Song for the day when you go over the Great Divide. Always give a word or a sign of salute when meeting or passing a friend, or even a stranger, when in a lonely place.

Show respect to all people and bow to none. When you arise in the morning, give thanks for the food and for the Joy of Living. If you see no reason for giving thanks, the fault lies only in yourself.

Abuse no one or no thing, for abuse turns the wise ones to fools and robs the Spirit of its Vision.

When it comes your time to die, be not like those whose hearts are filled with fear of death, so that when their time comes they weep and pray for a little more time to live their lives over again in a different way. Sing your death Song and die like a Hero going home.

-Tecumseh Shawnee Chief

Where there is love and wisdom,

There is neither fear nor ignorance.

Where there is patience and humility,

There is neither anger nor annoyance.

Where there is poverty and joy,

There is neither cupidity nor avarice.

Where there is peace and contemplation,

There is neither care nor restlessness.

Where there is mercy and prudence,

There is neither excess nor harshness

-St. Francis of Assisi

God Bless You

I seek in prayerful words, dear friend,
My heart's true wish to send you,
That you may know that, far or near,
My loving thoughts attend you.
I cannot find a truer word,
Nor better to address you;
Nor song, nor poem have I heard
Is sweeter than God bless you!
God bless you! So I've wished you all
Of brightness life possesses;
For can there be any joy at all
Be yours unless God blesses?
God bless you! So I breathe a charm
Lest grief's dark night oppress you.
For how can sorrow bring you harm
If 'tis God's way to bless you?
And so," through all thy days
May shadows touch thee never-"
But this alone- God bless thee-
Then thou art safe forever.

-Author Unknown

The Great Invocation

From the point of Light within the Mind of God
Let Light stream forth into the minds of men.
Let Light descend on earth.
From the point of Love within the Heart of God
Let Love stream forth into the hearts of men.
Let Christ return to earth.
From the Center where the Will of God is known
Let purpose guide the little wills of men.
The purpose which the Masters know and serve.
From the Center which we call the race of men
Let the plan of Love and Light work out,
And may it seal the door where evil dwells.
Let Light and Love and Power restore the Plan on Earth.

-Djwhal Khul & Alice A. Bailey

Benediction from Gloucester Cathedral

Go your way in peace.
Be of good courage.
Hold fast that which is good.
Render to no man evil for evil.
Strengthen the fainthearted.
Support the weak.
Help and cheer the sick.
Honor all men.
Love and serve the Lord.
May the blessing of God be upon you.
And remain with you forever.

The Canticle of Brother Sun

Most High Almighty Good Lord,
Yours are the praises, the glory, the honour, and all blessings!
To You alone, Most High, do they belong.
And no man is worthy to mention You.
Be praised, my Lord, with all Your creatures,
Especially Sire Brother Sun,
By whom You give us the light of day!
And he is beautiful and radiant with great splendour,
Of You, Most High, he is a symbol!
Be praised, my Lord, for Sister Moon and the Stars!
In the sky You formed them bright and lovely and fair.
Be praised, my Lord for Sister Water,
Who is very useful and humble and lovely and chaste!
Be praised, my Lord, for Brother Fire,
By whom You give us light at night,
And he is beautiful and merry and mighty and strong!
Be praised, my Lord, for our Sister Mother Earth,
Who sustains and governs us,
And produces fruits with colourful flowers and leaves!
Be praised, my Lord, for those who forgive for love of You
And endure infirmities and tribulations.
Blessed are those who shall endure them in peace,
For by You, Most High, they will be crowned!
Be praised, my Lord, for our Sister Bodily Death,
From whom no living man can escape!
Woe to those who shall die in mortal sin!
Blessed are those whom she will find in Your most holy will,
For the Second Death will not harm them.
Praise and bless my Lord and thank Him
And serve Him with great humility!

-St. Francis of Assisi

CHAPTER XV
STRUGGLING SPIRITS
THE GHOST OF CHOM

One of the more selfless aspects of mediumship is that of a rescue medium. Rescue work is not for the inexperienced medium or for those who wish to be entertained by Spirit. It is an extremely serious aspect of mediumistic work and should not be approached lightly. Rescue work can be very emotionally, spiritually, mentally and physically taxing on the medium. You never know what to expect in a rescue circle. There can be moments of great sadness coupled with instances of great joy and hilarity depending on the circumstances. It is wise to remember that Spirits retain their personality and the mind lives on after the change called death. To put it more plainly, if the person was a mean curmudgeon who never had anything good to say about anyone, he will not be transformed into an angelic forgiving Spirit upon his death.

    The purpose of a rescue circle is to assist earthbound Spirits who are usually struggling with the fact they have died and are now in the Spirit World. This is through no fault of their own. People have preconceived beliefs regarding the afterlife based on their individual belief systems, whether they be of a religious nature or not. People retain their beliefs after their transition and hence, this is their reality. Earthbound Spirits are not necessarily evil or mischievous, but most often are unaware of their condition. If a life is cut short by accident, foul play, suicide, war, natural disaster or any type of a sudden or violent death, that soul is hurled into the Spirit World without any comprehension of how they came to be there. Not all people who pass over in this manner are in need of rescue. This is most often apparent when a being does not possess any spiritual awareness or belief system. They find themselves in a dark place with little understanding or hope because the mind lives on and their reality is nothingness. They believed in nothing, therefore there is nothing. There are Spirits who remain earthbound because of a desire to cling to their earthly existence for a variety of reasons even though they are cognizant of the reality that they have passed into another realm. This type of entity can raise havoc in the lives of people in the form of a haunting, or varied types of psychic disturbances and phenomena. These physical manifestations are frequently a plea for help from a Spirit who may wish to move on into the Light but for their own reasons remain tied to the earth plane and do not know how to move on. Rescue circles are held specifically with the intention of assisting earthbound Spirits to move on into the

Light through the participation of mediums who work in concert with their Spirit Guides. The medium's Guides function as the beacons for the struggling Spirits that are in distress and who desire to find their way forward into the Light.

For example; if a person holds religious beliefs which incorporate hell, fire and brimstone in the afterlife, they will expect this when they pass over, in particular, if they feel and know they have not led a virtuous life according to the precepts of their religion. They may be frightened and become mired in fear and darkness in the Spirit World because of their mindset and belief. They are not aware of the Light or of the ministering Spirits who are able to lead them into the Light if only they would express a desire to move forward. All they need to do is ask for help and allow themselves to be guided by beings of a higher spiritual vibration.

The World of Spirit is a world of degrees of spirituality. A lower entity, (earthbound Spirit) cannot perceive a more highly evolved Spirit entity's vibration or Light. However, a more highly evolved Spirit can lower their vibration in order for the less evolved Spirit entity to see their Light and sense their vibration. Once the desire is expressed by the earthbound entity, the thought is received and acted upon by Spirit. Spirit does take care of their own.

The purpose of a rescue circle is to help earthbound entities at the behest of Spirit. A medium's personal Spirit Guides know when an individual medium is inclined toward rescue work and is willing to assist Spirit to lead struggling entities into the Light. (Not all mediums choose to perform this type of service.) It is desirable to have a minimum of three mediums involved in a rescue circle. After prayer and meditation, a time is set and prior to the circle, agreement is made as to which medium will take the rescue if it is deemed necessary. It is also easier for Spirit to communicate with the entity through a medium. This means the designated medium will enter into a trance state and allow his body to be temporarily used by the earthbound entity for the purposes of the rescue. This is sometimes required because the struggling Spirit is often unaware that they have crossed over and it is necessary for them to have the experience of being in a physical body once again for the rescue to be effective. The entranced medium will take on noticeable physical characteristics of the manifesting entity, for example; if the entity passed in a violent manner, they will often place the condition on the medium. They may be missing limbs or have experienced a blow of some sort or great pain caused by an accident. All of these conditions will be remembered and placed on the medium. The medium is transfigured by the manifesting entity and this is a very real experience for the struggling Spirit. The medium physically appears as a totally different individual while they are in the trance state. There are occasions when it is not necessary for a medium to enter into the trance state to complete a rescue. The mediums who are present in the room can clairvoyantly receive any needed information from their Spirit Guide and from the earthbound entity. They can telepathically converse with the Spirit entity and encourage them to accompany a Spirit Guide into the Light. When Spirit is present in a room there is an immediate and palpable shift of energy. The sensitive medium is acutely aware of this shift. When a Spirit manifests for the first time after his or her death, their presence is indicated by a burst of noticeably cold energy which is easily felt by those in the room. It is also not unusual in everyday circumstances for a person to feel a chill upon entering a room where Spirit is present. At times this is the means of recognition and a natural reaction for one who is sensitive.

The rescue circle is opened with a prayer, and the rescue work begins in earnest.

The second medium will clairvoyantly know when the earthbound entity has taken over the body of the medium taking the rescue. It is the responsibility of the second medium to communicate with the struggling entity. They will enter into a conversation and explain to them how they came to be in Spirit. The medium will point out to the Spirit they no longer possess a physical body of their own and they are now in the Spirit World. This second medium will tell the Spirit they are temporarily allowed to use the entranced medium's body. Within a short space of time the earthbound entity realizes that this is not a familiar body to him and after some conversation begins to understand what is taking place. The entity will be encouraged to look for the Light and to move towards it. Usually in rescues, the Light is the Spirit Helper of the medium who acts as a beacon for the lost Spirit.

The third medium functions as a battery during the rescue circle. He lends his energy to the process and keeps a watchful eye during the process to ensure that the rescue runs smoothly. Most rescue circles run without difficulty although they can be time consuming, in particular when you are attempting to convince the struggling entity that they have nothing to fear. Many souls are lost, completely bewildered and confused. You must be clear and patient in your explanations as you reason with them. You must convince them that they are indeed in Spirit, have nothing to fear and no need to be fearful of the Light.

Entities frequently will recall and relive their last moments lived on earth. As reality sinks in, this realization can come as quite a shock for some souls. While they are in the entranced medium's body, they will look around them and question the people in the room. Sometimes they ask for their loved ones, husband, wife, friends, parents and children. Remember, the personality does not change with death and some people (now Spirits), can be very amusing. You can never predict what will occur and not all Spirit entities are friendly and warm. Some can be quite angry and hostile. This may place a medium in physical danger. This is why it is advisable to have at least three mediums in a rescue circle. It all hinges on the type of earthbound entity you are helping. There can be some very serious and tense moments in any given rescue and conversely, moments of great exhilaration when a struggling earthbound entity realizes they can indeed move into the Light. It is wise to remember that earthbound entities are not all beings of Light and some Spirits may have been in the shadows for long periods of what we know as time.

In the meantime, the Spirit Guides who in most instances have lowered their vibrations, (which allows for the earthbound entity to see their Light and sense their vibration) patiently wait for the earthbound entity to express the desire and willingness to accompany them towards the Light. Frequently, loved ones who have predeceased the entity will come forward. They impress the medium clairvoyantly in order to prove their identity to the earthbound entity. They invite him or her to go with them and conduct him into the Light. Every being is a Light and it is to this Light we are drawn. As Spirits with a body, we are seen as a Light by others in the Spirit World. It is understood mediums are protected by their individual Spirit Guides with whom they work closely, particularly during this process. The entranced medium has temporarily stepped aside to allow his body to be used by the earthbound entity. He is extremely vulnerable and therefore must place great trust in his Spirit Guides.

In a rescue circle, it is Spirit that decides which earthbound entities are to be rescued, the medium has little say in the matter. I point this out to the reader because the medium does not say, "I am going to rescue so and so today", it does not work that way. The medium is being of service to Spirit.

Prayers for the dead are encouraged and your prayers can help lead a soul into the Light. The rituals for the deceased allow the Spirit to move forward into the Spirit World and are appreciated by the departed. It has been my experience in giving consultations that loved ones often thank people for their prayers and for the lighting of candles for their Spirit. Remember the consciousness lives on and these gestures of love do not go unnoticed by those who have gone on before. They are aware of the thoughts and prayers offered for them.

In July 2003 I received a telephone call from a former work colleague asking a favour. He requested a reading for a relative who would be visiting Montreal from Halifax the following week. His wife would accompany this relative to my home. I agreed to the reading and as is my wont, did not request any information from him except the name of the person coming to see me. For the sake of privacy, I have altered the names of the persons involved.

On July 22 at the appointed hour, I answered my door to find a white haired petite Italian woman dressed in black. She was introduced by my friend's wife as Aunt Anna and appeared to be in her early seventies. The wife left to return later, ensuring our privacy for the reading. Anna had not been to see a medium before and did not know what to expect. I explained how I worked, stressing every reading was an experiment and there were no guarantees. I then proceeded with the reading in my usual fashion. Approximately two minutes into the reading, I felt the energy of a very strong entity who clairvoyantly impressed upon me that he was Anna's son and provided the name Vincent, which was instantly recognized and accepted by Anna. It turned out that Vincent was her only son who had recently passed into Spirit, in his early forties. In the moments which followed, Vincent provided ample evidence it was he communicating to his mother through me. During this reading I noted that my Spirit Guide permitted Vincent to come very close within my auric field. It appeared to me that he was communicating directly through me to his mother. (This is the exception and not the rule during most readings. My Guide usually relays the information telepathically to me as it is provided from the communicating Spirit. Although, I will add, this has happened during other readings. When this does occur, I am totally at peace with it. I have full confidence in my Guide's decisions and I view my work as a team effort.) Vincent very clearly impressed me that he had died by his own hand. He had committed suicide by shooting himself in the head. Up until that moment, this fact was known to his mother and immediate relatives only, but not to myself. Vincent assured his mother that he was okay. He was evidently a very happy-go-lucky individual when he was on the earth plane. He was a loving and devoted son whose untimely death came as quite a shock to his family. He went on to apologize to his mother for causing her such deep pain and sorrow. It was a deeply emotional reunion between mother and son. Vincent did state he had his own demons to live with which his family knew nothing of. He particularly kept this from his mother. For him, death was his way out of this mental anguish and pain. In spite of the manner of his passing, I was pleased to witness he was happy and in the Light which allowed him to communicate as forcibly as he did in the reading. This was very significant for it demonstrated the Light is available to all who would seek it and that God in His compassion and wisdom welcomes all of His children into the Light, even those who commit suicide. In the Roman Catholic faith, suicides are not looked upon kindly and the belief that these souls are consigned to damnation for eternity is still prevalent amongst many believers to this day. Because of her belief, Anna told me she was concerned for her son's well-being in the afterlife.

She loved Vincent dearly and always would. I assured her that Vincent was indeed at peace, happy and in the Light. The manner in which he was able to communicate was clearly evidence of that. At the conclusion of the consultation, Anna left my home with a tape recording of the reading, which I hoped would bring her comfort and solace. I felt privileged to have been a part of this reunion between mother and son. In an October 19, 2010 telephone conversation between my former work colleague, Vincent's cousin and myself, he stated that Vincent was a really great guy, a fantastic human being and that his mother Anna is doing well.

I feel compelled to address the issue of suicide regarding ordinary people in everyday life from my viewpoint as a medium. It may be of some consolation to know that souls who die by their own hand are not consigned to an eternity of darkness in the afterlife and denied the presence of the Light. This was not my first experience when during a consultation a Spirit person who had committed suicide returned to communicate with their loved ones to assure them they are in the Light and to apologize for the pain and suffering caused by their manner of death. The act of suicide itself is the result of an unhappy individual who sees little point in continuing on in the world. At that point, life has become unbearable and he or she views death as a way out. Who can tell what finally triggers this action? Suicide is frequently not a rash act. I believe suicidal thoughts manifest long before the act becomes a reality. Having attempted suicide, this is my personal experience. The world was not a place where I chose to be at that particular juncture in my life. The actions I took then were meant to put an end to my anguish. People do not commit suicide because they are happy. It is a final and often fatal act of complete desperation. Still, it is always a tragic event no matter who, when, why or how. If a person can find the strength to hold on to the morrow, then a new day might bring a new light, less pain and things can get better. But alas, this is not always the case. **I strongly urge that no individual condone or encourage another person to suicide. You need to take care and carefully choose your words when addressing this subject in the presence of the young and impressionable soul.** Through the years of my work, whether in private consultations or in public demonstrations of clairvoyance, I quickly recognize suicide when it is within a person's aura. I believe that Spirit uses my personal experiences of life when I am functioning in the capacity of a medium. There is comfort in knowing that the Light of The Eternal One is always present, even in the darkest of times. There are ministering Spirits who lovingly tend to the souls of those who find themselves in the Spirit World as a direct result of suicide. There are Rescue Spirits who work in unison with those who choose to serve as rescue mediums and help to lead struggling or lost Spirits into the Light. When loved ones ask me what can be done to help these Spirits, my response is always the same. Pray for them, light candles and ask that they be led into the Light. I believe that in the majority of cases when a prayer or earnest thought is sent out, either by the suicide victim or by others on their behalf, the prayer is heard and acted upon by compassionate and loving ethereal beings of Light in the Spirit World. The struggling Spirit is shown the way into the Light and hence peace is granted to the troubled soul.

The subject of rescue work and earthbound Spirits is further addressed in The Medium Touch.

The Ghost of CHOM

One of my most significant experiences was my role in the Spirit rescue circle that has come to be known as, The Ghost of CHOM.

One day in March 1978 while working at Eastern Airlines in Montreal, I received a telephone call from JoAnne Rudy, an executive at the underground rock station, CHOM-FM. JoAnne was unknown to me then but is a personal friend of Ann Barakett, my friend and work colleague at the time. When I initially spoke with JoAnne on the telephone, she said, "I need your help to get rid of a ghost." I was naturally suspicious thinking this could be a radio station hoax. I asked Ann if JoAnne was serious and she replied, most definitely. In fact, it was Ann who had told JoAnne about me. I agreed to meet with her at the radio station's head office at 1310 Greene Avenue. I plied JoAnne Rudy with many questions at our initial meeting concerning the alleged ghost. I had to be certain this was real. During the course of our conversation, I learned from JoAnne she knew of one other psychic person only... namely Millie Gordon, however she had relocated to Vancouver. Considering Millie was responsible for starting me out on the spiritual path, this was my double-check. Though she was psychic, I knew Millie was not a medium. This was scary stuff and Millie did not do this type of work. I consented to help and agreed to meet the following week to perform a rescue.

In 1970, the radio station acquired an old three storey house located at 1355 Greene Avenue in Westmount, Quebec. The house was converted to accommodate a radio station which would be home to CHOM-FM. The former occupants were well-established business persons in the community and had resided in the house for quite a number of years previously. One evening the owner was found dead in his bedroom from a gunshot wound to the head. It was rumoured that he had taken his own life. The death was hushed-up for a while and the Westmount Police Department was very reticent to divulge any information concerning the death. When the radio station acquired the building, there was one room on the third floor which was still boarded up – apparently the late owner's bedroom. After renovation this particular room was converted into a record library and office, which was constantly in use. Eventually the cause of the man's death became common knowledge on the street. However, I was not apprised of any facts; who the person was or how he had died.

Apparently, soon after the radio station settled in, some members of the staff were disturbed by unusual occurrences allegedly attributed to the former owner. This became cause for concern. The entity became a habitué of the station and was referred to as, The Ghost of CHOM, the station's call letters.

This was the 1970's, the early days of this underground rock radio station. Several employees were known to smoke pot. JoAnne states she would frequently smell marijuana when entering the building and, occasionally outside as well. At the time, she thought it was patchouli. However, it turned out to be a mixture of pot and patchouli inside the station. JoAnne Rudy states that Daniel Richler, son of the late world-renowned author Mordecai Richler, worked at the station. Danny, raised in England was quite psychic. He saw 'The Ghost' walking up the stairs on a few occasions. He told JoAnne about it and assured her, "It is not drugs, somebody is here." Danny could not handle these apparitions and quit soon afterward. The Ghost was common knowledge to the listeners. Staff often spoke lightly of The Ghost of CHOM while on-air. However, some staff felt uncomfortable and quite fearful. JoAnne Rudy further states; "It was beginning to drive people nuts." JoAnne recounts the following in an August 21, 2010 conversation:

"Many of the people who worked in 1355 Greene Avenue had experiences that were unnatural" said JoAnne Rudy. "Of course, I attributed a lot of it to drugs, so I didn't listen. For a time, I did not believe them and discounted the matter. Later, odd things started to happen. I had purchased a hand-crafted pine mirror made by the fiancé of one of our employees, (Cynthia Blood). He was a gifted cabinet maker and it was a beautiful work of craftsmanship. The mirror hung in the hallway of the second floor of the station. The mirror was constantly broken. I actually brought it into a local hardware store to have it repaired on three different occasions. We'd replace the mirror, but at least once a month the thing would crack. I just figured somebody was throwing it on the floor or hitting it. It got to the point where I put it in the closet because I was fed up with it. The needle on the turntable lifted from the album while the announcers were in the studio. These were three big turntables. One night, the needle just scratched across the record as it played on-air. Listeners could hear the scratching sound as it quickly moved across the vinyl.

Footsteps were heard approaching the studio, however no one entered. There would be a sudden chill in the air for no apparent reason. Neil Kushner, an employee at the time, claims he was actually lifted out of his chair in the station's library. Incidentally, this was the former bedroom where the suicide had taken place. On another occasion, a late-night announcer was locked out of the recording studio. He left for only a moment. While out of the room, the door slammed shut behind him. There was no other individual around."

Apparently, there was a lull in the phenomena for approximately one year. No instances were reported. Then it suddenly commenced again with reports of mirrors cracking, creaking on the stairs as if someone was walking on them, but no one was visible. At times the room became unnaturally cold and a rocking chair moved on it's own. Due to the transient nature of the business and the laissez-faire attitude of the "hippie-type" employees of the day, they tended not to remain long in their jobs. There had been a turnover in staff, and management was at a loss how to handle the situation without causing concern among their newer employees. Only a few of the longer term employees were aware of the re-occurrences.

In her position as Director of Operations for CKGM-AM and CHOM-FM, JoAnne issued a memo stating the seriousness of the matter and confirming that this was not a joke. Since there were reports of unexplainable and unusual disturbances, she requested anyone having information regarding unusual happenings to personally inform her. I too inspected the memo to ensure it's authenticity.

These were the facts up until March 1978:

The owner of the station, Geoff Stirling was away in India visiting with his Swami. He called JoAnne in the middle of the night with instructions. He was tired of hearing these stories about The Ghost. He knew of such matters and instructed JoAnne to find a medium able to investigate these mysterious occurrences and conduct a séance, exorcism or whatever was necessary. JoAnne contacted me upon obtaining approval from the deceased's estranged wife.

We agreed to meet the following week. Our circle consisted of four members of station management, namely JoAnne Rudy, Nancy Byrd, Craig Cutler, John Mackey and two other mediums; Margaret Eaton and Eddie Barr, who were personal friends of mine. We had fasted and prayed as usual in preparation for this encounter. We entered the dimly lit office where most of the phenomena had occurred. We sat in a circle formation and prayed for guidance and protection for all. We waited and were quite certain that the entity was seeking help and would attempt to make contact with us. The temperature of the room dropped considerably. (This is not an unusual phenomenon when a Spirit entity manifests for the first time after their death. They bring the noticeable cold with them.) The coldness made some of the circle participants understandably apprehensive.

I became aware of a presence standing behind me as he came into my energy field. We had agreed that if it were necessary for someone to take on the entity's condition, I would. We were all aware of a change of atmosphere in the room and did not know what to expect at this point. This could have gone either way. It may be an uneventful rescue or turn into a battle with a very mischievous entity. We three mediums and the other people in the room were protected by our Guides, however one never knows what may transpire. I then permitted the entity standing behind me to enter into my aura. A feeling of great hostility overtook me as I looked at the people present. I had now taken on his condition and was seeing the group through his eyes. I felt as if I were looking at a collection of strangers and not too pleased to see them in my bedroom. My physical appearance seemed to be altering, and I was aware my legs had become much longer and I had taken on the physical proportions of a much taller person. This man was over six feet tall. This condition was visible to everyone in the room. The two mediums, Margaret and Eddie clearly saw the Spirit overshadowing me. I received the impression that I could speak a foreign tongue; that fact was later confirmed to me that this entity was Czechoslovakian.

The next condition I was aware of was the sensation that the right side of my head had been blown off and I felt I was no longer in possession of this part of my head. I was aware I was in direct contact with the entity who I mentally advised to remove these conditions from me, that he no longer required the use of a physical body since he was now in Spirit. I received the impression from him that he was ill at the time of his death, that he had been drinking heavily and his relationship with his wife had deteriorated. He had spent most of his time being depressed in this particular room which was his bedroom and had taken his life by placing a revolver to his head and pulling the trigger. He kept drawing my attention to the left side of the room. I went directly to one spot where he advised me telepathically this was the spot he had taken his life. I kept touching a particular area of the wall, now covered with shelves holding record albums. I was later informed by those present at the rescue, this was his bedroom and the spot I was drawn to was still covered with blood stains when they took over the building and remained so. When the radio station first took ownership of the premises, Westmount Police had the room closed off with yellow crime scene tape. Hence, station management knew this was the room where the former owner had taken his life. They had not advised me or the other mediums present of this fact.

I determined from the entity, by questioning him telepathically that he knew he was dead. However, due to guilt and his beliefs since childhood, he feared what was beyond because he had taken his own life. This was the reason he remained earthbound, clinging to his last memory of earth and wondering what those strangers were doing in his home, this familiar place where he could come to be safe. I mentally advised him to look toward the Light. I was aware of many Spirit Associates in the room who were waiting to assist him if only he could see their Light. Spirit cannot interfere with anyone's free will, so until he was willing to be helped, they would patiently stand by. Amongst these, appeared a woman who seemed to be in her late sixties at the time. Her white hair was pulled high on her head and she wore a gray dress. I sensed this was his mother who was in Spirit. He seemed to recognize her and I urged him to go with her toward the Light. In the first recounting of this rescue circle in The Medium Touch, I purposely left this part out because I felt it too personal a matter for the so called Ghost of CHOM to become common knowledge. There were many Guides and Spirit Associates around us that evening. I saw him in his green sweater and gray slacks walk toward the gentle looking woman who had reached out her hand to him and he moved toward her into the Light.

This is the main reason the rescue circle went so well. He did not wish to fight or cause any harm or disturbance to anyone in the room. He wanted peace of soul and her presence assured him that he had nothing to fear. His mother came to get him. He apparently saw the Light and his mother and willingly moved toward it. In a few moments the heavy condition lifted from me. I felt lighter within and knew he was on his way, no longer fearful of the unknown. I advised him telepathically not to stay attached to the earth plane. He could now move on, progress in Spirit and be released from this misery. God does not judge, He is all loving and all was well. He was free to go to the Light.

My colleagues were watchful since we are never sure of the turn a rescue may take. However, we felt the vibration of the room change and become lighter and warmer, as if a great blanket of tension had been lifted. We were able to perceive the presence of other entities who had now come into this gathering and we clairvoyantly delivered their messages to the staff who were sitting in circle formation with us in this now lighter atmosphere. I was able to inform the others how the room was furnished when the entity lived there, from the information he had given me. All that was necessary was for him to make contact and be made aware that help was available and that The Invisibles are always on hand to lead the way into the Light.

JoAnne shares what happened that night after the rescue circle.

She and her husband Hershel were scheduled to go out to dinner that evening with their friends, Anna and John. They came by the radio station to collect JoAnne and then drove to her home on Cote Ste. Catherine Road to pick-up Hersh. When they arrived at the apartment, it was shrouded in darkness. JoAnne rang the doorbell. No answer. After attempting another ring without response from within, JoAnne let herself in with her key. The apartment was in complete darkness. She called out to her husband by name. No response. Suddenly, from the kitchen appeared this "thing" yelling. It was Hersh, with a white sheet over himself playing a joke. He thought it was hilarious. JoAnne relates she thought this ghost business was all nonsense and she had to be nuts to have any part of it. That is, until several years later when in Vancouver he received a reading from my first spiritual teacher Millie Gordon. The experience with Millie made Hersh a believer. Whatever Millie told him, gained his attention.

JoAnne Rudy and I have remained friends through the years. I remember after the rescue, the gentleman in question's identity was made known to me. I recall at the time of the rescue he wore a deep green sweater. One day on my way home from work as I walked up the stairs leading to the Greene Avenue exit at Westmount Square, which was my daily route from work to home, it dawned on me I had in passing seen the man before. I recalled seeing him entering Westmount Square as I was on my way out. He was a well-known antique dealer in the area and frequently wore a green sweater.

In the Spring of 1981, Stase Michaels a well-known astrologer living in Montreal at the time, gave a consultation to the wife of the man, whom through his death became known as The Ghost of CHOM. They discussed the events which had transpired and the woman agreed to meet with me. When the subject of her late husband was raised, she said, "That is past history." That was her sole comment.

Following the rescue circle, there were no further manifestations.

April 26, 2011

Whilst I was in Los Angeles finishing this book I received the following email from JoAnne Rudy of Montreal.

JoAnne had evidently emailed John Mackey who was the General Manager of CHOM and one of the people present in the room that evening. JoAnne asked John in her email of April 25, 2011: John, remember when I set up my friend Joey to get rid of the CHOM ghost?

John's email response: Yes I remember Joey. What a night as he told us the story of the suicide, then proceeded to go around the table and tell us all about our lives: with me he mentioned my mother had lost my Dad in 1943, remarried. When I asked how he knew his answer was: "She is standing behind you!" Shivers! Told Nancy about her life in England and her love of horses. Geoff's brother-in-law (Craig Cutler) about his motorcycle accident. Weird!! However the ghost never appeared again, and the picture on the wall never had a break on the glass again!!! Still John!

I am acutely aware of the seriousness of guiding earthbound entities toward the Light. I take this part of mediumship very seriously. Rescue work as described above is conducted by mediums to help lead struggling earthbound entities to move into the Light. As a further matter of interest, the Rite of Exorcism as defined by the Roman Catholic Church is commonly performed by priests. These priests are trained as exorcists. Their work is to release souls who are possessed by evil discarnate entities, identified as demons. The Vatican's Exorcists, authored by Tracy Wilkinson, published 2007 is an informative look at exorcism in the twenty-first century. I found it of particular interest to read of Father Gabriele Amorth and other Catholic priests who perform exorcisms on a current basis within the framework of the Roman Catholic Church.

I read Father Malachi Martin's book, Hostage to the Devil when it was first published in 1976. I was very interested in what Father Martin, (a former Jesuit priest, exorcist and theologian) had to say on the subject of possession and exorcism. Through the years, I have followed Father Martin's writings and hold him in extreme high regard. I personally find his work fascinating on many levels and recommend his books highly.

Father Martin passed on July 27, 1999 at seventy-eight years of age in Manhattan, New York, USA.

CHAPTER XVI
AND... SO IT GOES

As I look back over my life, there are instances which have served to shape my beliefs and contributed to my way of thinking and most definitely, have provided me with a sense of belonging to something much greater than myself. The hand of God reaches out to touch His children in many ways and sends Divine Messengers in the guise of humans to help and guide us along the way. The Invisibles and Spirit Guides and those who have gone on to the Higher Life in Spirit, regardless of how short or long their journey here upon the earth plane was, watch over, pray and support us in our endeavours.

The Spirit World is not so far removed from this reality. It is simply a matter of dimensions and of learning how to pay attention and make a conscious choice to be mindful of the Light, wherever you may find it. If we look for the Light in others, then we will see it. If we open our hearts and minds to The Eternal One, we will find our way. We will be given the signs along the way. We will learn and grow from our life experiences, from knowledge and the affirmations of our faith. As we seek and find some answers, we commune with nature and become cognizant of the world around us. When we least expect it, the veil is lifted perhaps for only a second, but long enough for us to realize we are indeed more than what we know. We are more blessed and protected than we ever could have imagined. If we choose to serve from pure motive, then we will be used in the manner of Spirit's choosing: to heal, to comfort, to bring solace to the bereaved and bridge the gap between this world and the next. Here is a recounting of varied life experiences that have left lasting impressions on me and thoughts close to my heart.

By the time the 1970's came around, I started to work publicly. One Sunday afternoon while speaking at the First Spiritual Church, I was quite pleased to see my father Joe sitting with the congregation. Daddy certainly did not believe in Spiritualism or any of that spooky stuff as he termed it and occasionally referred to me as "a spook." It was a big step for him to enter a Spiritualist Church. It was a surprise to me to see my father there to hear me speak. When the service was over, I joined him at the rear of the Church. He greeted me with, "That wasn't bad." I took the remark for what it was worth and was glad he had come to hear me speak. Further to this, in a recent conversation with my sister Irene on August 28, 2010, I mentioned I was going to write about the Sunday that Daddy came to hear me talk at the Church. To my surprise Irene informed me she knew he had gone and she shared the following:

She clearly recollects the Sunday afternoon in question when our father dressed up in his favourite dark brown suit, which he wore on special occasions. Daddy did not say where he was going. He quietly left the house without a word. Upon his return later in the day, Irene asked him where he had gone. He then told her that he had been to the Spiritualist Church to hear me speak and said he was quite impressed with my talk.

My father passed away from a fatal heart attack on the early evening of August 5, 1980. On the night of August 6, whilst my father's body was laid out for viewing at the local mortuary, I was awakened in the early morning hours to see my father's Spirit body standing beside my bed. Daddy was wearing his normal attire; a familiar blue plaid shirt, gray trousers and suspenders. He looked well and was minus the little moustache that he had recently cultivated. I didn't think the moustache was flattering and had told him so. It was interesting to me he chose to appear "sans moustache". This was his way of letting me know that he was okay.

My mother Emma would occasionally come to a service. One evening I was sharing the platform with Margaret 'Peggy' Eaton, an excellent medium. I was seated on the platform behind Peggy, as she gave my mother a message, part of which had to do with her recently acquiring a new teapot. (Sometimes it is the little things that Spirit brings.) Upon Peggy telling her about the new teapot, Emma responded in the affirmative, "Oh yes, my son Josie gave me a new teapot." I happened to be the President of the Church at the time. At her response, many of the regular members of the congregation started to laugh, as did Peggy as she smiled and turned and looked at me, as if to say "Josie!" By now I was embarrassed and blushing. Speaking to the congregation later, I stood up with hand in the air and said; "By the way, I'm Josie." I had no choice, the cat was out of the bag. As a child my nickname at home was Josie. Today, it is used by my closest friends only, so don't get any bright ideas!

I've previously addressed the following in Chapter 8 of The Medium Touch and feel it is germane to what follows. In July 1974, my friend Gloria Gari and I attended the Funeral

Mass for our friend Jose Martinez who passed over suddenly following a short illness. The funeral was held in a small country Church in Sainte-Marthe, Quebec. It was a very sad occasion for all who knew Jose, particularly for his wife Noella and their two young children, Dolores and Manuel.

Gloria and I entered the Church and knelt alongside each other in the pew. For a split second it was as if we were encased in a time warp. We simultaneously looked at one another and were startled to see the other wearing a monk's brown habit. We simply glanced at one another and knew it was real. Gloria and I are longtime friends. I believe for a second we were transported through time and space into a previous lifetime where we were monks together. This experience impacted us profoundly. It reaffirmed a belief in reincarnation.

1975 found me in London, England working as a visiting medium at a Congress held by The International Spiritualists Federation of Healers. I was greatly touched when I received a reading from Mrs. Jessie Kessen, a medium who hailed from Scotland. She clairvoyantly brought through my Spirit brother Paul. I knew of Paul because he had previously come to me several times. Jessie also spoke of a female Spirit who had never touched the earth plane. (Mary, a stillborn child on September 4, 1950. Paul was a miscarriage in 1954). It is comforting to know that these pure Spirit beings who are part of my birth family consider themselves as such and do come through various mediums from time to time to remind us they remain part of the Crinita family.

By 1992 I was residing in Bethlehem, Pennsylvania. One evening the following took place. I had retired for the evening to my third floor bedroom as usual. At approximately 2:30 am I was awakened from a deep sleep. This is not unusual for me as it is when apparitions from Spirit generally manifest. I distinctly and clearly see these visitors. I sensed a presence in my bedroom. I found myself to be in a rare catatonic state, feeling groggy and unable to move. This is not a usual condition I find myself in when unexpectedly awakened by Spirit. I was certain of a presence and slurred out the words, "Who are you?" There was no reply. I asked, "Are you of the Light?" No reply. Still, I was unable to move and felt as if paralyzed. I became irritated. I forcefully asked again, "Who are you?" In response, I heard a deep and powerful male voice, best described as sounding ancient. This voice was not in my head. I heard it in my outer ear and not clairaudiently. It was real; it was in the room. It was audible and crystal clear. "I am Eirenaios" he said. I was beginning to wake up and gather my wits. Having been roused from a deep sleep, this experience had most definitely caught me by surprise. I asked, "Why have you come?" He replied, "Because we made spontaneous love a long long time ago." I asked again, "Are you of the Light?" – no response. I was becoming more aware. I asked, "Are you of The Christ?" He responded in a chortle, "I am older than Christ", (he seemed to find this question amusing). By now I was fully awake and alert. My mind was racing and I thought, "I have many questions for this one." I was intrigued and a little frightened at the same time, however not afraid. I said to him, "If you are not of the Light, I command you to leave." With that – dead silence and he was gone. (At this juncture, I believe my Guides made their presence known to him. This is why he quickly departed.) I jumped out of bed and ran downstairs to my living-room to try and absorb what had taken place. I had never previously had an experience such as this. I have heard my name called out loud during the night by Spirit. This was a full-out conversation with a Spirit entity and it spooked me a little. It was unfortunate in a sense because I was beginning to formulate questions for him in my mind – and he was gone, just like that. I was travelling to Toronto that week to meet my friends Elizabeth and Bill McIntosh. I shared the story. Not one of us could make much sense of it. It just happened.

In hindsight, I think it was rather interesting that someone from perhaps an ancient world was able to reach through time and space. I found his comment that he was older than Christ to be fascinating. As I became more in control, I was formulating questions as to who he really was and why he came. I felt he would have been a good source of information for me. There was so much I wanted to know, however he was gone before I could put any questions to him. I know this was not a malevolent being … this was a real experience.

It is my belief that an inner recognition of a kindred Spirit occurs when we encounter people in our current life with whom we have an immediate connection that defies explanation. It is because we have known them in some other guise, in some other time and place; and we connect once more to begin anew where we left off. Whether the connection be for good or ill, one is drawn within the cycle of reincarnation, in order to balance all that needs to be balanced in the greater scheme of things. This is far beyond our mortal understanding as we journey through time and space.

I hold that in the theory of reincarnation, the soul chooses to experience what it is to be a male or female, straight or gay, parent or child, et cetera, in various lifetimes. I do believe the soul travels the wheel of life in order to gain full understanding of what it is to be a human being. I do believe that the soul is not forced to reincarnate, it is entirely on a free will basis. However, once the die is cast, as a reincarnating Spirit, one may in rare instances experience a memory of things past in order for them to complete the purpose of a current lifetime experience. With each incarnation the slate is wiped clean and it is not common for people to remember their past lives on a conscious level.

In keeping with the law of karma that is the law of cause and effect, which is considered to be the paying back of debts owed. It is hoped that as the soul travels along the pathway of life that we clear the slate in preparation for another future lifetime. Karmic ties could be likened to the invisible threads which bind one soul to another through many lifetimes. I hold that before a soul reincarnates, they are made aware of any karmic debts owed and are presented with the opportunity of clearing those debts before they take to the road again in the guise of a new soul. As always the law of 'free will' prevails.

One of the most significant and uplifting events to occur in my life was almost thirty-eight years ago when my friend Francis Ivess gave me an authentic relic of St. Francis of Assisi. The history of this blessed moment in my life unfolded in this manner: My friend Francis' late father, Anthony, was at one time considering becoming a religious lay brother of the Redemptorist Order. During that time he became friendly with another young man who did enter the Order and became known as Brother Raymond. They remained friends throughout the years. Brother Raymond was assigned to the Holy City to work in the Reliquary in The Vatican. The responsibility was given over to the care of the Redemptorist Order.

Brother Raymond most likely was housed in the Church of St. Alphonsus Liguori, who founded the Order, November 9, 1732. In 1954 on Brother Raymond's return to Canada after twenty years, he brought with him a relic of St. Francis of Assisi as a gift to the Ivess family. It was given to me by Francis because of my devotion to the Saint. It has been in my possession since 1973. This relic was authenticated on October 28, 1935 by Archbishop Camelus Cesarano C.Ss.R. It is a cinder taken from the side of the Saint. This is one of my most treasured possessions and continues to have a place of honour in my home.

In October of 1976, I made my first visit to Assisi. It seemed to me I had been there before. It felt like home. This trip held great meaning for me and I have made reference to it in detail in The Medium Touch, Chapter 10. I erroneously indicated the date as October 1977, but it was in fact October 1976. During this visit our home was St. Anthony's Guest House run by The American Sisters. The Sister Superior of the house, Sister Rosita had kindly arranged a personal tour of the Friary of San Damiano as a favour. We were met at San Damiano by Father Salvator Butler, O.F.M. Father Butler, as it turned out was one of the world's leading experts on St. Francis of Assisi. He had recently completed an English translation of the book, 'We Were With St. Francis' which was originally written in medieval Latin and Italian. This book is a rendering of short vignettes from the life of St. Francis written by his close companions and sheds light on the Saint from the perspective of those who were his intimate companions known as "inter nose" meaning – not to the public. The book is a telling of their personal experiences with Francis during his lifetime.

When the tour of San Damiano was completed, Father Butler invited us into his cell in the Friary to converse further on St. Francis. I was pleasantly surprised to observe a silk hanging of The Buddah displayed on a wall. (Shades of Thomas Merton I thought to myself). Father shared further information on St. Francis and St. Claire - I was a captive audience. As an aside, Father expressed an interest in my family name. He was a Latin Scholar and felt the name Crinita might have been Trinita, in an earlier time.

Father Butler gave me a copy of We Were With St. Francis and inscribed these words: October 21, 1976. To Joe Crinita who I think is going to like reading about this Francis –

and get to like him too, and all the better because he knew how to thank the ONE who made all things beautiful for him. Salvator Butler, O.F.M. Father Butler was a most congenial and generous man, I liked him very much. Coincidentally, visiting Assisi at the same time was the Anglican Bishop, John R.H. Moorman, whom I was informed by Father Butler was the second most renowned expert on St. Francis in the world. I had an engaging exchange with the Bishop, a warm and pleasant man. Bishop Moorman authored several books on the Franciscans and on St. Francis, namely: St. Francis of Assisi' and 'Richest of Poor Men.

This journey was a spiritual feast for me. I encountered many wonderful religious friars and nuns and secular devotees of St. Francis. I was invited to read the Gospel at Mass in the Portiuncula and given a personal tour of the Friary at San Damiano and had the honour of being invited into Father Butler's cell. To add to the magic of this special time, I carried on my person the relic of St. Francis as I walked about his beloved city.

The events of Tuesday, September 11, 2001 will be forever etched in our hearts and minds. This global tragedy ultimately touched and affected millions of people on the planet. It was a turning point in our conscious reality. Everyone can remember what they were doing September 11, 2001. That tragic day left its mark on the world forever. I was at work at Travel CUTS Head Office at 45 Charles Street East in Toronto, Ontario speaking with my friend and colleague Borja Puentes Sanchez. Our General Manager, Heather Crosbie came into my office as we were speaking and said, "Two airplanes have just crashed into the Twin Towers of The World Trade Center in New York." It was approximately 9:15 am. Borja and I left the office and ran up to the corner of Yonge and Bloor Street. People were standing in the streets, shocked, watching events unfold on the giant outdoor screens. It was surreal. We watched in silent disbelief. I thought, "Could this really be happening?"

I was scheduled to give the opening address at the October 19, 2001 For Purpose On Time Community Conference held in Virginia Beach, VA. The Conference theme was: The Bridge to the Future. This was one of the most difficult talks for me to write and deliver to my American friends who are part of my spiritual family. We met to comfort and support one another. The experience touched me profoundly. In remembrance, I include it here:

THE BRIDGE TO THE FUTURE

And behold a darkness will descend upon your Spirit.

And for a time you will wander alone and be fearful of the morrow.

Whilst the Spirit travels inward to the source of its power and after a time of sorrow and contemplation - the veil will be lifted and you will remember:

That you are one with each other and the Universe.

That you are part of The Eternal One.

That even in your darkest hour you come from a place of knowing.

That you are strong!

That you are whole!

That you are a transformer, a beacon and Light bearer.

And again you remember: That the Light will not go out.

That your Spirit is the Light.

The living Light of The Eternal One that will illuminate the darkness and lead you through the clouds of unknowing, of uncertainty and of despair.

These are conditions of the world and have no lasting power over the Spiritual Warrior, or over any spiritual seeker and follower of the Light.

The Eternal One watches, listens and comforts.

When the soul is prepared to hear and receive the message,

We are then reminded:-

"I am here, I am always present and I will pour out my Spirit upon you to sustain you in your time of need and I walk with you in these turbulent times, to bring you to a place of understanding, of strength and perpetual love. So that you will know and be mindful, that you are a resilient and capable human being in possession of an eternal Spirit which will not be destroyed, for you are part of Me".

Always the Hierarchy stands and watches and although the Invisibles cannot interfere with the free will of humanity, they nevertheless can and do inspire those souls who walk in the Light. The supplications and prayers uttered throughout the Universe are carried to the 'Compassionate One' who pours spiritual strength into all who ask for guidance in the darkness of their individual sorrow. In the course of time we rally, feel our inner strength return and within the recesses of our being, a sense of knowing becomes manifest. As a spiritual being, we feel the healing power of the Spirit which fills every cell of our body and which has calmly seeped into our consciousness, helps us reaffirm that 'It is all right and this too shall pass'. The Light always banishes the darkness, as surely as the sun rises daily in the sky. We remember this and we are not afraid. For in the remembering we know and we sense inherently that this is so. Due to recent events, we have been compelled to look and search very deeply within our hearts and souls. No one has had an easy time of it. We have experienced a range of emotions from shock to disbelief, to fear, to sorrow, to anger and incredible sadness. Also there is a sense of pride, of admiration inspired by gallant heroes. Still many cannot adequately put into words that which has transpired and what we have been witness to. Because somehow mere words do not seem adequate as we search for meaning. Our mind and our Spirit have been assaulted by instruments of darkness and although we know where there is Light, there needs to be dark. Still we were not prepared. The unconscionable has changed us all forever. Nevertheless we will go forward. The world will not stop, nor will we be held hostage by instruments of evil who would dare to strike fear into our minds, our hearts and our souls.

We have come here to join one with the other as bearers of the Light.

We have come here to demonstrate that we believe in who we are and we have come to profess that belief.

We have chosen to come here because we integrate our spiritual selves into the reality of this world of which we are a part.

We have come here because we are committed to the Light and to our personal and spiritual growth, to make a difference on the planet and in the life of all whom we touch.

We have come here to comfort and support one another.

We have come here because we walk the talk.

We have come here to insure that the Light does not go out knowing that our personal Light matters in a world reeling from tragedy.

We have come here because we believe in the future of this planet. A future reflected by the Light not darkness. A future created by our individual and collective commitment to making this world a better place to live, simply because we are here and we care for the human family including all creatures with whom we share the planet.

We believe in a bridge to the future:

A bridge of love not hate.

A bridge of hope not despair.

A bridge of joy not sadness.

A bridge of peace not terror.

A bridge of truth not mendacity.

A bridge of Light not darkness.

A bridge of freedom not fear.

And we will build that bridge with our love, our hope, our joy and our very being as Light bearers to the future. We move into a future vision, a vision which we hold deeply within our heart, mind and Spirit. We now carry within a clearer understanding of ourselves and of one another. We have learned this through our personal and our collective sadness, out of pain we grow stronger, wiser and more compassionate, each one according to our needs and experiences. We are the creators of a future vision which will sustain us in our darkest hours and in times of need.

We are what we believe and that which we believe is reflected in the simple act of living day-to-day, by the act of being who we are and consciously choosing to be the best person we know how to be, moment to moment.

In times of crisis, the best and the worst of humanity becomes manifest. We are given glimpses of the reality of what it is to be a human being. For many it is an opportunity to become a far greater person than they would have aspired ever to be. Some are provided with experiences wherein they can unconditionally serve others to the point of risking or the giving of their lives in order to assist or save someone else.

We are inspired by the valour and dedication of people who in this time of great need, selflessly and relentlessly searched for signs of life in the devastation brought about by the forces of evil. We are inspired by their courage and by their Light, for in darkness they lead the way and are indicative of all that is the finest and all that is good in humanity. Out of the depths, they have given us hope and we honour their courage. Within the spectrum of humanity, we experienced the dual nature of mankind.

It is the ancient paradox of good and evil, the Light and the dark existing in the same Universe, the same world. This is a reality. It brings home the point that we must choose our behaviour and how we conduct our life is entirely up to us as Spirits with a body possessing freewill. All we can do is be aware that we can choose to become better than we are and strive to participate in life with a view to always seek the highest good in all of our actions. The path to enlightenment requires the individual devote his time and effort.

It is only through a constant conversation with The Eternal One that we can finely tune our inner awareness. In the silence of the meditative state, we learn to heed our inner guidance and from that guidance we find solace and comfort. It is through the stillness that our individual spiritual nature harmonizes with our personality and the two become as one.

As travellers in eternity and as spiritual devotees, we are aware that there will always be mysteries and that our faith will be put to the test. Because in the infinite scheme of things, we are meant to question and to challenge ourselves and be receptive to new awareness as they occur to us. Awareness is based on understanding and a sense of knowing on the heart level. We know this because our inner voice tells us so. We know this because we asked the question and not because we received the answer. We also know answers are not always forthcoming in the time and space which we, in our humanity deem appropriate as we learn to wait upon the silence.

When the time is right, from some deep part within our being, we hear a quiet still voice say, "Be still and know." In time of great trepidation our spiritual disciplines come into play and each one must look within to find their personal truth, their individual strength and understanding. From this comes the realization that it is what it is. The question then becomes, "What can I do?" and "Where do we go from here?"

As a result of inner searching we come to understanding and self-realization. From an inner sense of knowing, we can reach out to others and share unconditionally of ourselves and of our Spirit because we come from a place of certainty. A certainty based on our inner strength which has an unlimited source, that Source being The Eternal One. We talk of building bridges, we talk of future vision whilst we deal with the here and now.

Divine Order has it that we are all where we are supposed to be. That all is as it should be. As spiritual beings we have the ability to find our way out of the darkness that surrounds us and which for a while may cloud our judgment and our awareness. This is part of being a person. In our humanity we may stumble and fall, but we must be mindful that there are unseen eyes who watch out for us and guide us in the most subtle of ways, lest they interfere with our inherent free will.

We have already chosen to be here on this planet at this time.

We have already chosen to be here together at this time and in this place.

We have already chosen the Light over the dark.

We have already chosen courage over fear.

Let us be fortified with that knowledge and forge ahead.

To aspire to do good where and when we can.

To aspire to love unconditionally, simply for the sake of loving.

To aspire to practice tolerance.

To live our lives with integrity.

To do what we say we are going to do and keep our word in the Universe.

To pray unceasingly and meditate on the ways of the Spiritual Warrior so we can always remain in touch with the Higher part of our nature.

To not be afraid when confronted by evil and fear.

To use our inner strength as our weapon against the forces of darkness.

To be the one candle which glows in the dark.

To embrace our shadows knowing that they are part of our nature and our humanness.

Conversely, knowing that we are also beings of Light and that the Light is always triumphant.

To be happy with ourselves and to let our Light be seen as never before as we live our lives. To know that what we say and do matters.

To believe that our word is law in the Universe.

To call on the Invisibles including friends and family, those who have gone before us and to ask for their intercession and guidance.

To remember there are Legions of Angels waiting on us ready to assist, but the call must come individually from us.

Let us share our experiences of the Light, of our awareness of the miracles in our lives with others as we turn strangers into friends and companions. Know that others will find us for if we are sincere in our quest, we cannot hide who we are. The Eternal One watches and lovingly tends to each and every one of us and when darkness comes, it is only for a while.

We will not be left alone to wander and wonder in fear and in solitude without Light. This cannot be so for we are all part of the Great Spirit and the Light of Spirit knows no limits, no boundaries and no soul is left untouched or goes unnoticed.

You are the bridge. You are the vision. You are the future... and We are the Light and We are One.

So let it be and so it is.

I have long wanted to address the issue of spirituality and sexuality. As a gay man I feel it important to do so because I strongly believe the two are completely separate and one can live both with grace and dignity. Permit me to share some thoughts from my life experience, as I have personally travelled this road.

People are wired differently, this is what makes us unique. We are as different as the stars in the sky, the trees of the forest or snowflakes. Do not deride yourself or suffer unnecessarily by allowing yourself to fall into the trap of self-loathing or unworthiness. Be proud of who you are, hold yourself in high regard and do not deny your nature. Do not permit any religion, organized group or individual to intimidate or suggest it is shameful to be gay. Do not allow the mean spirited and narrow of mind to dim your Light. We are who we are... and be who you are. Take comfort in the thought that The Eternal One – The One who created trees, stars and snowflakes has also created human beings. We are loved, whether at times we feel it or not. God's love is eternal. Believe He lives within you and if you lose yourself along the way, He will find you in the darkest moments and lead you into safe harbour. He sees your Light even when you are unable to – and in your darkest hours He is ever present watching and waiting on you. He knows you - you are truly loved exactly as you are. To those souls struggling with their sexuality whilst finding their place in the world, give yourself time and do not despair – God is watching over you and will see you through, just as you are.

I am thrice blessed in this life. I have a very loving family who never questioned my choice to become involved with Spiritualism. The Crinita Family are a supportive, stalwart and giving bunch. (I might add some of my siblings are psychic as well, others skeptical). I've been favoured with many cherished friends in my private and professional life. I hold them dear. I have formed lasting connections with those whom I have come to know as my Spiritual Family on both sides of the veil.

A constant in my life since the age of fourteen years, is my idol Joni James. She has been there for me through the years. Since hearing her sing for the first time in person at the Seville Theatre in Montreal, I was a fan then as I am now. I initiated and ran Joni's Montreal Fan Club for a number of years. Words are inadequate to describe the admiration, esteem and love I feel for Joni. Her great God-given talent has served as an inspiration to me in good times and when I was in need of solace. Her gentle and golden tones have always seen me through and I am honoured to call her friend.

These are her words written for me on June 24, 2010:

To Our Darling Joey

The little dimpled cheek boy standing in the snow at the stage door in Montreal –

It was instant love for both Tony and I and has been ever thus since that time until now

Though Tony is gone to heaven

You've always been my total Joy – and delight

Now I am begging our sweet Lord to give you good health – so we can have more special times on earth.

Special friends are special people – and you are one of the most.

Forever – Joni James Acquaviva and Tony too.

Now Joni Schriever. Love, Love, Love.

I have been truly blessed by the calibre of spiritual teachers who have crossed my path, each one leaving me with grains of wisdom and gems of knowledge.

For the record, my spiritual teachers have all been Women. A Posse of Fantastic, Fabulous, Wise, Strong and Spiritually inclined Women who have guided me through the years. Is it any surprise my constant Spirit Guide Wana and two idols, Susan Hayward and Joni James are also women? Thank you Ladies for always seeing me through.

I would like to acknowledge two individuals who were members of my development class for quite a number of years. Eddie Barr was an accomplished artist and a very talented medium. Patricia Spells Palmer was an equally talented medium and inspirational speaker who also sat in my class for a few years along with Eddie. They have both passed on to the Higher Life. I am honoured to have played a part in their mediumistic development and to claim them as beloved personal friends. I look forward to our reunion one day in the world beyond.

I would be remiss if I did not mention my longtime friend and confidante Andree Duquette who passed to the Higher Life on January 19, 2009. Andree was very fond of the following quote regarding the misfortunes of life and used it frequently: "In life you have only two options, either to be a better person or to be a bitter person – there is no third option."

I strongly believe in the power of prayer, through prayer we can storm the Gates of Heaven.

My Prayer

Lord, help me to find my way to you.

Guide me through my life in all that I say and do.

In times of darkness and of fear,

Remind me that your Light is always near.

-Joey Crinita
September 21, 2009

Like all people, I know the process of mortal death is as mysterious as it is inevitable. When all is said and done, it is the final curtain – conversely, it is also the opening of the portal to eternity. The Spirit departs the body and returns from whence it came. Our loved ones and those who have gone on before await us on the other side of the veil.

I am truly honoured and privileged to be of service to Spirit. When I was most in need, Spirit altered the life of a young and desolate person and helped to transform my existence by their subtle influence. I sent out an SOS call which Spirit heard and answered. It is the meshing of my soul with Spirit which has left me immeasurably enriched. For this, I am truly grateful to The Eternal One. I wholeheartedly believe there is always a Light at the end of the tunnel. Even in the midst of darkness, the Light is still present. And so I pray... lead on kindly Light.

And... *so it goes.*

ACKNOWLEDGMENTS

Ron Sexton for encouraging me to write this book and for his unfailing support. Jean Sexton who has patiently and efficiently worked with me for the past seven months with continued good humour, a keen eye and a questioning mind. What can I say? Thanks is not enough for the editing, typing, the hours on the telephone and for years of friendship. Thank you Jean. Gillian Payne for not letting me abuse the Queen's English too often. Irene Crinita, for her wise, honest and perceptive input, and of course, for being my sister. To all the people who have contributed to this book, and so generously shared their experiences with me: Elizabeth and Bill McIntosh, Colleen Gregory, Gloria Gari, Carol Tucker, Francis Ivess, JoAnne Rudy, Elizabeth Bruni, Donald Royer, Sharon Lyn Hollis, Frances Lombardo, Joni James, Dolores Martinez, Gloria Crinita for also being my sister, and my nephew, Justin Crinita. A heartfelt thank you to all the people who permitted me to share the personal stories of their loved ones based on their private readings and experience with me. Noella Martinez, Sharon Davidson, John Reath, Jim Hawkins, Jean Sexton, Ilona Asling, Greg Asling, Gemma Zaccardelli and Vincenzo Zaccardelli. A special thank you to the following people: Joyce Love, John Berkheimer, Dorothy Santangelo, Karen J. David and Jonnie-Ruth Kuhn for unwavering support through the years. Many thanks to my longtime friends Dee Lois and Marvin Sward who for many years gave me a home away from home on Kings Road on my visits to Los Angeles. My friend Borja Puentes Sanchez who came into my life and touched my heart. Miss Joni James, always my hero who continues to lift me up by her beautiful singing voice and cherished friendship. To all those mentioned in this book who have now graduated to the Higher Life, I thank you for allowing me to be of service, to tell your story and for being a part of my life as family, teachers, friends and fellow travellers in eternity. To my Spirit Guides who have never let me down, and my Guardian Angel who does just that.

PAX ET BONUM

Giovanni Cimabue, circa 1278 – 1280

St. Francis of Assisi

www.ingramcontent.com/pod-product-compliance
Lightning Source LLC
Chambersburg PA
CBHW020731160426
43192CB00006B/182